BATTLE SCARS

BATTLE SCARS

A Story of War and All That Follows

Jason Fox
with Matt Allen

CORGI BOOKS

TRANSWORLD PUBLISHERS
61–63 Uxbridge Road, London W5 5SA
www.penguin.co.uk

Transworld is part of the Penguin Random House group of companies
whose addresses can be found at global.penguinrandomhouse.com

Penguin
Random House
UK

First published in Great Britain in 2018 by Bantam Press
an imprint of Transworld Publishers
Corgi edition published 2019

A CIP catalogue record for this book
is available from the British Library.

ISBN
9780552176019

Typeset in 11.5/17.25pt Adobe Caslon Pro Std by Jouve (UK), Milton Keynes.
Printed and bound in Great Britain by Clays Ltd, Elcograf S.p.A.

Penguin Random House is committed to a sustainable
future for our business, our readers and our planet. This book
is made from Forest Stewardship Council® certified paper.

1 3 5 7 9 10 8 6 4 2

For the men and women engaged in their own
personal conflicts with mental health issues.

This is my story.

The battles featured here occurred during the past decade in an unnamed warzone.

The names and locations featured in those operations have been redacted to protect the security of those involved and the practices of the British Special Forces. Some of the people involved in my struggle with mental health have also been disguised to protect their anonymity.

For my loved ones at home, the Killed In Action and survivors of war, everything else has been described as it happened . . .

1

Is this my time?

   Not here.

   I want to go home.

   I should be so lucky.

And we're back there now, the place where it all started.

The sky erupted. Bullets with a blossom. Vivid puffs of phosphorescent green that sparked in the desert terrain below and sharpened into small dots, arcing towards our helicopter through a hazy, pea-soup blur. The trippy, spectral visuals were tracers, their surreal glow created by the night-vision goggles, the 'NVGs', strapped tightly across my face. *Pop, pop, pop!* Hundreds of them, more muzzle flashes in lime, more shooters, more rounds, speckling the ground a thousand feet down, suddenly zipping closer as

I sat somewhere under the Chinook's whumping rotary blades. We had been spotted by a large group of enemy fighters, a couple of hundred at least, and their angry response was a rowdy launch of little lead wasps, each one approaching with an increasing velocity and brightness as they screamed by in their incandescent fury.

Anticipation grabbed at my chest. I was being wind-blasted from the air rushing through our windows, every glass pane on board smashed in to cool the oppressive desert heat outside – air conditioning, British military-style. The heavy smell of aviation fuel had clung to my nostrils for a while, but as the helicopter descended ever more rapidly, an all-too-familiar stench took over. Sweet and pungent, the desert environment had a whiff all of its own: a weird blend of human and animal sewage, vegetation, dirt and body odour, the filthy essences mixed into an intensely rich and warm perfume. I could almost taste the habitation, the stink of mud buildings, the straw roofs, animal feed, dirty water and tangy manure. The rot and detritus cooked in the hot daylight, and even at night-time the smells never stopped wafting across the sand. During missions that involved a slow approach by land, there was an almost undetectable change in smell as we advanced, and my senses were often attacked subtly by aroma, kilometre by kilometre. But dropping rapidly out of the sky in a helicopter delivered a swift shock to the system and the odours blasted and tingled the hairs in my nostrils.

After several years of working in arid warzones, this reaction had become a trigger point, a warning I was moving into trouble. In the military we referred to those instinctive feedback loops as 'combat indicators', a sensual sign of looming conflict. On the ground, one of these triggers might have been something that didn't look quite right at the side of the road, a dug-up mound of earth maybe, or a hint of some recent enemy activity such as the not-so-subtle planting of an IED by an amateur. It was always a subconscious alarm bell, and my body and senses seemed to come alive with the realization . . . *I'm in a helicopter, I'm surrounded by teammates, and know that smell* . . . a fight was coming. Goosebumps prickled my skin; Kylie Minogue sang softly, sweetly, into my earphones, my iPod Shuffle delivering a surreal soundtrack to a night-op turned to hell when it could have easily thrown out something more befitting of the vibe, like the angry riffing of Iron Maiden or AC/DC. And then, a blast of pain hammered at my legs, an intense throbbing that seemed to begin in my kneecaps and wrenched at my thighs.

Oh no.

No.

No, no, no. Please not a hit.

I peered down nervously and squinted into the gloom, but I hadn't caught a bullet or shrapnel splinter. Instead, the stress of incoming fire had tweaked my body's sympathetic nervous system, the fight-or-flight response, and I'd instinctively grabbed at my knees, my fingers locking around the quad muscles in a white-knuckled grip as I painfully clutched at the flesh. Blowing away a sigh of relief, I pulled back and tried to reassure myself that everything was going to be OK. *I'm not going to cop a round – not on this job.* Weirdly though, there was no release from the throbbing sensation in my legs, even once I'd grabbed at the barrel of my gun for comfort. I winced. It wasn't my knees I'd been clutching in terror: I'd been squeezing the soldier next to me, and he'd been squeezing me. We looked at each other, realizing that a surreal moment of accidental tenderness had briefly unfolded, the pair of us kitted out in body armour, ammo, shock-and-awe weaponry. We had been touching each other's thighs and giggled nervously like it was a weird first date. Two soldiers about to land in the middle of a gunfight, rounds pinging past us, our helicopters dropping into the heart of a village brimming with enemy fighters armed with AK-47 machine guns and rocket-propelled grenade launchers, both of us feeling embarrassed at a split second of unintentional intimacy. It seemed funny for a second or two – *unless you really thought about it.*

A shout went up from the back of the chopper.

'Three minutes!'

The call was echoed down the line of waiting fighters, from ramp to cockpit, every voice reaffirming to the next man that it was 'Go Time'. Three minutes during which nobody should be in any doubt that a proper scrap was about to kick off. Three minutes until we landed. Three minutes of helplessness, of not being in control of anything. With the Chinook's ramp slowly opening, I could assess our situation more clearly: Toyota Land Cruisers had pulled up underneath us, heavy machine guns mounted on the rear, the shooters on the back blowing the grainy green sky to ribbons. In response, our gunner popped off rounds, dragon-breath bursts looking to strike the targets below, but we were moving too quickly and it was almost impossible to hit anyone as we swooped down to 500 feet. I took a split second to check over my kit one final time: gun, ammo, radio; a frantic pat-down that always took place whenever we were about to execute a mission. I switched my iPod headphones for the standard-issue earpiece that linked every soldier working on the ground.

The buildings ahead sharpened in my night-vision goggles. The sturdy-looking huts, made from mud and straw, seemed to tumble over one another, unplanned and built seemingly without thought. Their edges were stacked along uneven lines and confusing alleys, and I could never understand how the rows stayed together. But the buildings' robustness under fire made them architectural wonders to me; sometimes the walls were several feet thick and it was often hard work to blow in the perimeters if ever we had to breach a compound.

There would be an engaging, if unnerving, chaos to entire settlements. The streets comprised disorientating, sprawling arteries of tunnels and alleyways; blocked-up squares used for dropping off human excrement; shop stalls and shutters – with no distinctive landmarks or signposts to help anybody negotiate their way from A to Z. Homes weren't laid out in neat little rows and cul-de-sacs like they were at home in new towns such as Milton Keynes or Peterborough. Instead they popped up without permission or thought. Getting lost in the thick of an urban firefight was sometimes an occupational hazard, and somewhere in that sprawl was our target in a top-secret mission.

An explosion jolted me violently and our helicopter jinked to one side with the shock. *Nowhere to run to.*

Avoiding the barrage from below was almost impossible now: moving around in the air too quickly would only burn the fuel we needed to get us away once the job was executed. *Nowhere to hide.* Tracer rounds peppered my field of vision along with the hypnotic, distracting blizzard of static electricity generated by the chopper's spinning rotary blades, weird little shards of light that shimmered in the green dark of the NVGs. I looked across and watched the helicopter next to us receive another rush of heavy fire as we began our touchdown.

The last thing we need is for one of the helicopters to fall from the sky . . .

And then, another shout above the noise: the ramp had been fully lowered. I could see the tree branches bending and rippling ahead of us in the downforce of our arrival. The buildings and cars, and enemy fighters, were in full view. We were on the ground.

'Time to move!'

Our cue to run headfirst into a tempest of bullets and bombs in a mission we had worked out only half an hour previously on the back of a fag packet.

I'm not a headcase. The sound of gunfire could sometimes put the fear into me as it would anybody else, but my stress was only ever temporary. Sometimes the rush of incoming rounds might kick-start a fit of the giggles, though. I couldn't tell you the number of times I'd been on a routine mission, resting, or drinking a brew with the rest of the unit, only to be sent diving for cover when the *phut-phut-phut* of incoming fire had cut through the chatter. In those moments my mouth tended to go dry; I would suck hard at my Camel-Bak water pouch, the adrenal surge kicking in as the whizzing rounds landed nearby, their impact hammering a pulse. For a few seconds there would be silence, a moment of composure and recalibration. *Where did that come from? Who the hell's firing?* And then, inevitably, the sound of snorting and chuckling; a bunch of soldiers crouched behind a wall, laughing at the screwed-up insanity of nearly getting dropped by a smacked-off-his-face farmer. Usually, the bloke had been armed with a barely working rifle and was taking pot-shots at us because he had nothing better to do. Somebody might whisper conspiratorially, *'Ooh lads, it's going off! Bloody hell . . .'* and then several years of combat experience would kick in. We'd fan out to points of cover and return fire, methodically clearing the area of hostile forces and angry agriculturalists, saving the teas for later.

There were even times when dodging a bullet seemed possible to me. Rounds didn't fly in straight lines. Instead, through a pair of NVGs, I was able to watch a gunman firing at us from the ground as we flew overhead, the lead slug corkscrewing from the gun barrel, at first emerging seemingly in slow motion, which sometimes created the illusion that I could easily sidestep it before it landed. Whenever that thought crossed my mind – and thankfully it rarely did – the bullet would almost always pass by instantly, at light speed, embedding itself into a surface behind my head.

God knows how I could laugh at near-death experiences like that, and I've often tried to figure out why, exactly. I've told myself it was most probably the result of nerves, excitement even. Perhaps it was an instinctive defence mechanism, some weird, primal human reaction. Or maybe it was a boy thing, like when a bunch of drunken football fans become hyped up for a scrap, singing as they lob bottles and firecrackers at the people charging towards them. There is always a little humour to be found in fear. It's screwed up, I know, but it was a true facet of military life. At home, the stories of us messing around while under fire always sounded weird, especially whenever I'd been reliving them at parties, or in the pub with friends and family. Explaining the laughing and gallows-joking to someone who had never set foot in a warzone often got me a funny look.

When it came to the AK-47, though, there was no fun, no games, and no time to mess about. The AK-47 was horrific because it was so aggressive-sounding. *Ferocious.* The angriest weapon in the business due to its bullet, a 7.62mm short, and when fired from the barrel it sounded like the bark of an angry Rottweiler.

Bark! Bark! Bark!

I ran off the back of the Chinook and shifted right.

Bark! Bark! Bark!

I knew we had to find cover in order to plan our approach effectively. I caught sight of a ditch just in front of the trees and sprinted towards it, engaging the unseen enemy fighters ahead with bursts of fire, running through the treacle-like mud as the noise ricocheted around me.

Bark! Bark! Bark! Bark! Bark! Bark! Bark! Bark! Bark! Bark! Bark! Bark! Bark! Bark! Bark!

More bullets. More noise. The sound of crackling gunfire and exploding grenades seemed to arrive from everywhere. Then a call came through my earpiece, a situation report to turn the stomach upside down.

'One friendly force, KIA.'

One of our lads had been fatally shot. We were a man down already, only a few seconds into the attack, and human instinct meant it was almost impossible to numb the fear that it might have been a friend, one of the lads, somebody who had kept my spirits up during a never-ending tour in the middle of nowhere. My mind was thrown through a loop.

Get me out of here.

I couldn't tell you what triggered the heady, emotional tumult that followed as I landed in that ditch and rolled on to my back, taking a second to catch breath. Maybe it was a physical reaction: my muscles burned from the death-or-glory dash across open ground, every step weighed down by ammo, grenades, body armour, radio, batteries and NVGs. Or it might have been news of the KIA. My thoughts spiralled at the Russian-roulette of the announcement, the nagging question of who it might have been, and how.

Is it someone I don't know? One of the new boys, maybe . . .

. . . Or maybe Dave.

My heart sank; I experienced a dark feeling, an almost imperceptible sensation bracing me for bad news – that it was bound to be Dave, one of my good mates in the group. He was a 27-year-old Royal Marines commando sniper from Portsmouth and not long ago the pair of us had killed hours by dossing underneath the Chinooks, our only real shelter in the sweltering sun at our desert base. As we drank endless cups of coffee, Dave and I had connected. We talked about our home lives a lot. I was in the process of divorcing my first wife, a break-up that had knocked me badly – not that I'd have admitted the full details of my emotional pain back then, even to Dave. And because he was single and up for a laugh, I'd found a lot of fun hanging from his coat-tails whenever we went out back home; the nights out had helped me to forget my relationship issues. Being a younger bloke gave the impression that Dave wasn't able to look after himself as well as the other lads in the unit, though that was a massive misconception. His arms were a sketchbook of tattoos, each one detailing a military tour or overseas adventure. After several months on base, his bristling beard and rough complexion, lit up by a pair of bright-blue eyes, had given him a feral look, like a wildling warrior from the TV show *Game of Thrones*. A weird intensity clung to him, as if chaos was only a pint or five away.

Please not Dave.

My mind refocused. *Forget it.* I checked my weapon. *Change the magazine on your rifle. Check your kit. Don't lose any kit . . . Do not lose any kit . . .*

There was a moment of realization. *This mission is bloody horrible . . .*

Then a flash of panic came in quickly afterwards. *I don't want to die . . .*

Not here. Not now.

I want to go home.

Please let me go home.

And that's when I thought of her for the first time in ages.

Mum.

2

Flashback: to a moment of innocence and security, a scene as far removed from the stink of cordite, sweat and fear in that ditch as I could imagine. There was Mum and me. We were sitting on a sofa, cuddled up as we watched *Top of the Pops* on the telly together. Me: ten years old, red pyjamas, silly haircut. Her: a dress from the mail-order catalogue, something hippy-looking – she used to like that stuff back then. I remembered us laughing at some big-in-the-eighties band. It might have been Duran Duran, I'm really not sure. But I know I felt protected there, safe, *loved*, sitting in our little council flat, the room warm from the small gas fire in the corner, my eyes drooping because bedtime wasn't far away. Home was relaxed and cosy – secure. I wanted to go back.

Take me back.

The present: a ditch. I was muddy, trapped in some battle-scarred village a million miles from England. I had become soaked through with sweat, having carried all that kit while shooting at enemy targets. I was getting shot at. A teammate gone, dead; maybe Dave, maybe not. My legs were on fire, my boots were heavy with mud. There had been a sprint through God-knows-what but it felt like superglue, just to get to a ditch as the firing and bombing exploded overhead. How was I still alive? *Everywhere bullets, shouts, chaos, panic. Bullets, shouts, chaos, panic.* And now I was freaked out, thinking of Mum, wanting to go home. *Wanting to cry.*

Am I a coward?

The reality check: I acknowledged the emotions as they hammered at my heart rate, it was a way of rationalizing a psychological paralysis that was threatening to pin me down. Gulping in a deep breath seemed to slow everything that was going on around me as I focused on our surroundings. But was I scared, really? Fear was an emotion that had struck me during the job in the past, but it had often kept me alive, sharpening my focus in chaotic situations. The feeling was always fleeting and I had usually been able to turn it off like a tap.

Not this time.

I tried convincing myself that maybe I wasn't scared at all. Was I unsettled by some other emotion? Might it have been the blurring boundaries between home life and war that had caused me to freak out and think of Mum? I listened to the *Bark! Bark! Bark!* of the AK-47s again, the rounds whistling overhead and hacking at the branches in front of us. They seemed to shake me, which was an unusual experience. I had previously found it fairly easy to zone out on operations because I was detached from the mundane, or painful stuff happening in England. The people I loved there felt distant, like Mum and Dad, or my daughter. The bills, family issues, and domestic problems seemed inconsequential too, because they were taking place thousands of miles away. But the infrastructure of base life had suddenly changed. Technology and social media unsettled our day-to-day routines and we all felt it creeping into our lives. On top of the usual letters and phone calls, emails from home were coming in every day; online photos and texts, too, when that kind of thing hadn't been available to us on previous tours. Our mobile phones were usually close by as we worked at the base. With those pinging intrusions came the tears, the stress, and the arguments that sometimes flared up between couples separated by miles of desert and mountains. The void seemed even bigger when dealing with time zones and unpredictable operational hours. For the helpless ones stuck at home, a sense of separation was only amplified by the countless sleepless nights spent stressing about the latest newspaper headlines on IED injuries and friendly fire. I had even heard some of the lads fretting about the way they'd left a Skype conversation with their parents, wife or kids. *Have I said the right thing? Did I make it all worse?* Shortly afterwards they would step on to a helicopter for another mission, feeling distracted or angry, which made those intrusions all the more hazardous for everybody.

Was that happening to me, too?

Previously I had sat in the back of a Chinook, worrying that my ex had been sleeping with somebody at home, and all because I'd received an email warning me as much. (Though we were in the process of a divorce, I was hoping we might patch things up.) I was moving into a gunfight but overthinking my home life at the same time. I readied my kit and seethed, the other lads joining me as the helicopter lifted up, my thoughts whirling at the uncontrollable possibilities happening thousands of miles away. *What's she doing?* I had visions of her sleeping with another bloke. *But who?* And it wasn't just her on my mind. I was also thinking about my younger brother, Mat, a Marine fighting in another episode of the war. *Please let him be OK*. His emails often bothered me, not because he was inexperienced or incapable, but because he was my little bro and I wanted to protect him. Now, for a split second in that ditch, my earlier home life had crept into the black-and-white of a battle when it needed to be the farthest thing from my thoughts.

I closed my eyes. I reminded myself of the realities of war, that loads of soldiers had probably thought of their families when pinned down in horrendous situations like the one I was experiencing. I remembered watching the opening scene from a haunting, bloody war movie where a kid who was probably only seventeen or eighteen years old had been cut in half by machine-gun fire. He was still alive, screaming for his mum, disembowelled and bleeding out in agony on a beach in World War Two as his friends lay dying around him.

Keep it together . . . Just keep it together.

The thought process seemed to steady me. There were some more deep breaths, some more internal chatter.

Come on, you're an experienced soldier. You can do this. You live for this. You don't really want to be just another civilian bloke, do you? Sat at home, drinking beer in front of the telly? You've got purpose out here; kudos, near super-humanity.

I had regained self-control.

You love this job.

The disorientating panic felt like minutes, but it would have lasted only a few seconds, and in that brief flash of chaos I had rationalized exactly what was happening. I was extremely stressed, emotionally overloaded, in the fight, and I had been presented with two options. One: lie back and give up, probably die. Or two: get my head together, remember why I was there in the first place and do the job I was being paid to do. I reached for clarity, remembering the person I truly was: 'Foxy', a Royal Marine commando from the age of sixteen; highly trained; part of the military elite, working from the shadows in the world's most dangerous warzones; Jason Fox, husband, son, oldest brother, dad to a beautiful daughter. I looked across at my two teammates, unrecognizable in their camouflage cream and NVGs, crouching down in the ditch beside me as they waited for a signal to push forwards. I was refocused on the awful reality and how to survive it. Mum, Dad, my brother, and the soon to be ex-wife had been compartmentalized. Forgotten. I could worry about my freak-out later.

Conflict rushed back into focus.

I looked up. More tracer fire zipped overhead like a meteor shower, the effect created by flare material in the bullets, and as the lead screamed towards its target, the rounds glowed in the dark. A rocket-propelled grenade exploded nearby and the air around us rippled with its powerful kinetic energy. I didn't wear ear protectors like some lads did; I found they reduced my spatial awareness and their noise-cancelling technology amplified every little sound while diminishing the louder explosions and bangs to a crazy, teeth-grinding *krzzchhh!* Even without them my hearing was still on edge, the senses heightened with adrenaline. I peered through the NVGs, my legs steadied for another charge across what could have once been farmland, churned-up mud that required me to lift my legs higher than normal as I raced across it. *There!* Several muzzle flashes and a burst of tracer fire revealed the positions of two fighters, the pair of them suppressing our movements with a barrage of bullets. I raised my gun and steadied myself.

Everybody on this mission is having their own little drama, I thought. *Everyone here is in a bad place.*

It was true, too. Some of the unit were engaged in contact with a group of enemy fighters that had found cover behind a clump of trees. Others were dealing with a cordon of gunmen hiding on the other side of the compound. I could hear them lighting everything up around me. Mayhem had crept into the mission, and as an older head in the group I was fighting with, I needed to use my emotions to lead. I had to let the stress of combat sharpen my thoughts, not hinder them. I pulled myself up, moving quickly over the exposed land with the others, into the darkness, towards the treeline, taking out two enemy gunmen as we moved. All across the mission, dozens of horror stories were being written.

I just had to deal with mine.

3

We were surrounded by hostiles. An intense gunfight had begun. Through the darkness I could hear more shouting in the distance. Crackling instructions on the comms only added to the chaos and every sentence carried more bad news and occasional flashes of misinterpretation.

'Mart's on the stretcher,' said one of the blokes moving alongside me.

'He's dead?'

'No, wait!' shouted another voice. 'He's carrying the stretcher, he's not actually on it . . .'

We seemed to be working on the worst of the worst, a mission where we were outnumbered and outgunned, all of us understanding there would be no let-up until our job was done. Not that any of us were in a position to down tools and quit anyway. There was no time-out option and no white flag to be waved. We were strapped in until the bitter end.

The sensation of chaos hadn't been unfamiliar to me. Missions I'd worked on took unexpected turns all the time, and for all manner of reasons – good and bad. Surprise was something to be expected in my line of work. I remember during my first-ever tour with the military, we had received intelligence that a high-value enemy fighter was holed up in a village and his plan was to wreck shop on the British Army lads with a suicide vest. We were sent in, and having arrived at the house where he was supposedly hiding, our unit encircled the area. An interpreter yelled at the guerrilla to come out, shouting and screaming warnings, but nothing happened. Everything seemed still, too still. We lobbed a grenade into an empty corner of the courtyard outside his home, a fairly aggressive way of coaxing the bloke outside, only to watch, surprised, as the door burst open and a family emerged with their arms in the air, blinking and coughing into the dust and debris. The good news was that nobody had been injured during the hunt; the bad news was that the target had gone – and his escape made us edgy as hell.

Rarely did we get bogged down with problems of our own making, though it wasn't entirely unknown. I'd been on missions where one or two of the lads had become carried away and tried to overreach, or act heroically, usually after a job was nailed and a sense of overconfidence had crept in. Whenever our guard dropped, trouble tended to follow shortly afterwards. I remember one patrol where we were required to investigate an outpost and we walked on to the area early in the evening, kicking in doors and searching buildings while the sun dropped. There was a gunfight, but nothing too rowdy, and once the shooting had calmed down, we collared a couple of interesting prisoners for questioning. One unit even located a bonanza of enemy hardware along the way, including laptops, mobile phones, explosives and rocket-propelled grenades. It was quite a score.

Sweet, I'd thought as we wrapped up the job. *That was fairly easy.*

Perhaps a little too easy . . .

Somebody shouted over the comms: 'Squirters heading north! Give chase!'

'Squirters' was a term we'd long used to describe people legging it from a scene. Often they were vigilante farmers or stray fighters, and hardly worth dealing with. In some countries they might even have been kids fleeing with guns or ammo – that's how screwed up my places of work were sometimes. Giving chase wasn't worth it usually, especially if our prime objective had already been completed, and we often just extracted ourselves from the scene. But for some reason, on that occasion, the whole team gave chase, all of us running into a field of head-high crops, not quite sure where we were going.

Our pursuit led us into the unknown. Within seconds I was disorientated, surrounded by tall plants, my feet squelching in gloopy mud. I had lost sight of the other lads. The group was divided and in the scratching, grabbing vegetation it seemed impossible to detail any points of reference or head for one visual target. Then I heard the first fizz of a passing bullet, followed by the crackle and pop of an automatic rifle.

The shooting had begun.

Whoever we'd been chasing had turned, found cover and was firing wildly into the undergrowth. Three of our lads were hit almost immediately in the melee and everybody seemed to be flapping, caught in a state of confusion. Wounded soldiers yelled over comms for assistance, while the rest of us desperately struggled to pinpoint their exact location or the whereabouts of the shooters. Luckily, nobody in the unit had been seriously hurt, but they were banged up badly enough for us to require a casualty evacuation (CASEVAC) with a helicopter as the squirters escaped into the wilderness.

We had ballsed it right up. Before giving chase into the weeds, our forces had been in control. Intelligence had detailed in advance the buildings we'd needed to search, also establishing the anticipated number of enemy fighters on the ground. We'd held all the cards and fulfilled our brief in double-quick time – then we overreached. During the ride home, one look at our three casualties was enough to deliver a sobering lesson in how not to work in the wilds. But it could have been so much worse.

It could have been here.

It could have been now.

In the desert, my mind in bits, the operation was falling apart. This wasn't a swift, glory-packed adventure, the stuff of documentaries and embellished stories in the pub. We were bogged down in a messy gunfight, outnumbered and surrounded.

Away from the ditch, my team pushed through the trees and brambles, cutting across an alleyway that led to the heart of the compound. Positioned at the end were two fighters, dressed in dark robes and headdresses, armed with AK-47s, firing blindly at anything that might have been moving in the darkness. Without NVGs they couldn't see us, but we could see them. The team halted and everybody pulled in close.

'Right, let's just calm this down,' whispered a voice behind me. 'This place is all enemy fighters, so we can pretty much rip through the whole compound.'

With a few rounds, our two targets were taken down, but at the noise another figure seemed to lurch from a doorway, running blindly towards me in the black, an AK-47 in one hand, a wounded fighter slung over his shoulders in a fireman's carry. He aimlessly squeezed off a shot or two, hoping to hit something – anything – in range, his frame staggering back with the recoil. Off balance, he didn't stand a chance, but when our returning gunfire dropped him to the floor my stomach flipped. Behind him was a kid. A boy just four or five years old, standing there unharmed in the murky-green haze. He was clutching a dirty teddy bear and was draped in a worn-out old football shirt that dangled around his knees like a nightdress. His eyes looked jet black and unblinking through our NVGs, his mouth shaped into a silent scream.

Our intelligence was off.

'Wait! *Wait!*' someone shouted. 'There are still civilians here. Think about what you're shooting . . .'

There was no time to grab the kid as he ran away from the buildings and towards the trees for safety, no time to drag him to a secure hiding place or to console him; our route to the compound was now clear. With our path free, all of us sucked up deep breaths and regained focus in a few precious seconds of respite. Everything seemed to slow down very slightly. I advanced down the alleyway, checking for more shooters, only for a game-changing signal to come over the radio.

'Assault Team . . . *Jackpot*,' crackled the voice. Or, as it's translated in the military dictionary: 'We've got what we came for.'

All of us looked at each other. *No way! That's it? Job done . . .*

The operation changed in a heartbeat. Our aggression, a shared mood that had driven us into the heart of a hornets' nest outpost, killing several gunmen along the way, was turned off. Immediately our new objective became escape, without the horror of anyone losing a limb, or worse.

Let's just get out of here.

4

Everything seemed to pile in on top of us.

The sky lit up like a firework show in algae green. The enemy was angry. There were even more shooters now, but who could blame them for getting riled up and attacking in numbers? We had landed on their turf, ripped through their base, snatched what would have been considered a prime asset in the war we'd been fighting and wiped out a bunch of personnel in the process. They kicked back in numbers. Rounds seemed to strike at us from everywhere, and over the noise and roar of a heavy gunfight new orders came through. I was instructed to lead a group of soldiers towards a suitable landing area for the helicopters coming in and my team moved away from the compound, into the unknown.

When I remember back to what happened in those next few minutes, hacking through some unknown vegetation, the scene always arrives to me in snippets, like torn fragments of a photo being pieced together. I know we walked along another irrigation ditch in some effort to gain protection from the incoming fire, but in the darkness I had no real idea of where we were going. It was guesswork and whenever we pushed in one direction, a voice in my earpiece warned me to stop.

'Wait . . . *Wait!* Point man needs to halt. Four blokes setting up an ambush twenty metres ahead.'

I was point man. I was their target.

We doubled back, but the same warning came through again and then again.

I later learned that four hundred fighters had swarmed into the area. There were also pick-up trucks that had been loaded with weaponry, and they were firing at us from a distance. Armoured positions were now smacking our location with rockets, while mobs of gunmen swarmed into the foliage around the village like dogs on a hunt, sniffing out exactly where we were in order to cut off our teams, one by one. Stress crept in, the type of crap-your-pants stress that entangles itself around the limbs, lungs and guts, and in the tension I felt myself shutting down again. Dark thoughts peppered my thinking as I pushed towards any potential landing spot.

I don't think I'm going to get out of here alive.

This is it . . .

There was something different this time, though. My apprehensions were more reflective and fretful, almost final. I imagined home, the security of England and my first daughter. The possibility of not coming out alive seemed to burn at the edges of my emotions. I remembered my kid's face. *That smile. Her laughter.*

I don't think I'm ever going to see her again . . .

My stress was tinged with guilt. She was only two years old and had a birth defect. I often felt upset about the lack of time I'd shared with her. That was only made worse by the fact that in the beginning I certainly hadn't been as close to the family set-up as I should have. I'd become too involved with my job, consumed by it, but the military would do that to a bloke. I also hadn't seen her as much as I would have liked at first because of the split from my wife and I was staying away from the house. I was emotionally wounded and failing spectacularly to handle our situation in the right way. Whenever there was the opportunity to spend any time with my kid, or when it was my weekend for childcare, I spun out. I couldn't understand the issues connected to her illness. Meanwhile, she couldn't understand the pain and discomfort that was overwhelming her.

I became frustrated, often losing it over whatever was going on at the time. Weirdly, I was able to manage the other types of chaos in my life quite comfortably – a Royal Marine Commando speciality – so I should have been well equipped for domestic turmoil, but I wasn't able to get my head around her condition and her vulnerability. Still, whatever happened, she was my daughter. I loved her and I found it impossible not to think about her, especially during a moment where the chances of me seeing another day seemed to be shrinking with every footfall.

Please let me see my kid again . . .

According to my comms, the enemy had closed in even tighter. I tried to think of an alternative route for escape, but there was no way we were sneaking past four hundred fighters to some unknown spot two kilometres into the distance. Some of the lads had been carrying a dead teammate around for the best part of five minutes, and under heavy fire, too. There was a swift change of plan: our Officer Commanding called in the choppers.

'We can't get to you, lads,' he yelled. 'Can you pick us up from where you dropped us?'

The instructions sounded funny, like a punter dialling through to his Uber driver, but the reality was terrifying. We had already made a dramatic entrance, so I understood that our landing zone had been 'burnt', and the guerrilla force hunting us down knew the exact position of our previous drop-off point – this meant they could lay down all manner of misery and fire on the helicopters as we scrambled towards them for safety. Situations like that had been a problem for us in the past because our enemy were very quick at adapting. They had to be. It wasn't as if they were a superpower or an established state; they were underdogs, a loyal force up against very powerful people with the very best resources available to them. Vast sums of money had been pumped into the research and development of the equipment and techniques used by the British military, so the people we were fighting knew the only way of competing successfully was to learn and improve. Just like an animal that needed to survive, they often built desperately from the ground zero of their mistakes. They were always capable of surprises, and while a lot of the lads I fought alongside wouldn't like my saying it, I was sometimes impressed by their updated modus operandi. *Hats off to them: they're keeping us on our toes out here.*

It was true, too. They were forever watching how we operated and reacted accordingly. The very first time we landed a chopper, they observed what we did from cover, noting where we arrived and how we disembarked. The next time we dropped off our soldiers in the exact-same spot they attacked, killing one or two of our lads along the way. On some occasions they would fire at us from hidden locations. On others, they would booby-trap the area around a landing zone with IEDs. Once *we* knew that *they* knew an area was capable of taking helicopter landings, we avoided using it, conscious that something was probably waiting for us. It was almost impossible to utilize the same landing-area twice.

Not that our pilots seemed too bothered this time.

'Hunker down, boys,' came the call over the comms system. 'We're coming to get you . . .'

It would be a seven-minute wait. Seven minutes for the lads to gather together and construct an all-round defence; a loose circle of fire that downed anything moving across our path while we awaited the helicopters' low throb as they moved into earshot. Seven minutes before I escaped the dark thoughts tightening around me as my mind seemed to unravel even more.

Please let me see my kid again . . .

I heard their bullets first, then the sound of a Spectre gunship arriving somewhere in the darkness, smashing everything around it, the crew on board firing and reloading a light artillery weapon. Normally an indirect tool, which lobbed shells on top of its target, it had been retooled into a blunter instrument. A gunner fired it straight down the throats of the enemy below and the noise, impact and tremors ripped through the air in a powerful sonic symphony: first, the whip of a shell exploding from its tubing, then the slow, shrieking bomb cutting through the sky before landing with a low, powerful *WHOOSH!* as everything was blown to shreds in a sensory overload.

It wasn't long before I spotted our helicopters through my NVGs; distant at first, then more distinct as the trippy sparks of static from the rotary blades moved into view. But all that sound had given our enemy a position on which to focus their fury. Pretty lines of tracer fire zipped worryingly close to our rides, though at least the attention had been briefly drawn away from anybody on the ground. We approached the landing zone as a group, a laser beam lancing down to indicate our pick-up position. The triangulated stream of light from the nose of one of the choppers illuminated the smoke and cordite curlicues choking the air, the lightshow resembling the inside of a warehouse rave as my brain flipped from intense stress to the blissed-out euphoria of possibly, *maybe*, getting out of this nightmare. We raced towards the ramp knowing it to be our only escape-ticket home.

And then I was inside one of the helicopters, on the floor, listening to the sergeant major – the man responsible for making sure that no man had been left behind – counting us in as the barking bullets lacerated the ground around him. At some point or another most lads would have talked of wanting his job, if only for the pay grade. In that moment, however, not one of us would have traded places with him. Standing in the open, ushering soldiers inside, he looked exposed and vulnerable to any approaching shooter. *No thanks, mate.* Working as the last man on the ground was like shepherding cats through a sandstorm.

He was yelling now: 'Assault Team, do you have everyone?'

I heard shouting, more yelling. More pandemonium.

'Lads, keep the noise down on the radio!' he screamed, before completing one final headcount and signalling the bird upwards.

It was done. The Chinook began to rise, its incredible lifting-power seemingly vacuuming us skywards with some unseen force as the aircrew rinsed the enemy with rounds, our two helicopter gunners screaming at one another in relief and excitement as we moved out of range. I watched them as they high-fived and hugged, an adrenaline-rush spiking through them, but I didn't have the strength to share in their relief. I was laid out in the darkness, spent, my skin covered in dirt, blood and sweat, my flesh cut to ribbons from the vegetation we'd been pushing through. Hot air rushed through the helicopter's smashed-in windows, buffeting me again. Overwhelmed with the not-knowing of how I'd got out, or who I was with, the smell of aviation fuel was back in my nostrils.

Lucky, lucky, lucky.

I bumped the body lying next to me and looked over. It was Johnny, a senior soldier with a few more years experience than me. He was flat on his back, breathing hard, sucking on a water pouch strapped to his kitbag.

'What happened down there, mate?' I asked.

Johnny shrugged. Like most of us, he had heard only the basics: our mission had been nailed; in return we had lost at least one person, though nobody seemed to know who, exactly. He looked buzzed, his eyes wide with endorphins. We had done it. We were heading back to base. We were safe again. I wanted to feel the same high, a rush that always arrived when I'd successfully finished a dangerous job, but I was unable to suck it all in this time. The adrenaline wasn't there. Instead I felt numb and detached. Something unknown had happened; the push of a button had taken place in that ditch and on that walk to the landing zone, and I had freaked out momentarily in a flat spin of emotions that had never struck me before – not that powerfully, or viscerally, anyway.

I'd been thinking about Mum in the middle of a scrap. I'd worried that I might not see my family again.

Am I a mess?

Have I lost it?

The idea might just have changed my life for ever.

The storytelling began as soon as we landed. It always did – descriptions of near misses and tales of war wounds.

There was also a body bag to deal with. It was just the one, though, and it wasn't Dave who had been zipped inside – *thank God*. I'd already clocked him as we tore our kit off in the hangar, the pair of us laughing in relief behind our facemasks of blood and dirt.

'Mate, I was convinced it was going to be you,' he said, pointing to the black, soldier-shaped plastic sleeve being unloaded from the chopper. He had no idea I'd shared exactly the same dark thought.

So who had *been killed?*

Nick. I barely knew the bloke. He was one of the new lads, not that it made his KIA any less of a downer. While decompressing and showering away the dirt and battle and blood in the living quarters, one of his teammates had tried to process the death as we'd stood side by side in the toilets, washing our hands.

'Nick caught a bullet to the head,' he mumbled, looking a little frazzled. 'I tried to patch up the wound, but as I held his skull my thumb slipped into the hole. There was nothing I could do . . .'

Talk about an emotional overload. We had been rinsed, every single one of us.

There's no aftercare following a mission like the one we'd just survived – there simply isn't the time.

No *How are you doing, Sergeant Fox?*

No *Has anything upset you today, Sergeant Fox?*

And no *Have there been any issues after losing it in a ditch, nearly accidentally dropping a kid, and thinking you might never see your family again, Sergeant Fox?*

War doesn't give a soldier the opportunity to reflect too hard on his or her emotions. Instead we relived operations step-by-step in a debriefing session, the group hopefully learning from our mistakes, while noting the tactical gains in our successes. There wasn't a process for the therapy a normal person required when stepping in and out of traumatizing situations like we were in. The stress I had to deal with on missions was the kind managed alone, lying in a bunk while trying to figure out how the hell I was still alive. As for the wondering about whether I was a coward for thinking of home and my family when I should have been focused on the job? Well, that was all on me too.

The actions and tactical planning that led to our mission, and Nick's KIA, hadn't upset me. I didn't feel any anger. All of us understood that death was an occupational hazard in our line of work. Yes, we were risking our lives, but that was what the job entailed. In the same way that a fireman puts out blazes, we sometimes attacked enemy targets in high-pressure situations. I saw it as just another mission and wasn't bent out of shape about it – I didn't know any lads that felt differently, not publicly anyway. I also never took any notice of the political contexts in which we were working. An elite military group like the one I soldiered within was a strategic asset called upon by government ministers in times of crisis. At certain moments we were placed into warzones to deliver on a tactical level, but we might also deliver on a political level. It wasn't really worth thinking about the parliamentary side too much because governments changed and prime ministers came and went, but our role remained the same.

I hadn't joined the military out of patriotic desire, anyway.

I loved Britain, for sure, but I went into the job for the personal challenges it would bring me. Once I'd worked on a number of dangerous operations, I sold the idea to myself that I was protecting the people I loved at home by preventing an enemy from actively improving their reach and training to a point where they might have been capable of inflicting widespread damage upon the UK.

I had also built up a strong dislike of bullies. I'd been that way since I was a kid, and I believed that I was stopping oppressors from doing bad things. I'm aware of the simplicity of that thinking, but it's how I rationalized the unpleasant work we were doing at times. A number of conflicts I'd been inserted into had been debated in the media, and people argued about their validity until they became blue in the face, but I had to believe I was fighting the good fight. As a collective of blokes, we never discussed the morals of going into war. My only focus was the square foot in front of me at any given time, and the seconds ahead. Psychologically, the job was broken down into lots of smaller components. The bigger picture was always to neutralize an enemy force, and I and the guys I worked with were methodical, efficient and professional. Beyond that, nothing else mattered.

*

I got back to the base's sleeping quarters and dropped my kit on the top bunk, collapsing on the soft bed underneath, my body sinking into the mattress. It felt good to free myself from the weight of the backpack, my combat vest and a heavy weapon. I loved lying flat out following an operation. It delivered a few moments of calm as my back stretched and clicked after the physical grind of running around with all that baggage strapped to my body. The tension and adrenaline pinching every muscle seemed to slowly subside and it wasn't long before I had drifted off with the exhaustion. But it wasn't proper sleep. It was so rarely proper sleep.

My eyes opened a couple of hours later. They stung with fatigue as my brain raced, the stress and terror of that night mission again impacting on my synapses like a hundred mini breakdowns – that flashback to my life circa 1984; me thinking of my kid as the enemy came down around us.

Am I supposed to be feeling like this?

Is this normal?

I questioned myself and briefly wallowed in the doubt and self-loathing. *Mate, you're supposed to be a highly trained soldier, not someone lying in a ditch thinking about their mum. What a loser.*

I rallied and my mood turned defiant. *Stress? Not having*

it. That's a get-out-of-jail-free card for some people, usually when they screw up or lose it. Not you. You know what's right and what's wrong, and when you make a mistake you 'fess up to it. You're not going to say you've messed up because of some awful past experience or something you've seen in a battle, are you? Anyway, it only lasted a few moments . . .

Pride inevitably followed shortly afterwards. It often did. *Don't bother mentioning it to the other lads. It's not worth it . . .*

I was fooling myself, though, and deep down I think I knew it, too. That ditch and those moments of uncontrollable terror represented my psychological tipping point, like the final drops of beer that caused a pint glass of emotion to overflow, spilling on to the table and pooling slowly in a sloppy mess.

5

When people imagine the symptoms of post-traumatic stress disorder they usually picture the Hollywood version: a handsome but roughed-up Damian Lewis-type experiencing night terrors, horrific nightmares and the sweats, his character waking from a terrifying dream or thrashing crazily in the bed sheets and screaming the house down. Or it might be the clichéd scene with a veteran cowering underneath a restaurant table at the sound of a car backfiring outside (or a screaming baby, a dropped plate – anything noisy and unexpected), the classic, stylized expression of trauma etched into their face as he or she relives a gunfight or IED explosion, the mind unable to tell the difference between the present and a grim and gory past.

But PTSD isn't like that, not always, and not for me. It was slow-moving, sluggish. It crept into the corners of my life, enwrapping my mind and body, emptying me as I became detached, disorientated and indifferent to the things that ordinarily would have brought me happiness, such as my family, a football match on the TV, or a few beers in the pub with mates. Intensifying anger, anxiety and a lack of sleep only added to the internal dread that life had become a pretty rough ride.

Heavy slime, or gloopy treacle, oozing into every emotion and thought, clinging at the skin and adding pressure to the internal organs: *that's* what PTSD really felt like. It first clawed at me a couple of weeks after that helicopter ride to base, at home, in the not-so-Hollywood location of Poole High Street – a drab, pedestrianized strip of grimy chain stores, bookies and boarded-up shop fronts. I had been standing at a level crossing as I stared into a depressing parade of shop windows lit up with Christmas decorations, the street busy with shoppers, my mind a warzone away, back in the cluttered alleyways and squares of a hostile desert outpost, in the heat and in the stink of sewage and sweat. I was frozen. The world in Poole rushed around me at a million miles an hour. People with umbrellas, people wearing cagoules, people walking dogs all passed by in a blur, like one of those album covers where the lead singer of a band is captured in razor-sharp definition while a whirlpool of faceless figures swirls around their image. Only I wasn't a rock star; I was a soldier out of war, and not twenty-four hours previously I had been in the scorching sun at our camp, covered in sand and grime, packing up my kit, laughing with friends, feeling exhausted but looking forward to the long journey home. Now I was having an unsettling, almost out-of-body experience in the December wind and drizzle of Dorset. I felt light and wrenched from reality, the connection to my physical self somehow yanked away. Not that I understood the realities of my condition; I didn't have the first clue what PTSD might have felt like at that time, and it wasn't exactly a condition I'd have expected to take me down. Stress disorders weren't something that affected battle-hardened soldiers like myself – not that I knew of, anyway.

So what was happening to me?

Feeling a little bit moody at home wasn't a new sensation. In settled and safe domesticity, life sometimes seemed underwhelming and after a week in England I usually missed the chaos of war – ironically there was a weird order in conflict. War had defined lines in black and white, but in real life there were too many grey areas that messed with my head. In war, I knew that the enemy wanted to shoot me dead, so I had to shoot them first if I wanted to survive.

Even as I write that, I know it must sound horrible to people who haven't experienced combat, but it was a fairly simple rule to comprehend in the anarchy of a battlefield. I even liked the places we operated from. Dusty villages made up of claustrophobic alleyways and a confusion of maze-like streets, the perimeters dotted with food stalls and hanging linen. They seemed otherworldly, like something from a sci-fi movie, and flying over the desert in a helicopter, the burning fires visible beside the Bedouin tents below, was always a beautiful sight – until somebody decided to shoot at us.

It was only once I'd returned to The Real World that the frequencies of life wobbled at a different intensity. The rules were less defined, blurry, and the grey areas were difficult to deal with: an ex-wife that I still loved but knew I couldn't be with; a daughter sick with a birth defect, her distress breaking me into pieces whenever I saw her; a girlfriend who wanted to be with me, but I wasn't sure if my heart was in it. Then there were the texts, emails and bills to manage, and weeks and weeks of mind-crushing normality. Home life often felt destabilized and fraught with pitfalls, but this time my unease was different, an imperceptible nagging that something was off, a dark, unacknowledged shift – an ominous sensation. My dissatisfaction with the grey of The

Real World had hit me much earlier than usual, and with a worrying twist, too.

Could it have been the tour?

The realities of my latest stint in war were brutal: a grim, lengthy shift that had rattled my unshakable self-belief and left me drained and nervous. That had everything to do with the nature of conflict back then. The British military were fighting in several locations where the War on Terror had evolved into a series of intensifying guerrilla conflicts on different continents. The group I fought alongside had been called in to operate across all territories. Our work was secretive, highly skilled and demanding, and the load was taking its toll on some of the soldiers. The tempo of operations was high – too high – and the mood in the desert camp was dark when our squad landed several months earlier. Just days before our arrival, the soldiers we'd relieved had been attacked by enemy fighters. Apparently one of their units had walked into a daisy-chain IED that had ripped them apart, killing one and injuring ten others, the medical list comprising lost limbs, eyes, even the last thing on earth a man would want to say goodbye to. It was a horrifying mess, and when we arrived bright-eyed, bushy-tailed, eager for some action, we saw that the surviving lads were in a bad way. It would be just as dark by the time we left.

'We'll take you out, but we've had a rough time,' said the Officer Commanding as we worked through our handover details. That told me everything about their state of mind in the war we were fighting. He was a grumpy, bear-sized dude who looked like he would ordinarily have had little issue engaging with the enemy. Reticence was something that wouldn't have come easily. 'We've had one bad knock,' he continued. 'Fingers crossed we don't have another . . .'

Apparently the scrapping had become even hairier than ever before. Skirmishes were more frequent now and as a result the unit had been decimated; they were exhausted, morale was low. Nobody could blame those boys for wanting to get home without an extra KIA statistic or one more life-changing injury to worry about. The incumbent men had been pushed through the mill and wanted to get away; we were eager to get started. But some time later I understood their heavy mood. We were the ones feeling low and it was we who didn't want to tempt fate as our home date approached. By the end of that tour, we had experienced a serious casualty rate.

And some of the injuries had been horrific. A couple of blokes had been shot in the arms and legs, and there were life-saving procedures in the base's surgery. Others hadn't been so lucky. During one early-morning patrol, a small group of gunmen spotted us as daylight broke and took pot-shots from the top of a nearby hut. We ducked down into a slight dip in the terrain and set up an all-round defence, a small, tight circle of men covering every possible angle, but the bullets peppered the ground all about us, puffing up blasts of sand with the impact. There was a shout; one of the lads had been hit in the arm and was crawling towards a nearby derelict wall, the wound leaving a bloody trail in the dust and dirt. We gathered behind him, engaging the enemy as we moved, before crouching below a small pile of broken bricks. Almost as soon as we had found cover, the shooting died off. I took a second to make a headcount.

'Danny, Mooro . . . Where's Ben?'

And that's when I saw him: he was face down on the floor, a weird gurgling noise coming from his mouth and throat. Before we could call out, Ben somehow pulled himself upright and I spotted the ugliness of his injury. Blood and gore was splattered over his body armour and gun.

'Oh no.'

With two men down we had no option but to call in a 'Pedro', a CASEVAC helicopter worked by US forces, which was kitted out with all the drugs and anaesthetics needed to keep a seriously injured soldier alive. Surgeons were able to patch up the critically wounded on the fly, before getting them into a more stable environment. The Pedro pilots were fearless, too. They would happily swoop into a hot landing zone to scoop up the limbless. Often I would see them waiting at the base, radio on, whirring up their blades as the first sniff of enemy contact crackled over the comms. Some people thought they were reckless because their attitude was always 'Let's go,' regardless of the risks, but they had a determination to retrieve injured lads, wherever they were. We loved them. Whenever we had to dial up the Pedro call sign, they would show up all guns blazing.

Ben made it out alive, somehow, though his career was well and truly done. Not long afterwards Danny, an extreme-sports freak only in his mid-twenties, followed him home, though his injuries were the result of a split-second decision rather than an ambush. In the middle of the night we had been flown way out to the back of beyond, miles from our base, to search a small village for enemy leaders. Our group was dropped off a few miles outside the settlement and we walked in under darkness. I was tired, really tired – we all were – and as we located the small house where we understood one target was hiding, confusion kicked in. We knew the route to the building would be chaos because they usually were – doors led to cubbyholes, alleyways led to blocked-up doorways – and once we got inside those places the crazy architecture was often disorientating. Sometimes a room that led to another room would then open out to *another* room, and all of them were positioned in a straight line with no other entry points to be found. While I liked the weird vibe of the areas we were scrapping in, the not knowing the flow of a building unnerved me sometimes – it was like the TV show *Crystal Maze*, but a more hellish version. Often a hunting party couldn't get to the final room unless they had travelled through the three previous doors. That caused a lot of stress when planning how best to attack a compound safely. The general rule? Speed was key.

We needed to kick through the place quickly to maintain the element of shock. Our forces were gathered in a small courtyard. There was a door at one end and our hostile was somewhere behind it, perhaps surrounded by guards, perhaps sitting alone watching the telly or kipping – we sometimes got lucky and discovered very dangerous people in very mundane situations, but only if our footwork had got us in there quickly enough. We approached the home cautiously, quietly. Danny was point man – it was his job to kick the door in and to step forwards, which was always a hairy role because he would be the first person to cop a bullet if someone was waiting on the other side. A good point man had to be fearless, controlled, and, most of all, decisive. There was no room for hesitation or over-analysing. But as we gathered around the doorway, Danny paused. He was waiting, waiting, waiting. Maybe it was the fatigue. Maybe he was just having a bad night in the office.

One of the other lads hissed into his ear: 'Dude, let's go. Take the initiative.'

But it was too late. The upper hand we'd had before was lost and as Danny smashed the door down and stepped into the frame, his rifle pointing into the darkness, a loud burst of gunfire roared out. The shots rocked him to the floor like he was a heavy bag of shopping, and in that split second there was no doubt in my mind that he was dead. The poor fella could easily have taken three or four hits and the blood bubbling from his throat didn't look, or sound, good. In what must have been a fraction of a second, every-body stepped over his body and engaged the gunman, killing him in a flurry of bullets as a medic dragged Danny out of the way and worked on what was left of his neck.

Somehow Danny made it, clinging on to life in the heli-copter back to base, where he fell into a coma for ages. For months afterwards the poor sod was stuck in a hospital at home, living through a machine that worked his lungs. *One breath in, one breath out.*

These were the peak moments of stress that happened during that tour, but our work had been relentless throughout. There were operations just about every night and the engagements were often long and intense. Meanwhile, our night-time rescue mission – the one that had caused me to wobble so severely – had gained notoriety among the men working alongside us and the wider coalition forces. News reports spread word about the raid and everybody wanted to claim that they were a part of it. Some of the American pilots who were flying the helicopters had been shocked at its intensity, and one of the crew later retrieved an empty gun casing from the job; they commemorated their survival by having it engraved. Another was awarded the Distinguished Flying Cross, while some of our lads were awarded Military Crosses for their efforts in the field. A few young blokes who went on that tour are still in the British military now, but some others packed in the job afterwards, all of them affected by the slow, painful grind of those months in the desert. I certainly became more cautious in the immediate weeks after that particular battle. I thought long and hard about approaching rooms and how I was going to burst into them; I was a lot more methodical than normal. My reluctance to take risks was a new sensation for me.

Normally I went on tour knowing I'd be returning home in far better shape than when I'd left, both mentally and physically. I'd eat well, train well and work bloody hard; we rarely drank booze while we were out there and I always came home satisfied that the job had been successful. But that short period in my military life was very different. Everybody lost serious amounts of weight. We were drained, emotionally crushed, which was why expert soldiers became so close. The intensity of our work was incredibly stressful on the body and brain, and we had nothing else to occupy ourselves with between missions other than talking and opening up. Usually we gossiped about the mundane stuff at home, the normal things we couldn't wait to do, like an afternoon in front of the telly for a daytime marathon with *Trisha*, Jeremy Kyle and *Deal or No Deal*. From the sweat of a dusty bunk in a scorching hot tent, a bunch of men packed in together, even the idea of a stroll through the supermarket for a weekly shop felt restorative, like a sunny day on an idyllic Caribbean beach. From the desert, Britain sparkled in the distance, an oasis. Now, standing in the rain of Poole High Street, everything decorated in cheap fairy lights, home looked like hell.

And I had a bad feeling about everything.

Normally I would have been excited about my next assignment, itching to get back into battle almost from the minute I landed back in the UK. The fast turnover of war often required soldiers to go on tour every ninety days, but my next stint wasn't for several months and there was a long list of tasks to be completed in the interim – training, insertion practice (where I would be leading teams that were diving on to mocked-up enemy boats), a bodyguarding course, counter-terrorism drills, a commanders' course, and a lot of cool stuff where we played with boys' toys. On paper, all of it should have been exciting, but for some reason I just wasn't digging it. Part of that was to do with being at home – I missed the military life abroad. Despite the risks and stresses, the job gave me purpose and a sense of satisfaction knowing that I was keeping the people that I loved safe at home while working for my country in a role that carried kudos. I was an *elite fighter* – and everybody knew it, too. I was also an adventure junkie and the thought of action usually excited me. I had liked being scared; it made me feel alive. But now . . . *Not so much*. I was fed up at the thought of domestic training and I sensed a creeping mood of unease, some indeterminable worry that I couldn't quite pinpoint.

What's happening to me?

Where am I?

I was a zombie. I heard the chatter of town life blowing around me, the patter of rain hitting the pavement, laughter, and the *bleep, bleep, bleep* of a nearby pedestrian crossing, but I was rooted to the spot, unable to shift my focus from the future to the present. I was transfixed on my mood and the dark thoughts that seemed to envelop me. They felt like a looming black cloud out at sea, growing in size and advancing inland towards my position. I sensed panic rising and I wanted to run away, to escape, but to where? My body was heavy, as if my boots had been planted in quick-drying cement. It was as if any forward movement I might attempt would take me closer to the approaching cloud. I had to get out of its path, to hide, but I was trapped, boxed in by an idea I'd never really considered before.

I didn't want to die.

6

The following morning I walked on to base wondering, *Do the others feel the same as me?* It was hard to tell. The deeper thoughts of a battle-ready soldier were necessarily shut away, closed to the rest of an alpha male group that was institutionalized to prey on weakness from the offset, rooting out those lads incapable of completing the gruelling training phases taking place across bleak mountain ranges and, later, in the jungle's unforgiving humidity, where ticks, flesh-eating infections and foot rot were adversaries every bit as dangerous and demoralizing as an enemy attack. In those conditions, the soft-hearted fell away quickly. Only the mentally strongest qualified and joined the more expert section of the military where emotions had to be steadied. There was no room for moaning, anxiety or cowardice when things got really rough.

Man up, they said.

Get over it, they said.

Get some balls about you, they said.

Was the next tour my mortal P45? This thought had popped up briefly over the past day or so, but I could feel it pinned to my back now, like an unwieldy piece of combat kit. Maybe the idea was manageable, something I could push away. Besides, I knew the aftershocks would be far-reaching if I were to admit to the other lads that I felt a little banged up. I didn't want anybody to think that I'd lost it, or that I was getting soft. I certainly didn't want to be branded as such, or have my reputation tarnished, which is what would happen should rumours start flying around at the base. Were I to push for promotion in the coming years, I knew that any admission of mental stress would damage my chances of success, and even if I had thought something was wrong with my head, I wouldn't have admitted it to a psych nurse for fear of it being marked on my record, a permanent chink in the armour. For fear of my Officer Commanding thinking, 'Shit, Foxy's seeing a shrink? He's done then . . .' For fear of being rejected by the other men. For fear of being binned off the job.

But was this normal? Was I supposed to be feeling this way?

I settled into work with the lads at the base's equipment

cage, squaring away my kit from the tour, trying to scratch off the mud and grime that had drifted into the grooves and edges of my radio, my gun sight and my sunglasses. I looked at the others sitting around me, wondering, *Have they ever had the same worries?* I knew that soldiers weren't shut off entirely. Emotional intelligence was a key component of working with an elite military unit, but that was because we had to *control* our feelings. Aggression had to be turned on and off like a TV set. Hotheads were no good in a battle when a moment of crushed pride might result in the whole team getting killed. Meanwhile, moments of fear had to become an ally: the emotion was an indicator of stress and acknowledged as a very real and natural reaction, but ultimately I used it to sharpen my thinking and then it was compartmentalized and forgotten afterwards. I often noticed that whenever we soldiers talked together we usually went through the issues that were bothering us, maybe something about our wives or girlfriends, the kids, maybe money troubles, but it was done without feeling. The language was always fairly impersonal and the conversations never went too deep because to show sensitivity was to look weak.

A metal door clanged behind me. One of the new lads had stepped into the cage with us. I recognized his face but couldn't pinpoint the name – I'd noticed towards the end of the tour that I was struggling to remember minor details like that, which was frustrating the hell out of me. He began retelling an awful story to nobody but everybody about his ex and I recognized his harsh tone from the countless chats I'd had with teammates as we killed time between missions. The story described the collapse of a relationship, something that would have been a deeply emotional experience, except the words were cold and aggressive, as if he had been recalling another mission.

'Yeah, so that was that done then, I binned it off,' he concluded, like he was discussing his latest car breaking down, or the news of a boiler packing up. And as I sat there, laughing along with the other blokes at the awfulness of another grim, collapsing partnership, I contemplated what these same people might have thought about my moment of paralysis on the High Street.

But was I really different from any of them?

Throughout my military career, I never considered the idea that my mind might go before my body. I don't think anyone does. I also never used to acknowledge mental health conditions as being real. I had long dismissed the symptoms of PTSD as being nonsensical excuses for cowardice or weak will, and I hadn't believed in the issue of psychological problems within expertly trained soldiers, anyway. As a younger man, I even viewed the associated conditions of mental health as a cop-out, an excuse for any individual who wanted to cover up their failures, like those blokes who'd showed up at American draft offices dressed in women's clothes in order to escape service in Vietnam – a cover-up. Nor did I trust the idea of psychiatric care. Could somebody really pinpoint a person's problems by laying them down on a fancy sofa and asking them to open up about their mother-issues, to shift blame for their actions and mistakes on to a shaky upbringing? Whenever I had screwed up previously, in or out of the job, I'd raised my hand and admitted responsibility. *That will be my attitude again. I only have to refocus the stress – it will be a fleeting emotion, anyway.*

So I wasn't going to start crying now, not after a little wobble, something that was probably nothing in the grand scheme of things. Besides, reaching out for help wasn't something we did in the British military. If one of us had a personal problem we were expected to shut up and deal with it alone, which was a good attitude to have during the middle of a battle when there was no room for moping about. But that wasn't going to help me now, and I knew that even thinking about asking for advice would be a hurdle I'd find difficult to overcome. There was another worrying reality: I didn't want to experience a moment where I couldn't look the other lads in the eye because of my shame, or a perceived sense of inferiority. So I was going to man up and get over it. I was going to get some balls about me and forget about the dark shape forming on the horizon, the blackness growing ever closer, a nagging sense of dread, the treacle and the slime oozing into my body and mind.

That cloud. A darkness formed a violent and bloody world away.

7

My days back at the base in Poole became weeks, and with them the nagging, unanswerable and ever-amplifying worry, *Where had the buzz gone?* Nothing I could tell myself was ever enough to deliver a satisfactory resolution. I couldn't explain why my purpose in life suddenly seemed so uninspiring, or why my future felt so threatened. And I daren't ask for advice from anyone around me. I was alone, drifting in a vacuum where the thought of operating on tour with the military caused me to shut down. I became vacant and hollow. I felt detached, as if I were looking down at myself as I stumbled through my life at home, or during my working shifts on the base, training and drinking with the lads, while pretending to everybody that I was OK – even lying to myself if I really had to. I was a mess, not knowing what was wrong and certainly unwilling to consider the possibility that my mental health had been shot to shreds. Even saying those words out aloud back then was enough to rile me up. *Mental health. Post-traumatic stress disorder.* Those phrases really gave me the hump.

My environment was hardly conducive to moments of quiet reflection or self-discovery. Despite the fact that my missus and I had broken up a while earlier, I had kept the news quiet and was able to hold on to my place in what was called the 'married quarters', a two-bedroom terraced house on a crappy little estate positioned just outside the base. It was a perk ordinarily given to the hitched soldiers in the job, but I had the whole place to myself for only £100 a month, all in. It was a great way to save cash, but some of the other couples living in the street hadn't taken too kindly to my being there. I was a newly divorced bloke and having fun. Always on the beers and up for mischief, I even left the front door unlocked so other single soldiers I knew could use my place if ever they needed to. One Sunday morning I came home from a heavy session to find a weird scene unfolding in the spare room. A mate had pulled that night and had brought the girl back to mine for some privacy, though he hadn't bothered to tell me. When I walked in on them, bleary eyed, it was as if a little snapshot of domestic bliss had appeared in my house. She was wrapped up in a duvet, watching *Hollyoaks* on the telly, with a fresh cup of coffee on the go. He was hunched over the end of the bed, running through a series of reps with the dumbbells I often dropped there, his face screwed up with the strain. And when his one-night stand eventually noticed me eyeballing their strange scene from the doorway, her look of shock quickly turned into one of despair, as if to say, 'Yeah, mate, he really is doing that.'

Then there was the sex. Some of the lads had wives at home. Others were with long-term partners, and the rest of us were hooking up with local girls in Poole. Months away from intimate contact often proved a rough grind and some soldiers became grumpy while they were working under stress, a million miles away from Britain; or nervous, especially if they were worried about what their partners might be getting up to – it wasn't uncommon for someone to return home only to discover that their significant other had done a runner.

Before flying out on that last tour, I'd met a nice girl called Sarah. A cute blonde with a posh accent, Sarah was a real social type who was forever planning nights out and organizing parties. Our early dates had crackled; she was exciting, and everything had gone so well, especially the sex. But our relationship was cut short by another episode of war, and as I packed my combat kit again, I remember feeling fed up that I had been dragged away so soon. Another few weeks together would have been cool and I fully expected our short-lived union to fall apart while I was away. Luckily, Sarah was even keener than I was, sending texts and flirty emails to read as I waited between missions on that long stretch away. Even though I was still a little heart-bruised over a painful break-up with my ex-wife, I'd become excited about where things might lead with Sarah, and once I'd landed home she was on my case, looking to pick up from where we'd left off.

Sarah said she wanted me to meet her friends. Shortly after returning home, we arranged to get together at a club called Aruba, on the pier in Bournemouth. But when we eventually met up, the crowd Sarah had agreed to hang around with were even posher than her – proper blue bloods with some serious cash. That was fine, I was usually comfortable mixing with anyone socially, but something had changed. I quickly became unsettled once I'd realized that the only thing they were interested in was the unfolding war. They wanted to know about the gunfights and body bags. They asked about the various scraps that had brought 'Breaking News' headlines to the TV on a daily basis. They dug for gossip. I became uncomfortable when ordinarily I'd have made a fun night out of it, humouring them without giving away any national secrets – discretion was key in my job. Instead I closed down every casual conversation almost as quickly as it had begun, and wouldn't talk about my experiences. I wasn't interested in the war chit-chat, not with people who hadn't experienced it for themselves, and while trying to catch Sarah's eye I spotted a couple of familiar faces at the bar, some lads from the base. They were laughing and joking, smashing the beers back, and I slowly gravitated towards them, hoping for some respite, however brief. But almost as soon as I'd introduced myself, Sarah had collared me, dragging me over to meet yet another stranger. She frowned, probably noticing that the toing and froing had annoyed me, and because my attitude came across as mega-stand-offish. I understood why: to Sarah it seemed like I only wanted to drink with people that were like me, and she must have thought that I wasn't interested in her, or her mates, at all.

There is a cliché that's spouted about the disparity between military and civilian life; the thought that the men and women who haven't stepped foot on to a battlefield *just don't get it*. Sure, I know some blokes who won't mix with people who haven't served in warfare, because they're under the impression that they'll be misunderstood, or judged for the work they did and the lives they led. I felt different. My attitude regarding civilians had often been more under-standing: *I was the one who didn't get it.* I looked around at Sarah's friends and thought, '*I don't get them.*' It wasn't that they hadn't understood my life and circumstances – I didn't expect them to. I just couldn't tune in to the frequencies of a normal social occasion as I would have done ordinarily. For some reason, I felt awkward. Engaging with new faces on a normal level was a sudden hardship, a mission, and every conversation became weird and uncomfortable, as if it didn't really mean anything beyond the surface level.

I needed to feel uninhibited and relaxed for a while. I wanted to be free from the social niceties needed when meeting a bunch of strangers for the first time. I usually buzzed off drinking with new people, but instead there was an urge to blow off steam with lads that were like me – *the ones I really understood.* Aruba was a place that my team-mates had talked about longingly during our conversations about home life, usually as we dossed around the base. But when that rose-tinted fantasy had arrived, the reality of me drinking there with Sarah and her friends just couldn't cut it. Instead, I wanted to unwind with the people I had been fighting alongside for six months. I needed to relive the feeling of super-humanity that had fuelled our work. I had to maintain the kudos of being an elite soldier. Perhaps I felt more secure in that environment, or protected. Certainly, the thought of going back to war had unsettled me during those first weeks in England, but for some reason I still wanted to revel in the battles I'd survived. I needed to see if I could enjoy the high of action again. I was also annoyed by the idea of being just another bod in a nightclub, drinking crappy lager. After several years of combat it had undeniably happened: I was institutionalized.

I wasn't the only one. After only a couple of weeks at home, Christmas having been and gone, the common complaint at the base was that people were already bored of home life; they grumbled that their wives were driving them crazy or that they'd been in a massive argument with a girlfriend during the festive break. The men I knew sometimes found their escape by working in the equipment cages, squaring their kit away late into the night, not because they wanted to but because they couldn't face returning home to the mind-numbing normality.

One night I spotted a younger lad working there when everyone else had finished for the day.

'You packing it in soon?' I asked.

'Yeah, deffo, Foxy,' he replied. 'I'm just tinkering around for a bit, sorting my weapons out . . .'

Moments later I heard him chatting to his wife on the phone: 'No, babe, it's really busy at work. I'm going to be here for a couple of hours at least . . .'

I'd understood his behaviour only because I recognized it in myself. As a younger soldier working my way into the highly skilled units of the military, I had immersed myself fully into the culture and the job, and it quickly became all-consuming. Had I been a single man, that would have been OK, but I was newly married, and not long after I had successfully made it through some of the more advanced elements of training, my wife fell pregnant. I should have been supportive. Instead I was neglectful and disinterested in my domestic life, just hell-bent on being a success in the job. There were missions at home and abroad, increasing responsibilities and tactical or technical updates, and I was expected to be good at everything. Everyone around me had been good to work with but there was a competitive element within my group, and everybody wanted to move up the ladder and earn more money as quickly as possible. Neglecting my work in any way would have screwed up my career. I went on courses and stayed late at the base when I should have been helping out at home. Unsurprisingly, my wife became miserable, fed up with my bad attitude. I couldn't blame her; she was having a shit time.

When our first daughter arrived it was discovered that she had a birth defect. At first everything had been cool. My wife had gone through a C-section, which went well. But my baby girl was small, really small, and at first she struggled to take in oxygen. The nurses panicked, moving her into an intensive care unit immediately, and she later spent several months moving between hospitals in Southampton and Poole as the doctors tried to help her. Despite the severity of our situation, I acted like an idiot. I saw family life as an inconvenience at a time when I really wanted to get my career on track. I was non-committal and nowhere near the family man I should have been. If I wasn't at the base, or studying on a residential course, I was serving away or working on a mission within the UK. A lot of the time my missus didn't know what the hell I was doing, which must have done her head in because it wasn't as if I'd been pulling cats from trees or styling hair. I was working in dangerous conditions that easily could have got me killed. The work rate was unbelievable, too. Some people thought that soldiers in my line of duty swanned around all day, only moving into action during moments of intense conflict, but believe me, the job was draining, both mentally and physically. When it came to my family, I was a shadow, and the nurses in the hospital resented me for it. I didn't like them very much either.

When my daughter was well enough to be at home, the troubles continued. My thinking was all wrong and I raged internally about having to help out with our new baby. *Bloody hell, I'm just getting my teeth stuck in to the job I've always wanted to do and then this happens. I'm trying to bring money in for the family – why should I be at home?* It was a selfish stance to have taken – I realized that much later – but the counterargument was that I'd had little room in which to strike a balance between the military and home. The career wanted every piece of me, as did my family, and I had trouble locating the middle ground. The arguments became intense. We both said things that we would later regret.

The war life never seemed to let up, either. In 2005 I completed my Junior Command course, a cycle that promoted me to the rank of corporal. Not long afterwards I was voluntarily flown out for a nine-month grind abroad where I trained local forces looking to contain a growing insurgency threat. With the British military involved, the training imparted upon those dudes was as good as anything I'd experienced in the UK. We conducted live firing drills as helicopters swooped overhead, eventually helping the troops to tear up a series of heroin labs while apprehending the big players in a flourishing narco trade, which eventually proved to be a lost cause.

I then extended the tour, which really upset my wife, but when I came back everything seemed to be cool for a while. Before long, though, I was away on duty again, getting into scraps with local guerrilla forces. Up to a point, the attitude among the locals towards us was fine. I remember a few rocks being thrown our way once, the missiles lobbed by a gang of bored kids. But the high jinks were short-lived and eventually the conflict intensified. The people living there began viewing us as an invading force; they believed we were looking to take over, and became angry. There were riots, ambushes and IED blasts. Those attacks changed the British Forces' role for years to come. The scuffles seemed to increase in frequency and intensity. I remember one mission in 2007 when a simple job to destroy an anti-aircraft gun was ramped up into a six-hour shoot-out. A year later, we were scrapping all the time, our encounters were making the national news, and everybody at home understood the danger we were in – most of all my wife, who was thoroughly fed up with the stress of caring for a sick daughter along with the headlines that may or may not have directly involved me. My phone calls home began to feel empty. I scanned the last Valentine's Day card I'd received from her to find some deeper meaning in the writing, but there was none. Before long, we had broken up.

The split put me in a bad place. For ages we tried to mend the destruction, but resolution seemed impossible and I realized my bad attitude during those first few months with a newborn baby had caused a lot of irreparable damage. Inevitably, one of us was bound to meet someone else, and the news she had started a new relationship came to me during the build-up to a mission. We had flown to base for some quick maintenance fixes on our helicopter, and with 45 minutes to spare I commandeered one of the vehicles that were always on standby for us, driving past the camp's precinct of Westernized junk-food outlets and into a welfare bank that was equipped with laptops. The emailed news that she was seeing someone had been delivered anonymously. I called her, a barney breaking out almost immediately, but our dispute was interrupted by a shout from outside the building: *Foxy, we're going!* And I moved into the operation, fuming.

Relationships for soldiers like me – and their partners – often seemed like rough work, and it would be the same years later as, yet again, domestic happiness proved harder to navigate than warfare, and during that Christmas in Poole, the balancing act had seemed almost impossible. On the rare occasions that I'd agreed to some quiet time at home with Sarah, I became uncomfortable because I wasn't very good at giving affection. I was terrible at it, in fact, and I wouldn't tolerate any kind of grumbling – about her work, her issues with an annoying mate, her feeling tired – even though I was probably moaning a lot myself. I felt uncomfortable in very comfortable situations, such as a night in front of the telly with a bottle of wine, and I would find a way to escape or to screw it up somehow. When the rows inevitably followed, I closed down. I couldn't be arsed to talk about the flare-up or to locate the catalyst for what was causing me to feel that way, but big arguments hadn't been an uncommon occurrence in my past relationships, either. Whenever I was preparing to go away on tour, a simmering disagreement at home, when I was married, would often explode into something much larger. Whether I had started it, or my ex-wife had, it didn't matter. The stress of an impending period of time apart caused tension, which led to arguments, and then to tears. I was also terrible at de-escalating those situations because they seemed so inconsequential compared to the conflicts I had to negotiate at work, and so I let them drift, unresolved, leaving the root cause to fester for months on end. Weirdly, when risks were amplified, when bullets flew around during missions, I switched on. Whether that mentality was a character trait that had made me ideally suited to a life in war, or if a life in war had made me that way, is still a mystery. I was trained to manage all sorts of nightmare scenarios in combat, but nobody had trained me how to react in a crisis at home.

I was the same whenever my parents became emotional – I shut down. Mum and Dad had been very understanding of my career choices. Mum had been in the Wrens, and despite the fact that she had a very worrying nature she was very pro-military, having served in the Royal Navy from the age of seventeen. Her dad had joined the Navy during World War Two as an engineer and retired as a lieutenant in 1977. Meanwhile, Dad had served in the Marines like me. His dad, my grandad, had been in the Royal Signals while my nan was in the Women's Royal Air Force. She often told me about the terrifying occasions during the Battle of Britain when she was dive-bombed by German Stuka planes and had to run for cover. Despite those shared experiences, Mum got really upset whenever I went away on tour. Before one trip, word filtered through that one of my mates had been blown up and killed after stepping on an IED. My brother was also in the military and had been away at the same time. The culmination of all of that must have freaked her out and she started crying as I went to leave.

I brushed her off. 'Mum, what are you crying for?' I said. 'Stop it!'

I was out of order, but it did my head in whenever the family became emotional. Maybe it was a coping mechanism.

With Sarah I'd been behaving in much the same way and we had broken up within a month or two of my being back at home. The fall was instant, and I quickly locked myself into a destructive cycle, using booze to blot out my psychological issues, to help me ignore the emotional trauma and temporarily escape that heavy, looming storm cloud that now seemed to trail me wherever I went. Working out intensely in the base's gym during the day often helped, too, because it gave me enough of an endorphin-rush to reduce the depression. I was able to function at work, though on most mornings I got up at five thirty, hungover, a banging headache forming as I groggily attempted to grasp at the events from the previous evening, shying away from what might have happened, feeling terrible but craving the next opportunity for a boozy session, all the while moving through the day's tasks with ease. I found it easy to go on benders in Poole because loads of young lads lived on the base and they were always up for having a heavy night. Escapism through alcohol was an all-too-easy exit route for me, and I leapt for it whenever I could.

Masking my drinking was easy, too. I was in really good shape because of all the exercise I'd been doing; if I couldn't work out in the gym for a solid three hours, I broke up my sessions throughout the day. That was easy because keeping up a supreme level of fitness was a major part of our job (no Officer Commanding wanted a porker on their team, someone who might become physically exhausted during a raid) and there was ample time to train. After the day was done, I returned home and ate a healthy meal, always making the same thing – some lean protein, like salmon or chicken, with some vegetables, something I could cook up really quickly. If I hadn't planned to head out for the night, I would drink a bottle of wine on the sofa and go to bed, doing it all over again the next day. At those times I often spent way too much time alone, swamped in solitude and living in my own headspace, which probably wasn't a great place to be. I was fast becoming an emotional mess, unhappy with my present, confused by the recent past, and nervous about what might be an unwelcoming future.

The only things stopping me from falling deeper into a mentally dark place were the bonds between the lads in the job, the booze and the exercise, but ultimately those habits and routines were merely papering over the cracks. Deep down I was in turmoil. I rarely slept well, which I initially attributed to the rhythms of war and the work routines we'd operated under whenever we were on tour. Getting up in the middle of the night at the news of fresh intelligence, running a hectic night-op, then grabbing small chunks of rest on the helicopter back to the base, had screwed up my body clock. After those missions had finished, once we'd landed safely, I'd usually drop off my kit then go to breakfast with the lads in an attempt to unwind from the latest gunfight. We then showered and went to bed, grabbing three or four hours' sleep before waking up to train, and to plan the next mission.

My mind was too busy to relax and I believed those unsettling processes might have carried over into my home life. But I had also developed a really short fuse. It took very little for me to blow up in frustration, even at the smallest setback. Violence never surged to the surface, I was only ever irritable and angry, but before long I was nicknamed 'Flashy Foxy' because of my explosive temper. Every outburst gave me another excuse to hit the booze again as I was dragged, oblivious, into a spiral of self-destruction.

8

Remaining focused was important. I knew I couldn't piss away my career and there was plenty to be getting on with back in Poole. The admin was overwhelming, new kit had to be picked up and integrated into our working practices, and there was a timetable of courses to be completed.

Still, something wasn't quite right. I usually enjoyed the work, for sure – I was doing cool stuff, as always – but this time my head felt fuzzy and my attitude was bad. The adrenaline wasn't there like it had been before, and I knew it, too. I could see it in myself, and the understanding that my enthusiasm had slipped began to piss me off even more. I'd never struggled to motivate myself for work previously, but now I was forever whinging, which wasn't a good look. I was a senior figure in the job; a lot of the younger lads looked to me as an example of how to work. But I didn't care.

I couldn't give a crap about what I was saying during instruction sessions. I bitched and griped about some of the practices we had to execute as part of the preparation for our next tour. I questioned the logic behind some of the courses we had been asked to attend. Rather than putting on a show of maturity and dedication for the less experienced lads, I tore everything down. I declared the work to be 'shit', and I realized that I liked moaning more than ever before. It became a cathartic release for me, as it was for most soldiers. We've long been regarded a cynical bunch anyway, and there's often something to complain about, though not all of it is warranted. But now I was complaining about *everything*, when the position I occupied required me to be inspirational. I also needed to stick up for the people above me, blokes who were making the decisions I might not have necessarily agreed with. My overwhelming feeling was that the joy had been sucked from the gig and I was unhappy with work as well as my personal life. *But why?* I had wanted to be a soldier and a member of the British military from the age of fourteen, and yet I was digging deep to find the happiness and satisfaction even when we did cool stuff. The feeling of excitement had gone from my life and the realization depressed the hell out of me. The thought of being depressed then destabilized me even more.

Every course, every task, seemed to muddle into one whole, and I found it hard to concentrate on what I was doing, my thinking dulled by some unknown chemical reaction. My bad moods came to a head when I was tasked with leading some younger blokes on a counter-terrorist exercise in conjunction with the police. The lads were new to the job, excited to be part of the elite and raring to go. For some of them, this was their first opportunity to join a rapidly paced operation where people were fast-roping on to buildings and firing while wearing the scrapping kit – combat vests, respirators and balaclavas.

Their adrenaline levels were up, and everyone talked excitedly as we blue-lighted our way up the M3 from Poole to London. Some of the newer faces were edgy, not because anyone was under the impression somebody might die during the day, but because it was the first time they'd worked under the highest levels of expectation. Executing was the key factor on that day and the biggest fear was screwing up in front of the other men during what was a very technical operation.

In the firing session, we were called upon to move down

corridors as a team of guys, taking out open and closed entry points, both as individuals and as a body of men. There were specialized moves for each task and they had to be nailed to perfection.

When the action started, we kicked in doors, fired rounds and completed a fairly routine day without too many hitches. However, given this was the British forces, there was always something to be critical about, and anything less than perfection had to be deconstructed in detail. Afterwards, the group gathered in a big assembly room, everyone sitting on what looked like school chairs as a sergeant major walked around while giving the wagging-finger treatment to those soldiers who hadn't quite performed to the expected level, or had made a minor mistake.

'Listen, you've screwed up on a few things,' he said. 'In a real-life situation you can't do that, there's no room for error and life will get messy. I'm going to hand over to Foxy who will talk you through some of the stuff you need to improve upon . . .'

The words hit me like shrapnel. I had been daydreaming and felt sluggish, as if I'd just been woken up from a deep sleep. *What did he say?* I had been wallowing in how bored I felt. *I can't be arsed with these operations any more.* The monotony of familiarity and routine had kicked in. *I'm just doing the same crap over and over again.* And the excitement of jumping in and out of action and dealing with a pretend terrorist attack was lost somewhere. *This is a pain in the arse.* The thrill had gone and the loss of enthusiasm had put me into a stupor, but the sergeant major's introduction was a rude awakening and I was dazed by it. As I rose to my feet, I was unsure of where I was, or what we had been doing.

I had lost my military mojo.

I looked out at the faces staring back at me as I composed myself and ran through a mental checklist of everything we had worked through during the day: *the car ride to the target site; the entry points to the building; the men descending on ropes above me, under the roar of the helicopter's rotary blades; a blur of kicked-in doors and shouted instructions, gunfire and explosions over and over and over.* I could see the emotional high of military action sketched across their faces as they watched me opening and closing my mouth, mumbling vague criticisms of their work. They were buzzed with the excitement I'd once felt on the job: revved up, high at the operation they had just completed, living the fantasy of it happening for real one day, them charging across a city and bringing down a gang of bad dudes before they had the chance to commit some atrocity, or major attack. All of the soldiers had arrived from conventional military backgrounds and completed advanced training, some of them more recently than others. I also knew that nearly all of them, had they been any cop, would have wanted my senior position if ever I decided to move on.

My attitude?

You can have it right now. Just take it . . .

I was indifferent. I had suddenly lost the will to compete. And that was the most threatening wound to any soldier of my expertise.

9

There were others more roughed up than myself.

Danny was in a bad way and there was nothing that could be done to emotionally turn him around, not by me and certainly not by anybody else we worked with. Once he'd emerged from his coma at the base hospital and been flown home for a period of intensive medical treatment, the doctors had delivered a crushing blow: he was paralyzed from the neck down, with no chance of ever walking again. He could forget a miraculous reprieve, or some stupidly expensive operation in the States. Danny's spine had been wrecked by a bullet, and though the medics had somehow managed to work simultaneously on his vertebrae and his vital signs as they helicoptered him away to safety, his world had changed for ever. An impressive military career was done and Danny would never get to carve across an expanse of fresh powder on his skis or snowboard, which was the thing he'd loved the most away from his life in battle. The rest of Danny's days must have seemed pretty horrendous to him back then. God knows what that must have done to his head.

He was respected, though; which, while not being anywhere near a cure-all tablet in crisis situations, meant a lot to a soldier in Danny's line of work. If a bloke was regarded as being good at his job and capable of working on the battlefield under the most extreme circumstances then it became a badge of honour. Often, it was enough to cover up a multitude of sins. Everybody knew that the lads were capable of doing bad stuff while they were away on tour, like neglecting their families at home; some men had short fuses and were forever getting into scrapes when they were on leave. All of us had character flaws – I know I did – and some of the blokes fighting alongside me were really horrible people – headcases I'd have hated bumping into away from work. *Proper nightmares.* (Small spoiler: not everyone in the job was on best-mate terms with one another – not like it's portrayed on the telly. It's quite the opposite in fact.) In war, though, short tempers, violent streaks and domestic issues didn't matter as long as everybody worked for each other and we were able to implicitly trust the blokes alongside us during a gunfight. The worst crime was always to create suspicion or doubt. Inside the bubble of the military, there was no room for failures or for people who were prepared to pull the wool over a teammate's eyes. There was no time for backstabbers.

Some of the team I'd regarded most highly in the job were people I couldn't stand personally. But Danny wasn't a bad bloke, he had a good working reputation and at the relatively young age of twenty-five he was already an interesting character, in military terms. Danny had been able to operate both efficiently and ruthlessly on missions while somehow staying mates with everybody around him. The group had warmed to Danny almost as soon as he had passed out from training, and now he was attached to a tangle of tubes and drips on a hospital ward in Poole, his lungs expanding and collapsing through a machine, paralyzed from the neck down.

Even though Danny was the one in pain, I sensed a weird anxiety in myself as I drove to the hospital to visit him one afternoon. There was something about talking to him again that unsettled me. As I walked towards his room, I knew he was going to be mega-happy to see me and I'd heard he'd been enjoying a craic with the other lads. But what would Danny be like, really? What state would his head be in? I felt confused, not sure of how to act, or whether to discuss his injury and the life he'd once had.

What could I say to a bloke whose life had been ripped to pieces by a bullet?

'Mate, how's it going?' I asked quietly, pushing open the door to his room and assessing his immediate situation: the hospital furniture, his surroundings, a stack of magazines and books on the nearby table. A clipboard with pages of undecipherable notes hung at the end of his bed.

It didn't look good. Danny was in a bad way. His skin was pale, bandaging covered his throat and his body was hooked up to a bank of beeping machines, drips and a ventilator. Unable to move for months, his buzz cut had grown past his ears. When I'd last spoken to Danny we had looked fairly similar: short hair, the whites of our eyes reddened and our stares sunken by battle fatigue, we were tanned from the desert sun and had beards of varying length. For a pair of blokes situated in the middle of a warzone, over weeks and months through the tour, we would have appeared in fairly standard shape – tired, ragged, but still up for it.

Danny looked up. His eyes flickered with excitement, a broad smile breaking as he stifled a laugh, which must have yanked on the gruesome wound across his throat. The last time I had seen him was a grisly nightmare and the events seemed to rush back to me at once. The shot had dropped him to the floor like a sack of bricks, blood bubbling from the hole in his neck, a medic frantically trying to stem the flow of red as we instinctively looked for our target. I honestly thought Danny was dead; I certainly never expected to see him again, let alone talk to him or shake his hand – nobody had.

A few days after Danny's shooting, the Officer Commanding called our team together at the base to update everybody on his condition. The prognosis was troubling. By rights he should have been gone already.

'It was bad,' he said. 'Really bad. We're not sure if he's going to pull through . . .' Tears had welled up in the OC's eyes, which none of us had ever seen in such a senior officer before, but it was testament to how highly regarded Danny was.

As we talked through the attack, I couldn't tell you how Danny might have felt about never having to experience war again, but I had a pretty good idea: he probably would have done anything to get back out in the fight, because blokes like him, and me, usually missed war when they were at home. There were good reasons for that desire, and it wasn't the killing or the violence. A bond developed between men, and women, working together under extreme circumstances – like fast-roping ninety feet out of a helicopter on to the bridge wing of a targeted tanker, with another 200 foot drop below that, the wind yanking at the cord, bodies barely attached to the line as they shot down into the darkness. In war, every moment of conflict seemed scary, some more than others, and during those flashpoints unions were formed, connections between colleagues that were made all the more vibrant because of our intense surroundings. We often referred to that sense of union as 'The Brotherhood', and when we were away from it there was an unexplainable feeling of loss.

But during war itself, The Brotherhood was almost unseen. It fed into the subconscious, but the day-to-day conflicts and skirmishes still became hellish after a prolonged period. When Danny had been shot, our group was near to the finish of a very long tour. The first half had been great – we were all keen. The following month or so had been challenging – but we were still good. By the end all of us had started counting down the days until leave and I was enviously watching the soldiers who were finishing their shifts and flying out of the war towards home, thinking, 'the lucky bastards'.

That's where we were when Danny's injury had happened,

shortly after the helicopter mission, our boys approaching the end of one of the longest tours any of us had ever done, all of us having tempted fate with the amount of near misses we'd already experienced during a succession of conflicts and gunfights. Like the warning that 30 per cent of car crashes happen within a one-mile radius of the driver's home, because of fatigue and a false sense of security, we were now vulnerable. Knackered. Maybe some of us became prone to switching off. After all, England was in sight; our guards were down so accidents happened, which was depressing. There were so many times during my career when, after learning of another fatality, I'd hear the words: 'And he only had a couple of days left 'til leave . . .'

'Do you remember what we talked about just before I was shot?' said Danny, voice rasping, his vocal cords lacerated.

I reached through the places and dates, where we were, what we might have been doing . . . *The TV room!* A daytime mission had just been aborted and a few of us were taking shelter from the sun. We were hanging about in the base, killing time, talking darkly about what we would do if one of us were unlucky enough to get blown up and lost in a coma.

'Shit, yeah, mate. I do . . .' It had been a heavy

revelation, something that movie directors would probably call 'foreshadowing'.

'I said that if it happened to me and I'd lost an arm or a leg, I'd want the life support machine turned off, didn't I?' he said, wearily. 'But when I came around and figured out what had happened, that was the last thing I wanted. Then I remembered the chat in the TV room and I freaked out, thinking a message might have been passed down the line, you know, about what we'd talked about – that I'd want them to turn the machine off. At first I couldn't talk. I could only move my eyes. And every time I saw a nurse walking towards me, I went into a flat spin, because I couldn't communicate. I was terrified they might switch me off for good.'

It's impossible to gather together all the personal emotions that would have taken place in my head during a frantic incident like the one that wrecked Danny's life. It had only lasted for a split second. As always, I'd experienced a rush of adrenaline at the sound of gunfire, but there wasn't enough time to register the emotional surge; the noise dominated my thinking. Was there a sense of relief at eventually getting the target we had been sent there for? Probably, but there was no backslapping that night, we didn't have the luxury of time and our gunfire had stirred the rest of the village; wall snipers began laying rounds down on to our position, and with two men required to drag Danny's lifeless body from the scene, we were suddenly stretched. I could hear it kicking off in another building on the other side of the outpost, too. Really, there was only one brutally honest assessment of how I would have felt in that situation, where someone alongside me had been shot: it was a rush of excitement, in a very short, concentrated burst.

That reaction wasn't a freak occurrence. In the past, whenever a teammate had been hit, dropped to the floor, shouting and screaming for help, I would think, *Bloody hell, this is real – but it's a buzz.* Then the reality of my situation always kicked in, my training too, and I would turn off any surplus emotion. Distracting thoughts were extinguished, such as whether the injured were OK, and if they were going to live or die. Even when friends were killed in action, any feelings of loss were sidelined; the grieving always came much later and never really for long. I often brushed the heaviness of death aside by thinking, *Right, that's shite – let's crack on now.* Bottling it up was yet another coping mechanism for a human mind caught in horrific circumstances, but during that chaotic minute or so, walking away from Danny's crumpled form, our job done, something else had welled up, a feeling I had forgotten. It was coming back to me now.

For a moment there, I had been frightened, really frightened.

That was another moment of vulnerability. Even after that freak-out in the ditch . . .

As I sat with Danny, telling him about the remainder of that day, I seemed to be reliving the emotions of those mental few minutes. I had later crawled behind a wall for cover. The gunfight had been dialled down a notch, our battle simmering to a few small pockets of contact, the gunshots ringing out from the other side of the village, but despite my relative safety I felt a strong urge to become *even safer.* I wanted to be in a position where I could see everything going on around me – the movements of any approaching enemy soldiers; where my teammates were; all the exit points – without being spotted by anyone else. I was scared, really scared, and I had an overwhelming belief that I was about to get shot. It was the wrong thought, for sure, one that could have brought up all kinds of issues of self-doubt when I really needed to be calm and controlled, where my decision-making had to be tight, but I couldn't stop the weird tide of vulnerability from washing over me, wave after wave of it. Even though I'd been surrounded by The Brotherhood – a crew of expert fighters, each one kitted up with all manner of shock-and-awe weaponry – it hadn't been enough to reassure me.

Later that morning, as we were flown to camp, I had tumbled into a deep sleep, my Bergen rucksack propped up on the helicopter floor as a makeshift pillow. After what felt like only a few seconds of rest, I was woken by a couple of the blokes shaking me violently. In a dazed state, my first reaction was to assume that another gunfight had kicked off and that somebody had attacked us, so I lurched upright, but the chopper was still, silent apart from the sound of footsteps clanging down the landing ramp. We were back at the base, the boys were packing up. I was half asleep, my eyes barely open, but the two lads looming over me seemed freaked out.

'*What?*' I snapped.

'Mate, we've been trying to wake you up for the past five minutes,' said one of them, laughing nervously. 'We thought you might have been dead! You looked pretty out of it . . .'

I pushed them both away as I stood up and collected my kit together, murmuring a thank you. I figured I was OK; a headstrong, indestructible individual. A little bit beaten up by the latest operation but not exhausted or broken down by a gun battle.

While sitting alongside Danny's hospital bed, the first

suspicion of my current mental state had kicked in. Was the sensation, the fuzziness that I had been carrying around with me all these weeks, actually terror, after all? Fear had never clung to me before, I was able to shake it off and move on ordinarily. But this time, was that weakness staying with me? I tried to forget the idea. I told Danny about the rest of the mission, a two-kilometre walk to another supposed enemy compound just as the sun had come up, the entire unit running through the heat thinking, *What the bloody hell are we chasing here?* And once our target, a large, ramshackle building, was identified, the team kicked in a door, only to find it had been a farmer's barn. It was full of cows and sheep. After calming down some fairly humpy locals, we were picked up and flown back to base.

The pair of us laughed at the story, but I was unsettled. With hindsight I should have seen the hazard lights flashing. I *was* wiped out. I *was* on the edge. And what I'd experienced was an unnerving sense of fragility played out amid the backdrop of war. My subconscious was warning me that I was in trouble and now the self-doubt was huge. *Why him and not me?* And *When will my turn come?* The Russian-roulette nature of our work had messed with my subconscious.

As I sat there in the hospital ward, chatting with a man who would never walk again, I was struck with the strange sensation that Danny would probably have quite liked the idea of going back to war. But I couldn't have imagined anything worse.

10

I understood that The Brotherhood was a pretty big deal in our line of work. It wasn't a union, or members' club, but a feeling, and a weird thing to explain to anyone unfamiliar with the rhythm of war and warriors. Whenever I tried to describe it to someone outside of the job I often compared it to a life jacket, something that had kept me safe during moments of turbulence, but I also remembered it as being a warm feeling, as if I had been wrapped up in a safety blanket. It represented a sense of security, and that understanding of stability came mainly from my position in war. I was surrounded by some of the best soldiers in the world, a group of people considered as being the elite in what they did, and I could rely on them whatever was going on, in any situation. And the fact that I was considered part of that elite group, and the idea that other people could rely on me, too, felt life-affirming. In those moments of self-doubt that can strike even the most confident of soldiers, I told myself, *Mate, you're good at a job where you have to work in some of the hardest situations any person could face, and you're considered capable of performing to the highest level. Love it.* That always gave me a boost.

Bonds of that nature could be found in all walks of military life, but nowhere else was there a group that had become as intensely linked as The Brotherhood that surrounded *me*. I had started out in the Marines, in around 1993, as a rough-around-the-edges teenager, and back then I thought it was an awesome unit to be a part of. And it was. Everybody was tight and there were a lot of friendships to be made, but it was a big organization and not everyone was expert – only a small minority were considered to be in that category and they often went on to bigger and better things. With hindsight, everything in the Marines was a little loose, but later, as I advanced and was introduced to the rigours of combat with the military elite, my role became more senior and there was kudos and there was camaraderie. My new teammates were better, faster, and stronger. *We were harder to kill.* I had some worries about going on to the ground for the first time. I knew I'd taken on a dangerous job but in those frantic opening seconds of my first gunfight, I wouldn't have wanted anyone else alongside me but the other guys in The Brotherhood. It was a close-knit weave and I was happy to be enmeshed within it.

Once a Royal Marine joined the elite ranks, he was made to feel welcome almost immediately. There was some grief dished out to newcomers, of course; a little joking but nothing too serious. As long as he was able to execute the job then he would find himself ensconced in the group pretty quickly.

There was no leniency for new faces, though. I had considered myself to be the bollocks for a while, but that was knocked out of me very quickly, my euphoria quashed by a wave of responsibility. The pressure to get up to speed was immense. Endless amounts of kit were thrown at me and I had to learn the intricacies of every part, like how to manage my assault vest and where I wanted to attach various pieces of equipment. How I wanted to fill each pouch was a constantly evolving task.

Amid the early chaos, I was given the role of optics rep, one of many important jobs, where I was to look after the military night-vision goggles, while making sure we were abreast with the latest advancements in optical gadgetry. If I'd missed the latest update in technology, people soon wanted to know why. If somebody borrowed a set of binoculars for a mission and didn't sign them back in to the inventory, it was my neck on the block. The equipment in storage was so expensive it was hard to get my head around.

The responsibility unsettled me at first. When I met with the former optics rep during our handover, we exchanged notes on the working practices. There was an aide-memoire – basically some laminated sheets of paper stuffed into a binder – detailing how everything worked, and I was filled in on the intricacies of the job. I had wanted to progress through the military ranks for the adventure and the action, but one of my many roles was clerical, dull as crap and ultimately stressful. In fact every bloke had a job to do that was administrative. It helped to ready us for promotion where our roles might become more logistics-based, but I wasn't the most methodical person at that time and I realized my attitude would need to change pretty quickly. Disorganization would prove costly, both for the group (when we were working – in or out of combat) and for my reputation among the lads, so I gave myself a psychological kick up the arse. *You've been given this job because they trust you to do it properly. Mate, you proved yourself in the training. Get on with it.*

And then I heard the dreaded words from our Officer Commanding.

'Right everybody, we're travelling tomorrow. Make sure your dive kit is ready.'

My bloody dive kit? Already?

One of the training sessions often bestowed upon the best Royal Marines Commandos in the British military was the boarding of mocked-up enemy boats on the move, and clambering on to them was a highly skilled task. Those sessions were demanding as they involved working with a small team, each of us swimming for a few kilometres at a time in icy temperatures while carrying heavy pieces of kit. The hardest part, however, was climbing on to the target. Scaling a ladder in churning, tidal waters with a heavy load strapped to your back was bloody hard work, and once we'd climbed aboard we were to fire live rounds at mocked-up enemy figures – it was warfare, after all. On the morning of my first week of dive training, it was snowing heavily. The flakes seemed to ping off the water, pooling into small, icy islands, and there was a sense of impending doom amongst the lads. Everybody understood how awful the coming days were going to be as we placed layers of warm kit under our dry bags (the military term for a dry suit), which we knew would weigh us down even more. Nobody said a word. The mood was bleak.

Once we had made it into the water I was battered by

the waves, and after reaching the destination it took me ages to climb the ladder. I was hyperventilating even before I'd hooked on to the side of the boat, and once I had climbed the first few rungs, a huge wave swept me to the side, twisting me at forty-five degrees, the ladder spinning and turning me this way and that. I tried to straighten my position but the tide kept pulling and churning, yanking me in circles. At one point I was hanging on to the underside of the ladder while trying to hook my legs around the rungs. I thought I was going to peel off; my arms were in agony. And then I saw the other divers working alongside me. They were scaling the ascent like it was no big deal, a pair of ninjas moving at rapid speed. When I'd finally made it to the top, one of my teammates hissed a not-so-subtle warning at me.

'You need to sort yourself out, Foxy,' he said darkly, advancing across the deck of the boat, though I couldn't see who it was through the facemask.

The comment jabbed at my insecurities a little bit. I decided to square myself away on the ladder over the coming weeks and I eventually became a good climber, but my issues ran deeper than a physical challenge. Back then I was aware that one of my weaknesses was a real fear of failure. I hated the idea of blowing it, and there were moments when I wondered if I was capable of keeping up with the velocity of elite training. Not long after our dive week had finished, another incident proved equally humbling, though I'm still convinced I'd been set up by the group as part of some weird induction prank. We were working on a live firing exercise on an old ship, moving from room to room, blowing stuff up and clearing cabins. At one point, forty blokes had squeezed into a room, all of us heavily armed. We were due to blast through a door before moving into the next area, firing as we went, but just as we'd set ourselves for the explosion, my shotgun jammed. I tried to re-bomb it, kneeling down and raising a fist to buy myself some time.

'Hold,' I whispered. 'Hold.'

I tried to force the ammo back into the tubing, but it wouldn't fix. *The bloody thing had stuck!* Thirty-nine highly trained Commandos were waiting behind me, poised for action, and yet I was struggling with the basics of reloading my weapon. I could hear the whispers of frustration. They were growing louder.

'Hurry up, mate . . .'

'Dude, what's going on? We want to move . . .'

There was a shout. Everybody froze. The senior officer running the training exercise strode over and grabbed my gun angrily.

'Let's have a look at this,' he snapped.

I heard him cracking open the barrel and popping the cartridge shells. There was groaning and griping around me.

'There's something wrong with the shotgun,' I said, defiantly. I was convinced it was faulty.

The instructor pulled out his flashlight and shone it into the rifle, sighing loudly. My heart sunk. He figured I had been in the wrong.

'Oh really? Maybe it would help if you'd put the rounds in the right way,' he said sarcastically, as the other lads shouted angrily.

'Who is it?' yelled one voice.

'Come on, which one?'

The instructor leant down. 'Who is it?' he whispered.

It's Foxy.

The abuse started immediately.

'Foxy? You knob!'

'*Muppet!* Bombing a shotgun back to front?'

Then I heard Chris, a mate from the Royal Marines, laughing loudly, pounding at the side of the ship with his fists, but I understood he was ripping into me more out of relief than anything else. I knew that because had the roles been reversed I would have done the same. We had been friends for ages and I was the dude who had screwed up in front of the other elite soldiers, big time, and not him; I was the unlucky one, though I'm still unsure whether the balls-up had really been my fault. (It was as if my instructor had decided, for a laugh, to make out the blame was with me, a new face, rather than the weapon.) Every now and then I tried to re-bomb a shotgun with the ammo pushed in back to front, just to check, but it was impossible. The cartridges wouldn't fit.

I had been stitched up good and proper.

11

I left Danny in his hospital bed, and I knew I'd been fearful, that my confidence had been rocked. *But how? And why?* I was so confused. Those sensations were new for me, in and out of war. I'd always revelled in combat and the heightened emotions that pulsed through a scrap or operation, and I was comfortable taking risks in my everyday life; I was rarely stressed out over issues away from battle. Meanwhile, the belief I was about to be killed had never struck me before, not even during my early gunfights, when everything had seemed so very unfamiliar.

My first full-on scrap had taken place seven years previously. Back then, I had been eager for it to happen. There was adrenaline and a moment of shock as the bullets roared around me, but nothing in the way of terror. I remembered that the shooting had come seemingly out of nowhere, which was probably how it went for most soldiers. Enemy fighters rarely allowed British forces the courtesy of a fair warning, or time, in the minutes leading towards a dust-up, and my introduction to fighting took place in a middle-of-nowhere town in a middle-of-nowhere waste-land as my unit made a routine patrol. We were working with a bunch of local soldiers, coaching them through the military basics in the hope that they might take care of their own business eventually, but there was a strange mood about the place. The area had been described as 'law-less' by senior officers; the Brits had never worked there before and in the days leading up to our arrival we'd received intel that local guerrilla gangs had been alerted to our activity and were unhappy. There had even been a propaganda campaign warning us that if we were ever to show up, we could expect to 'have the hell spanked out of us' (or words to that effect). I was always excited by threats – usually it meant something rowdy was coming.

Bloody hell, I thought, revelling in the potential of a bat-tle. *It might get tasty out here.*

Our work was due to last for a few days and the atmos-phere was fairly benign at first; civil, in fact. Very little seemed to be happening. A couple of local leaders even came out to meet us on the back of a pick-up truck, presumably to relieve their boredom. Dressed in robes, waving and smiling like representatives from a local tourist office, they guided us around the streets, pretending to be surprised by our appearance, claiming they were 'so delighted' to meet us Brits, cheesy grins and all. Nobody took that crap on face value, though. It was understood that a stack of AK-47s were positioned within reach, and everybody remained alert, but the atmosphere was still fairly agreeable. When we later stumbled across a small cache of opium, we left it alone for procedural reasons. In that neck of the woods, it was understood that modest batches of gear were used for currency.

I knew the matey vibe wouldn't last for long. A couple of days later, our team arrived in the same town at sunrise for more patrols and quickly became marked by 'dickers' on mopeds. They raced through the streets and alleyways at high speeds, churning up heavy plumes of dust, their noise changing the mood among the lads. I felt the tension rising without anything of note actually happening, but when we were later sent into the maze-like thoroughfares for a series of searches and door-knocks, the edginess intensified. Various major stashes were discovered: we found drugs in one hole, guns in another. Shortly after midday, several calls came through that two pick-up trucks had been burning around the streets with a mob of blokes in the back. One report claimed to have spotted machine guns, and despite the intensifying events I felt frustrated. In the afternoon sun it had become swelteringly hot and dusty. Meanwhile, the local soldiers I'd been working with had hardly proved themselves to be the sharpest knives in the drawer. I found myself explaining a number of basic procedures to them over and over as we set up a fairly simple defensive position in a large courtyard. Grumpiness set in. I was getting down, fed up. *Bored*.

Bloody hell, I thought. *Nothing's happening. I'm trained up for warfare. I'm itching to get into some sort of scrap . . .*

I turned to Mark, the other British soldier who had been working alongside me for the day, and moaned, 'Mate, this is mega-boring . . .'

He nodded, laughed, and sat against a wall, finding a sliver of shade in the heat. Mark was older than me and much more experienced. He had probably suffered this routine a million times before. Meanwhile, I should have known better than to tempt fate.

Dude, be careful what you wish for.

Our situation changed in a heartbeat. From across the town I heard the faint, skittering but oh-so-distinctive sound of gunfire. *Bup-bup-bup-bup-bup-bup-bup-bup.* Our troops had been dispatched into different locations across the settlement and some of them must have stumbled into a dust-up. *That pick-up truck, most probably.* Radio-crackle alerted us to an incoming communication: 'Contact! Wait out!' yelled a voice. And suddenly the rounds became amplified; they had moved closer. *BUP-BUP-BUP-BUP-BUP-BUP!* Our group was surrounded by four walls, each one probably twenty feet in height, which protected us from any stray fire, but I could hear the zipping bullets as they whistled overhead and bit into the dusty brickwork behind us. I readied my gun and ordered the local troops to fan out towards each of the several streets leading from the courtyard. The area we had positioned ourselves in was set at the heart of the town and all arteries fed into it.

Another call came through on the radio. This time we were informed that the other units were making their way to our centralized location and we should hold our position. I looked across at our defensive set-up and threw a wobbly. I couldn't believe the God-awful ineptitude of some of the inexperienced locals working alongside us. One lad was looking around absent-mindedly, slack-jawed, his machine gun drooping towards the floor, but as I started towards his space, yelling that he needed to get some brains about him and face forward, I heard the sound of an approaching engine. A battered pick-up truck with several enemy fighters hanging from the back had turned into one of the roads leading towards our position and was racing towards us, picking up speed.

Oh no . . .

For a second, I seemed stuck, rooted to the spot in surprise.

I was actually OK being bored, doing nothing, in a courtyard surrounded by idiots . . .

Here we go.

But the driver ahead seemed just as shocked by the encounter. He slammed on the brakes and reversed into a U-turn before heading away, with the guerrilla fighters positioned at the truck's rear directly ahead of me. Several of them shot wildly during the retreat, their bullets kicking up the dirt around my feet, and as I returned fire the bloke to the left of me fell to the floor, his gut torn through with bullets. The guy to my right was also rolling around, screaming in agony while clutching a wound in his leg. Somehow I had escaped unscathed. When I looked up, I caught a glimpse of the same clueless local soldier, still slack-jawed, his gun lowered. The idiot was staring back at me in disbelief.

'Shoot, you moron!'

The noise of gunfire was deafening. I moved across the road, meeting Mark, the pair of us blasting the speeding truck as it disappeared from view, overwhelmed by a rush of euphoria, relief and the just-under-the-surface stress of my first scrap. I had hit at least one enemy target and was struck by a huge surge of adrenalized satisfaction as the noise and dust of the skirmish drifted away. I'd dodged death, which left my head buzzing in disbelief, and I had fought effectively under heavy stress rather than spinning out. Right then I knew I had the potential to operate well with the people around me.

I'd always understood that how I handled fear in battle would define me as a soldier. If I treated it as a negative emotion, something to be avoided at all costs, I might fail or make a reckless decision. In those frantic seconds, I could have easily crapped my pants and gone into a flat panic – most people untrained in battle would have lost it – the stress then contagious among some of the inexperienced men we'd been working with. Everybody would have flapped and our casualty numbers might have been much, much worse. Instead, I had used the fear to focus myself; it helped me to remember everything that I'd needed to stay alive in a gunfight. Working on the edges of emotion had felt all right; more than all right, in fact. There was a weird realization that I had actually enjoyed the battle, but I couldn't figure out quite why.

I'd understood one thing, though: scrapping it out in The Brotherhood seemed huge. *Proper.* I had *meaning*, I had fought the good fight and defended my country while protecting its people at home.

The other British lads soon piled into the square, bullets cutting overhead. Several local soldiers had been hit, but our boys remained unscathed. I counted them all in as they jogged into our formation, arriving from different entry points, taking up positions in all-round defence and awaiting the next attack. We weren't safe yet, but just having everybody around me – people I could trust, fighters I knew wouldn't look back at me slack-jawed when I ordered them to do something – delivered a huge sense of security. A warm, fuzzy feeling enveloped me. As we all gathered behind a derelict wall for cover while planning out our next move, I felt The Brotherhood's security blanket for the first time. Those flashes of self-doubt and insecurity that marked my early weeks in training were replaced by a sense of quiet confidence. I *could* cut it in combat. I *was* capable of scrapping alongside the best.

I had officially joined the ranks.

*

I'm sure there's at least one bloke in The Brotherhood who might have felt indebted to me for saving his life. I honestly couldn't tell you who, or why, though. It was part of my job to bail out whoever was alongside me if ever they found themselves in trouble. The difference between living and dying during a battle might have been nothing more than me getting the drop on somebody before they'd had the chance to shoot at one of us. I probably dragged teammates away from a bullet, or pulled a colleague back from an IED device, simply by placing a hand on his shoulder, but the details are so sketchy because the actions were always instinctive. Thought rarely came into it.

The moments where The Brotherhood rescued *me* were less forgettable. I remember patrolling one village with narrow alleyways and high walls, as part of a group that was working under darkness. I stepped around the corner and heard a whisper behind me, a recognizable voice. It was one of my teammates.

'He's got a gun . . .'

I was confused. *Yeah, we've all got guns . . .*

And then the barking rang out. I was face-to-face with a murder hole, a small circular gap in the brickwork with enough space for a gun muzzle to poke through. The shooter was shielded by heavy stone and could fire freely without risk. It was an assassin's dream, like shooting fish in a barrel. Bullets ricocheted around my frame. Instinctively, I pressed my back against the wall, like a circus performer pinned to a wheel as a knife-thrower landed blades all around them. I was able to shoot back, but I knew a one-in-a-million shot was required to catch a target that tiny, and in the chaos I couldn't see an immediate escape route or any form of cover, until a voice shouted out from across the alley.

'Foxy, over here!'

Two of my teammates had crouched down behind a tree. The call snapped me out of a mental freeze and I moved my arse over, tap-dancing across the alley in a cartoonish dash. I ducked down alongside them, our hiding spot safe from the sniper's angle of attack.

'Cheers,' I said, breathing hard. 'So what's the plan now?'

'Reckon we should walk around to the other side of the building and lob a grenade at the bastard inside?' offered one bloke.

Excited by the idea, I nodded, and we edged our way to the rear entrance of the murder hole, which was at the back wall in a small brick hut, then threw an explosive through the window, our shooter looking the other way. When the bangs, smoke, and dust had faded, our point man announced he was going to clear the room. It was my job to run through the door afterwards, which was now hanging from its hinges, before taking down whoever was inside – if he was still alive.

'Are you with me?' the point man asked.

Yeah mate, we're with you.

We raced into the crumbling building, guns up, but in the rush there was a near disaster. One bloke, Warren, had a 66mm rocket-launcher strapped to his back with an elastic cord. The weapon extended beyond his shoulders and was much wider than the door frame we were running towards, and before the rest of us had time to follow him in, both ends of his weapon had caught on the outside of the wall. Warren must have been three feet inside the building before the elastic yanked his arse backwards and twanged him to the dirt. Fortuitously, our target, when we found him, was dead. We sat in the smouldering remains of the murder hole, a corpse slumped by our feet, laughing our heads off at a calamitous two minutes of action. Sometimes, cracking up was the only thing stopping us from freaking out.

12

To my mind, a solid, battle-ready soldier needed a good sense of humour because there was plenty to unsettle the mind, or damage one's confidence, while working in war. Having too much time to think as we waited for the next mission to begin could be tough. And we were forever waiting for the next mission to begin – waiting, and waiting, then waiting some more. Operations cranked into gear: the men readied their kit, a chopper's rotary blades started *whump-whump-whumping* and the adrenaline amongst the group peaked, everyone telling stories and cracking jokes . . . only for the mood to suddenly cool off.

A whispered rumour spread amongst the team. *The target has moved.*

And then, inevitably, we were told to stand down. *Anyone fancy a wet?*

Talk about a massive downer. Life between missions could be mind-numbing, a never-ending roller coaster of boredom and inaction at the low end, which was later punctuated by *Is-this-my-time-to-die?* anxiety at the higher frequencies, usually as we readied ourselves for battle. The waiting had become one of the unifying factors of base life. The Brotherhood was close not only because the intensity of fighting was so stressful on the body and brain, but also because there was so much time to wait between missions. We had nothing to occupy ourselves with other than talking and opening up – well, as far as the blokes were able to. Sometimes we spoke about the nice things at home, like our family, the kids, or the football, though that got boring pretty quickly. Inevitably, we talked about the bad things, too – the break-ups, the divorces, the feuds – and there was always a lot of that to chat through, all of it in that familiar, unemotional tone. Life with The Brotherhood made the tours much more manageable.

In war, the mind moved at a thousand miles an hour. We ran in and out of compounds, not knowing if the next footfall might trigger an IED blast, shredding our limbs and manhoods to a bloody pulp. We sprinted from ditch to ditch, the rounds whipping over our heads. We convinced screaming, hysterical colleagues that a grisly leg wound was 'easily fixable' for their weekly five-a-side football match in England, when in actuality it was hanging off at the knee with next-to-no-chance of ever being stitched back on. When my brain moved at those speeds for extended periods of time, it adapted. It settled into a rhythm. It wanted to work at a thousand miles an hour in the downtime, too, which was dangerous because blokes with a mindset like mine looked for distractions in dull situations. On the base, in our rest periods, we would thrill-seek and search out something that might take the edge off our boredom.

For example, the single lads found a lot of temptation in the female members of the British military. Whenever we wandered across the base, or hung out at the mess or in the gym, girls often came over to say hello, ask questions or flirt. And because me and most of the blokes I worked with had our own rooms, it was fairly easy to sneak anyone inside for a bit of fun – as long as we were discreet. Most of the time, the Officer Commanding turned a blind eye to any sex noises echoing around the corridors when we were off duty. They understood that we needed to let off steam, and as long as it didn't affect the working practices, our misbehaviour was considered harmless.

There was only one year in war where I was actually

single and happy to mess around, and for those intimate moments I would leave whatever awful battlefield I was stationed in, escaping the violence and stress. During that time, sex on a military tour became a release, and I came to the realization that killing and shagging were the two most extreme things a person could do, instincts that operated at opposite ends of the primal spectrum: love and hate; creating life and ripping it away. Performing those acts so close to one another brought a sense of balance, for me at least. When I later left the military, I picked up a book which confirmed my feelings. Cheerily entitled *On Killing: The Psychological Cost of Learning to Kill in War and Society*, I'd bought it because I knew that war had messed with my head and I wanted to learn how. In a chapter entitled, 'Killing at Sexual Range: The Primal Aggression, the Release, and the Orgasmic Discharge', the author explained how fighting and sex had long been linked. In the animal kingdom, it was why the toughest lion got all the mating privileges, but when it came to warfare, the author reckoned killing and shagging were both 'rites of manhood'. He claimed a lot of soldiers liked firing a gun because it gave them a sense of sexual power. The book even revealed how one Vietnam vet admitted he'd left the US army because he was becoming 'consumed' by killing in the same way a person might have been consumed by sex.*

'To some people carrying a gun was like having a permanent hard-on,' wrote another vet. 'It was a pure sexual trip every time you got to pull the trigger.'

But killing never felt like a sexual release for me. It was a part of the job. And sex for me, when it happened on that one tour, was also different. It wasn't about love. It meant escapism, a distraction from the stress that played upon my nerves during night operations and during gunfights.

Inside the sleeping quarters the mood was no different. There was a rowdy type of misbehaviour at play. 'Door Wars' was a game in which the sole intent was the humiliation of a mate, because laughing at one another helped us to pass the time more quickly. Somebody might have lost a few teeth during a scrap and their inevitable rinsing would begin, long before they'd even disembarked from the helicopter, gums still pissing blood. Pictures of hillbillies with rotting, wonky gnashers were downloaded in an office, printed off and then stuck to the victim's door. If the new decor wasn't noticed immediately, the rules of the game

---

*Lt Col. David Grossman, *On Killing: The Psychological Cost of Learning to Kill in War and Society* (Bay Back Books, 2009).

meant that those pictures stayed in place for the entire tour. This was bad news for Dave. One day he admitted to shagging a ladyboy in Thailand. Within hours, a portfolio of some seriously hardcore porn had been plastered to his quarters. Dave was so tired that when he returned to his bunk the new artwork went unnoticed. Despite his grumbling, it remained stuck to his walls for months. Though secretly he probably quite liked it.

Other games had a more deep-seated meaning; they involved trust, which was vital in war and a binding component within The Brotherhood. There were plenty of unwritten rules amongst the men, on or off tour, and there were plenty of things that you could or couldn't do. It didn't bode well if someone lied to the group for any reason. White lies and little fibs were fine, but full-on untruths caused big problems. They were known as 'integrity shouts', and losing one meant losing the faith of mates and colleagues. This idea was rooted in discipline: how was I supposed to rely on the person fighting alongside me in an ugly contact situation if they had bull-shitted people at the base? Unsurprisingly, those incidents were very rare.

To enforce that ethos, games between the lads, such as 'Queen's Eyebrows', became code-of-honour pledges that everybody took really seriously whenever they were played, mainly because a soldier was effectively swearing upon the Queen's life. If his promise, or claim, fell through, he'd have to sacrifice his eyebrows as punishment. Robocop was worse: we would shave off the front part of someone's hair – that always exposed the liars (but it also put people off taking up the challenge in the first place).

From the outside, these rituals must have looked pretty stupid, but the games were considered a code of trust for anyone working within The Brotherhood. Disrespecting the rules meant trouble, as one of the group – a Scouser who we'll call Gavin – found out to his cost during a long tour. Throughout the team, Gavin had gained a reputation for being really lazy. Completing some of the more boring administrative details on the job had seemed beyond him at times, and the lads were forever moaning at Gavin for not making the teas when it had been his turn.

'It'll be different this time, I promise,' he said shortly after arriving on base. 'I'm pulling my weight.'

'No way,' shouted one particularly annoyed soldier, after the bold claim had been made. 'You need to "Queen's Eyebrows" that.'

'All right then, yeah,' said Gavin, defiantly. '"Eyebrows!" I'm not slacking off on this tour.'

Gavin was inevitably caught out just a few days later

when he claimed to have cleaned up the specialist vehicle hangar. In actuality, he hadn't, and the place was a tip. He then threw a strop when somebody mentioned the forfeit.

'I can't walk around without any eyebrows,' he moaned.

Gavin then attempted the unforgivable: he tried to weasel out of the bet, even claiming not to have taken up the wager in the first place, and that was a massive problem in a group as tight as ours. One by one, Gavin lost allies within the team. Refusing to shave his eyebrows off was annoying, but his dishonesty – by claiming he hadn't agreed to 'Queen's Eyebrows' in the first place – was viewed as a massive betrayal. Some of the blokes even wanted to knock him out for denying the agreement and arguments raged on for days until eventually we all pulled together for a meeting. When Gavin arrived, it was like he'd been dragged into his own murder trial.

And he was going down.

'Here's what's happening,' said one soldier. 'If you won't let us shave off your eyebrows, we're going to come up with a punishment of our own and you'll have to accept it, whatever.'

Gavin nodded reluctantly. Why he was so bothered about his looks seemed weird to me – vanity was so misplaced in war – but over the next day or so, we put together what was cheerfully called 'The Box of Doom', a suggestion postbox in which anybody could present ideas for a suitable punishment. The list, when it was read out, sounded hilarious.

Lick the sniffer dog's bollocks for five minutes.

Wear the dog's electric collar and get zapped for fifteen minutes – continually.

Get your ex-girlfriend's name tattooed on your cock (in prison ink).

One of the suggestions played on his psychological triggers. Gavin had the fat gene – it ran in his family and he was paranoid about piling on the pounds. The note suggested banning him from the gym for a week, with an extra dollop of justice delivered in the form of a family-sized chocolate cake, which Gavin would have to pay for and then eat in the staff mess every night for seven days. He went into a meltdown, before finally, hilariously . . .

Screw it, kill him. He lied.

The note had been fairly tongue-in-cheek, but there was a serious undertone to it: *We have no time for mistrust.* Having somebody alongside us that we couldn't rely on – a hothead, some dude with authority issues, *a liar* – often became an emotionally cancerous situation within the group. Once the rot was discovered, suspicion ate away at everybody's confidence and it could be difficult to cut out the tumour.

Gavin eventually paid the price with 'Bog Prison'. Every day for five days he was locked into the local contractors' Portaloo during the hottest point of the afternoon. There was only one toilet in the block and a queue of impatient people often snaked through the base as Gavin suffered in the heat and the stench of a cubicle that looked like the hellish hole from *Trainspotting*. His cell time always lasted an hour, and as the sweat poured off him Gavin gagged and retched inside until one of the team gave him a bang on the wall to signal that his time was up. Whenever he emerged, hurling his guts up in the sand, a mob of local workers would glare and curse at him angrily, only adding to the indignity.

'Do I really have to do five days of this?' he blubbed after his second shift.

But Gavin already knew the answer. Not taking the forfeit would have meant losing the lads' trust for good, and that would have been the biggest punishment of all; a rejection that everybody in The Brotherhood was truly scared of.

13

Working through the seemingly never-ending training sessions in Poole made me feel hollow. I was messed up, confused. Triggered by the reality of a forthcoming tour, I couldn't figure out whether I was coming or going. Making simple decisions, both at work and home, was a struggle, and I felt unable to pinpoint the exact catalyst for my upended emotional state. I'd become distracted and spaced out, but all my problems, every troubling symptom I'd experienced, could easily have been attributed to war fatigue rather than a more serious condition.

A lack of sleep. *I used to work all hours on raids, running on fumes. Why would I expect to settle down to eight hours of uninterrupted kip every night when I got back to England?*

My short fuse. *Well, combat will do that to a bloke.*

My inability to hold down a relationship. *I'm having fun.*

The heavy drinking. *I'm having fun!*

My indifference to work. *I'm tired. It'll come back. (It had better come back.)*

That looming cloud, steadily approaching over the dark, churning English Channel. It's getting faster. *It's getting closer.*

Every personal issue could be easily explained away, except for that weird, gloopy ominous feeling, *that shape*, a sense that something wasn't right. The realization of what it might have meant was shrouded because I was in a state of denial, a result of my fearing both for the immediate future and a loss of face with The Brotherhood. That unknowing mood was unusual for me, because while I wasn't an outwardly sensitive person – the job had hardened me – I was emotionally intelligent. For the most part I could understand what I was feeling and why. If someone had annoyed me, the reason became clear very quickly. If I felt stressed, I usually understood the cause. But when it came to realizing what was wrong during that period, my awareness seemed lost, and the first understanding of what my feelings truly represented, when it arrived, jolted me harder than the bark of any automatic weapon.

My moment of understanding happened in a meeting, rather than a simulated warzone or some fast-moving counter-terrorism drill. As part of my UK work I had to attend a command course, two weeks of lectures and assessments that were given to various team-leaders-in-waiting from all branches of the military. Most of the attendees viewed these events as an essential but slow-creeping death-by-PowerPoint process in which we were taught how to plan, and lead under high stress, though there was always extra pressure for those more experienced people in attendance, of whom I was one. I understood that we'd be torn to shreds if our work didn't meet the organizers' incredibly tough standards. I sensed an edginess at play from the very first session.

Even before I'd arrived at the venue, I knew I'd have to learn a tonne of new procedures and practices, though some of the lectures did look genuinely interesting. During one component we used a computer programme setting out different combat scenarios. Our challenge was to decide how best to negotiate those flashpoints using the assets available to us, such as personnel, artillery and drones, so we could kill bad people effectively. A lot of what we were learning was dull, however. Having attended lectures from several military and intelligence big-hitters from Cobra, the Ministry of Defence and the Metropolitan Police, my next stop was a presentation in Trauma Risk Management

(TRiM). This programme was designed to teach a commander how best to alleviate pressure on the people around them. If something bad had happened, such as an IED explosion, it would be a team leader's responsibility to assess the people involved – those not seriously injured in the blast – with a series of questions: *How do you feel? Has the situation freaked you out? Can you carry on with your work?* There was nothing too invasive in the questioning, and if a soldier seemed OK his commander was supposed to check in with him after three months, and then another three months later on. At that stage any symptoms, such as a propensity for violence, were considered fine in isolation, but a combination of issues meant trouble. Not that I was paying too much attention at first because this was a procedure that might have worked well in a civilian environment but during a scrap where people were getting killed and soldiers were fighting at intense levels, there wasn't the time to make those enquiries. I figured it to be a waste of effort.

I don't care about this.

PTSD: what a load of bollocks.

I just want to pass this course so I can have a team of elite troops to worry about in the first place . . .

But in that bland room full of computers, flat-screen TVs and projectors, I recognized the first indication that I might have been suffering from the onset of serious mental health issues. Three experts had been tasked with holding the TRiM presentation, one of whom was the Royal Marines' welfare officer.

There was also an Army psychologist and a psychiatric nurse, a position that was, by then, established across the military. The Navy had a specialist that worked from our camp in Poole and all three of them batted off one another, explaining various stressful scenarios while detailing how a senior commander should recommend assessments to any one of their unit presenting a combination of negative symptoms. The checklist rang alarm bells:

'They might be exhausted by a lack of sleep, even when they're at home.'

'Some people might develop a nasty temper and will react to even the slightest provocation.'

'In some cases, people suffering from PTSD will struggle to hold down their relationships because they might have become detached and irritable.'

'Heavy drinking is a sign they're masking the issues.'

'People can become indifferent to the things they once were passionate about.'

'In that mindset, there's a general feeling of unease and insecurity.'

After the list had been concluded, I leaned over to a mate. 'Bloody hell,' I whispered. 'I'm ticking a few of these boxes.' We both laughed, and then the inevitable denial followed almost immediately afterwards.

Not to worry, though, I thought. *I'll just crack on.*

But that list soon played on my mind. As I drove home, I realized I was nearer to the end of my time in Poole than I was to the beginning, and the start date for our next tour was becoming more real. A few days after the course had finished, my unit were told of our responsibilities for the next trip. Intel was drip-fed to us about what could be expected while we were working in combat. Ordinarily, my excitement would have soared at the news of another chunk of time spent away with the lads, in action, but this time I felt weighed down by despondency. The lethargy and grumpiness I had experienced during those training courses had transferred to everything to do with my next tour. Whenever I considered the logistics of my time abroad, or what I could expect, my mood became lead-heavy. I felt stuck, unable to breathe, that black cloud now dominating the horizon. It was almost making landfall.

But why?

And then a few nights later the truth revealed itself as I tried, and failed, to fall asleep.

The cloud was fear, a dread of the forthcoming tour. And it wasn't temporary.

That truth was inescapable now. I realized that I'd become terrified of what might happen on returning to that place, to war, and my concern wasn't fleeting or controllable like it had been on previous occasions, but permanent and consuming. I hadn't been able to dial it down and I was unable to shake the awful feeling that I might die, that I wasn't invincible any more. The bullet to Danny's throat and my attempt to find the safest hiding place in the fallout to our gunfight was part of it. Other horrors and injuries, like the daisy-chain IED explosion that had wiped out a bunch of the men we'd been relieving on our arrival, had also shocked me, when ordinarily those incidents wouldn't have bothered me that much. Then there was the helicopter mission: one man KIA; that kid and his dark eyes, a mouth shaped into a blackened scream in my NVGs; the sensation of being hunted by the enemy as we attempted to locate our landing zone; and the thought that I might never see my family again playing on my mind as I crept through the vegetation, taking down hostile forces. The terror of combat and the aftershocks of death had made a permanent dent and I suddenly felt like a different person, as if a new, weaker me had arrived, but I wasn't sure how that would affect me going forward.

There was acceptance. I realized that my previous attempts to shrug away the dark mood of recent months had been nothing more than a stab at denial. As I lay there, anxiety rattled me and I worried about my performance and focus on the next tour, given my mental state. During several dark minutes I freaked out that a mistake from me – some hesitation, or second-guessing at the wrong moment – would result in one of the other lads getting hurt. I even felt the guilt, and I imagined the resentment amongst the other blokes when the news of my cock-up had got around. The most frightening thing of all, though, was that now I felt very, very alone.

Was there someone in The Brotherhood that I could talk to? Dave, maybe. *Probably.* But the paranoia that he might let slip, tell someone else over a few beers, made it too much of a risk. Also, to my mind, asking for help seemed like an admission of defeat.

I wasn't alone in feeling that way. Senior officers had once tried to check in on the returning soldiers after a tour and therapy sessions had been arranged. We had landed in England on a Friday and spent a few days in the house with our families before the personal admin began – trips to the dentist, doctor's appointments, that kind of thing. Then it was announced that mental health meetings with a psychiatric specialist had been scheduled for us. Everyone experienced the same feeling of annoyance: *What a waste of time – we're elite soldiers!* I figured it to be a needless distraction and just wanted to hurry up and get on with my real job.

We still had to go through with the sessions, though. The questions were invasive and a little too much for all of us. *How do you feel? Has anything you've seen affected you? Have you been feeling violent towards your partner or friends?* Nobody understood what the higher-ups were trying to gain from those interviews or what the implications of our full disclosure might have been.

Ultimately the therapy didn't work because nobody had wanted to admit a weakness to their superiors. And admitting to a problem would have made us feel pathetic. There was a little suspicion too. When the attending soldiers eventually gathered and spoke about it on the base afterwards, it turned out that everybody had clammed up (or so they said). Any plans to go forward with the exercise were later abandoned by the people in charge.

But now terror had taken over everything; it was a new enemy. I was fearful of what I had experienced in war and how it might affect me in the future – my judgement was skewed. I was fearful of what might happen to my career if I placed my symptoms down on official records. I was fearful that the lads, if they found out how I felt, might view me as weak, or that my position in The Brotherhood could come under threat – my existence and purpose in life felt jeopardized. Most of all, the fear that I was now capable of being really terrified was all-encompassing and I was caught in an ever-tightening circle of confusion. My environment – a macho, alpha-male collective where the idea of having a stiff upper lip and not complaining was key – had paralyzed me. What I really needed to do was to reach out and ask for help, but lads like myself weren't encouraged to open up, or to express sadness or upset, to our peers. Instead soldiers would hit psychological rock-bottom then brush it aside.

'Yeah I'm all right,' they'd say. 'Who gives a crap?'

My reality was that the people on base were probably the best equipped to locate an escape route for me because they had experienced identical horrors. Yet I couldn't ask them because no one else would have admitted to sharing those same insecurities themselves. I realized I was even more worried about their opinions than the idea of going back to war.

I had been taken hostage psychologically.

14

I'd been forced towards a tipping point and had to act decisively – no second-guessing, no hesitation – in a situation where sharp thought felt like a diminishing skill.

I know that I was pissed off with being pissed off and something had to give, but remembering the exact trigger point, a moment or epiphany convincing me to approach the unit's psych nurse in Poole, is a reach, and the details are fuzzy even now. Maybe I'd been reminded of his work during another long, dark night of the soul where I'd replayed the checklist of PTSD symptoms over and over in my head. Or perhaps the TRiM programme had been brought up in some casual conversation with the other blokes in attendance. My shame at being indifferent to training would have shoved me towards resolution, for sure – guilt was something I struggled to deal with. Either

I was going to have to address the brutal fact that a life of excitement now seemed utterly joyless, or I'd have to quit the job, because it wasn't fair on the blokes I served with, especially the younger ones who would have traded places with me in a heartbeat. I can only assume there was something about my situation that made me feel it was OK to open up, or ask for help, even though I remained unconvinced about the value of mental health care for soldiers like myself, but there seemed to be no other choice, not if I was to survive this scrap. *I didn't want to leave The Brotherhood.*

It had been a cold, wet morning when I called the psych office, but every day was miserable back then. If someone had asked me to recall the weather of any given month throughout those weeks in Poole, I'd have sworn it had been the same pretty much every day. *Overcast. Damp. Grim.* But come on, it couldn't have been, not for every moment of one whole year, even in England. Yet to my mind it had tipped it down constantly and the coastal skies had been black 24/7 from the minute I had landed back in the country.

I walked across the sports fields at the base, my shoes becoming wet in the damp grass, a finger hovering over the psych nurse's number on my phone. I was torn. I needed advice, help, but I didn't want to ask for it. The stress eventually outweighed my trepidation. I called the number.

Someone picked up almost immediately.

'Hello, this is the psychiatric department.' It was a man on the other end of the line, and I recognized the voice. It was the same nurse that had taken the TRiM course.

'Look, you don't know me,' I said. 'My name's Foxy, I'm a sergeant just about to go back on tour and I'd really like to see you. Are you in now?'

'Yeah, of course,' he said. 'Why don't you come over?'

I think I was taken aback by the immediacy, even though I'd asked for an appointment. I assumed there would be more of a process, an introductory chat before meeting in person, but I agreed to walk over, calming myself as I traipsed through the rain in an attempt to gain some semblance of control on what felt like a chaotic situation.

Mate, look: you're in charge here. Just say it's informal, that you don't want anything documented. You can orchestrate the whole thing because no one else in The Brotherhood will really know and you can just sort out your problems with the psych nurse. He's bound to be a genius with a toolkit of tricks and techniques.

You'll come out a different bloke.

The walk took ages. I was on a mega-downer, fearful of asking for help from a complete stranger – a shrink. I stepped into a doctor's reception room – with its beige walls, bland decor, a few chairs and a table sprinkled with books – like a normal dude getting his blood pressure checked. But I felt vulnerable. As I waited, I flicked idly through a magazine and landed on a story that explored the experiences of every man who had set foot on the moon.

Buzz Aldrin and Charlie Duke were mentioned. The feature explained how some astronauts had retired at a relatively early age and had initially struggled with the next chapter in their lives; finding purpose beyond the extreme existence that once defined them had proven painful. There were plenty of demons for them to deal with, too. A few NASA explorers, it turned out, came back from space and went to religion, others to booze. It sounded a lot like the ending of a military career to me. I knew that a lot of the soldiers leaving The Brotherhood had gone the same way, and while the chances of me turning to God were less than zero, I'd heard of mates who had become born-again Christians overnight; blokes you'd never think could do it. I was probably more at risk from exit-strategy number two. I'd been boozing up, and I knew some seriously experienced mates who had got themselves into cocaine and downers after retiring from the military. The human condition was so weird. There's not a lot of room for mediocrity, and when you've taken down a militia leader in a gunfight like I had, what do you do for an encore?

I relived that moment in my head, to remind myself of my once superhuman status. *I remember doing the bloke in a courtyard on one of the patrols. It had been a mess. There was fighting going on left, right and Chelsea. He had come around the corner, running towards me, his rifle up, ready to fire. But instinctively I'd shot him from the hip, catching him with a bullet straight to the head and he'd dropped instantly. It later turned out that the dude was a high-end commander in the forces we were fighting. Everyone said what a score it had been and the news was written on the noticeboard at base:*

'Good effort, Foxy – rinsed the bloke we were after.'

And then after an hour, it was wiped off. Forgotten. No one really talked about it again . . .

So, how do you recreate the buzz of that, Buzz?

My thoughts were punctuated by a voice from the other side of the room.

'Mr Fox?'

I looked up and saw the psych nurse gesturing me into his office. He shook my hand warmly and sat down behind his computer.

'Hi, I spoke to you a moment ago on the phone,' I said, following him. 'You don't know who I am . . .'

'Oh, I do,' he said, smiling.

The announcement took me by surprise. 'Right ... Really?'

'Yeah, I know people about.'

The possibilities flicked through my head. Could my name have come up in a previous conversation about what I was like? Or had he gone through a list of people that had recently returned from tour? I shrugged it off. I wanted to blurt my issues out quickly.

'Look, there's a tour coming up and I'm not feeling good about it,' I said. 'Something doesn't feel right. *With me.* I want to get rid of the feeling, but I want to keep this informal. I don't want our chat to go on my record.'

He nodded. 'I won't take any notes . . .'

I felt relieved.* Of course, I was cool with him scribbling down a few things as a reminder for any future meetings because, essentially, I was one of his cases, but the thought of my emotions and mindset being formalized permanently on record felt potentially destructive.

'Not for now,' he continued. 'But if we carry on then at some point we'll have to.'

---

* I later learned that a couple of blokes had sought out private mental health care in order to keep their problems off the records.

'Yeah, of course, but for now . . .'

The nurse nodded and explained his process. We would talk informally, he said, and then he'd assess my situation and any treatments I might require. I thought, *Well, this is exciting. I can keep this quiet and there's going to be a few things we can do to sort me out.* My mood brightened. I was immediately optimistic that I might regain my military mojo.

'Look, you need to make some time to come and see me for a proper chat,' he said.

I nodded, and once the formalities were over I arranged to visit him the following week.

I felt as if I'd taken the first step towards fixing my head and that life would become a lot easier from here on in.

And then a heaviness set in again soon afterwards.

War was hell, but reliving it through the viewfinder of my own emotions felt even worse. The nurse was somebody I could work with, though. I liked him – he was approachable, understanding – and when I walked into my next session a week or so later I assumed he was about to wave a magic wand over my head and correct every emotional combat wound. We talked about the forthcoming sessions and he repeated how he intended to get to the bottom of what had caused my fearful state and would then recommend a course of treatment. That sounded fine to me. But first he wanted to know when I'd experienced that opening sense of uncontrollable terror, or any of the other symptoms that had bothered me since returning to Poole.

'It was a night mission, on a helicopter,' I said. 'We'd been shot at by loads of enemy fighters as we landed, one of our lads was killed, and when I rolled into a ditch all I could think about was that I wanted to be a little kid again, curled up next to my mum on the sofa . . .'

I offered it all up, him scribbling the occasional note on to a pad, me recounting everything that happened during that operation and then the days, weeks and months that had followed. The nurse asked me how I'd been generally since that final tour and I mentioned my moods, a general sense of fuzziness and an inability to sleep. 'Essentially I've become nocturnal,' I joked, but it was true. I had spent eight years of my life working at night then fighting fatigue for large chunks of the day, and it had dented me. I recalled how I often envied the senior American troops. They fought on shorter tours and were allowed to sleep during the day while the Brits worked on planning missions. In briefings, if somebody wanted to chat to one of the Americans for intel or assistance, they'd be told, *Forget it, the*

Yanks are sleeping. And so we'd wait until five in the afternoon when their alarms would go off in unison.

'And how was your childhood?' asked the nurse. 'Did anything bad happen?'

Here we go, I thought. *Time to drag the family into it . . .*

I shook my head. 'No, it was fun growing up. I might have got whacked a few times for being out of order . . .'

'Tell me about that.'

Well, there was one time I had been a dick to my younger brother, Mathieu, I explained. I'd thrown him through a classroom window at school in a fit of anger. Mat had it coming, though. He had been winding me up for days, and during break-time he pushed me to the edge. I grabbed him by the blazer collars, lifted him off his feet and slung his body towards the school building. I hadn't expected the window glass to crack under his weight, but it exploded everywhere upon impact and Mat crashed through it, skidding across a floor as he landed, somehow unscathed, laughing his head off.

I was in trouble at school and at home, but that was nothing new. Apparently I was a worry from the second I was born, in 1976, landing prematurely with a collapsed lung and dying twice during the procedures to drain my chest in those first few days – I was ahead of the game before my war had even started. I think I went on to cause my old dear a lot of stress. I had two brothers: Mat, the window-smasher, who would go on to join the Marines, and Jamie, who was nine years younger than me. Having seen up close what his brothers had endured in the military, and suffering all the stories, Jamie ended up taking the safe route and moved into running nightclubs and bars in Marbella.

That was a smart move, I thought as soon as I'd told the story, grimly observing the cold, clinical surroundings of a medical office. I understood where the nurse was heading with his line of enquiry and it only played into my suspicions of mental health care – *everyone tries to pin it on the family*. But my life as a kid hadn't been bad, not in the slightest. I'd deserved that clip around the ear for throwing Mat through a window. Dad had been a bit heavy-handed when he'd cuffed me afterwards, but I was no different to any other lad from my generation – we got smacked every now and then. Mum was small, only five feet tall, and quite a timid character, but she used to whack the three of us when she had to as well. Once we'd got bigger, she wouldn't have dared – not that we would have done anything to her. Overall, we were good-natured boys, and apart from the odd broken window, or those occasions when I'd thumped

Mat for trying to beat up little Jamie, we were fairly harmless.

I knew Dad had helped us to channel all our energies positively. His spell in the Marines meant he was able to teach us practical skills, such as map-reading, which I found really interesting, but I also really enjoyed it when he told me about his career in the military and showed me the photos from back then. And then there was the sport. When we lived in Luton he went on to establish very popular youth hockey competitions in Bedfordshire and I became pretty handy with a stick myself.

As a younger kid I was skinny and got picked on a little, but it was nothing too bad and it probably helped to toughen me up. I had mates, I was fairly popular, and the boys that used to rough me up were often a lot older. None of that had left any scars, mentally or physically. I was over six feet tall by the time I'd moved into my teens and because of my height I could handle myself if anybody ever took the mickey.

I carried on . . .

After leaving the Marines, Dad moved around from job to job and had a sketchy time. He worked at Rentokil for a while and we lived in Basingstoke. We then moved to Yorkshire, where he joined a car company set up by his mate who then did a runner with the cash. We were in financial trouble for a while after that. The family had been living in a big house in Skipton but we had to move to Keighley. It wasn't the best of times, because Dad was so broke he had to work on a farm for food while Mum struggled with Mat and me. The farm owners couldn't afford to pay him in cash, so he'd work for slaughtered chickens and pigs instead, until he eventually landed a security job in Luton. I must have been around three years old at the time and we relocated to a nearby village called Houghton Regis, which was a bit of a sprawling mess of nothing and Mum and Dad weren't happy. As I got older I could tell, though they did their best to keep it together in front of the kids and as a family unit we were pretty tight. They took us on camping holidays to Cornwall or Scotland, which I loved because we could do lots of outdoor activities. Years later, once all the sons had moved away from home, Dad left.

As I got into my teens I realized I wanted a job that was big on adventure (apart from a brief period when I quite fancied being a graphic designer for some reason; I wasn't cut out for it). I'd liked Dad's stories and those old photographs, so maybe the Marines might be an option for me as well? The idea was only solidified when my exams didn't go too well one year, and at the age of fifteen I decided to sign up with the military. I completed all the application forms at the careers office and my entrance was set up from there, though the process wasn't entirely without its hitches. When I'd initially met with the recruitment officer from the Marines, he asked me to perform a series of pull-ups. I flunked the initial exam and was told to return in a few months, during which I eventually hauled myself into shape. Once I was on the recruitment course (the Potential Royal Marine Course, or PRMC), I steadied myself for a period of physical pressure, which was handy because we were thrashed for a few days in an initial selection process to prove we were up to what the Royal Navy described as 'elite amphibious fighters' where everybody involved was required to pass vigorous gym tests before running for hours through muddy fields. Only the recruits standing at the end were able to move into commando training in a couple of months, one of the toughest courses in the British military. I remember Dad being proud once I'd passed, but his joy was tinged with doubt. I think he questioned my persistence. *Does he possess the minerals to follow in my footsteps?* Dad sometimes doubted my commitment directly, which put my back up, and when it came to passing my basic training I used his criticism as a form of motivation. It became a battering ram to push me through to the end.

Dad might have been right about one or two things, though. During those first few weeks, while I found the physical aspect of recruit life fairly manageable, when it came to the required personal admin, I was undoubtedly inexperienced. I was one of two sixteen-year-olds in the group and the blokes around us were in their mid-twenties. They had lived a little and were able to function for themselves. I'd only lived with my parents and had no idea how to polish a pair of boots to the required standard or prepare my uniform correctly. I was totally lost: ironing away the creases from my shirts took forever and because I was wasting so much time on general kit-maintenance I lost out on sleep. I became tired during the day. The physical challenges that had seemed doable during the early phases became much harder when I was hanging with fatigue. Even being on time or operating in a vaguely organized fashion seemed beyond me for a period, and in the early stages I was sometimes late for briefings, quickly discovering that, in the Marines, when a meeting was set for 15:00 hours, to arrive at 15:00 hours was to be late.

There was one occasion when I even became visibly upset in front of the recruit troops' drill sergeant. It had been our first kit inspection and as I struggled to pull on several layers of clothing, I sensed him standing there, glaring at me, my vision masked by a tangle of fabric and strapping. A sense of crushing embarrassment came over me as I gulped back the lump in my throat and yanked a jumper over my head like a right idiot. Psychologically I was a bit lost, and a lot of the time I felt like an embuggerance to the older recruits around me, eventually phoning Mum in tears, griping about how hard it had all become. A quick pep talk from her and one look at the photo of Dad pinned to my bedroom wall was enough to reset the focus I needed to pass.

I'll show you, I thought.

I didn't prove my genuine commitment to the senior lads until around ten weeks into the course, and it was a consistent show of dedication and skill on a daily basis that did it. Only then did I finally feel accepted into the group. Life seemed to click for me almost immediately afterwards and the role eventually instilled a sense of discipline and focus that meant I was never late for a military briefing again. I was given something to strive for, a purpose, and as a teenager life was full of potential.

I had joined up at the end of 1993. The course had taken 32 weeks and at the time I completed it Britpop was huge – Blur and Oasis (I loved Liam and Noel) had kick-started a massive party around the UK, but I was missing out on the action, moving into 40 Commando, a group which the Royal Navy described as 'a battalion-sized Royal Marine unit'. I was also into Shed Seven, The Jam and The Waterboys, and whenever I hear the indie band Suede I'm always taken back to my training days, running around in the mud and wet, climbing rope ladders and crawling through pitch-black tunnels. Suede's lead singer, the skinny, foppish Brett Anderson, would probably be morti-fied to learn that he'd once inspired a young lad on his route to fighting in some of the world's bloodiest conflicts with one of the military's most battle-hardened outfits. A lad who was now laying down his life-story to a psych nurse in a clinic on a military base.

15

In the psych nurse's office, I pulled back from teenage nostalgia. I didn't want to become distracted. My stresses were nothing to do with home, or Mum and Dad, or Suede. I was being taken further and further away from the root of my problems and I became frustrated. The nurse seemed a nice person and I was warming to him, but I quickly realized he wasn't quite as tuned in to the military life as he should have been. I had to explain everything as we went along – what a Chinook was, what NVGs were, and so on. It was annoying. I also had the sense that he was looking for some other possible cause for my problems, as if he was concerned that my issues might be pinned solely on combat; it seemed he wanted to find evidence of me being screwed up *before* I joined the military, which I hadn't been. War was the catalyst and I knew it. I'm sure there were other issues at play, such as those in my personal life, but nothing weighed on me as heavily as my last tour on the job.

Overall, though, I hadn't felt too annoyed as we concluded our first chat. I believed the nurse was formulating some bulletproof plan for me. *Here it comes*, I thought brightly, as he wound down the session. *The magic wand*. But instead I was delivered a nasty shock.

'We should definitely talk again, Jason, but I'm deployable and I'm needed elsewhere,' he said, putting down his pad and pen. 'I have to go away for a few weeks.'

'You can't go away,' I said, panic rising.

'It'll be fine,' he said. 'I want you to see another psychiatrist while I'm gone: a Dr Beckelmann. He's based down in Portsmouth and he's great. He's used to working with people like you, but I also want to talk to some people here because we need to take the next tour away from you. And to do that we should make these chats a little more official . . .'

My tour was gone? As the words landed, the news of a reprieve from war began to spin me out, but I seemed instantly lighter in mood too, as if the cloud, that dark mood weighing on my shoulders for months, was rapidly retreating from view, temporarily at least. A little stunned, I nodded, agreeing to a meeting with this Dr Beckelmann, but as I walked across the wet grass of the Navy's sports

157

fields to my two-bedroom house, I began to feel guilty, as if I was letting the other blokes down by not fighting alongside them. Fear followed shortly afterwards as I was struck by a less reassuring outcome of my cancelled commitment to the British military.

What if that's it?

What if my work is over, for ever?

I was obviously put on the planet to be a soldier. It's what I'm good at – or at least I was, once. But if the treatment doesn't work, and I can't even do that . . .

Where's my purpose?

What's my encore?

As I relaxed at home and processed the day's developments, I realized there would be no quick fix for my problems. I learned that Dr Beckelmann was a civilian doctor working on the MOD payroll and was based at the Department of Community Mental Health (DCMH). There was no way out of it, either, though I later settled myself with a reminder that the first session may have been only a small step forward, but it was a step forward all the same.

A week later, having arrived at the Department of Community Mental Health, I remember thinking Dr Beckelmann must have been on a good pay packet because he looked considerably better dressed than the nurse on base. He was a big, portly bloke, thick-set, like an ox, but he wasn't fat – I could tell he was a bit of a unit under his suit. He was well presented, too. A neatly ironed pink shirt with white trim was offset by an expensive looking set of Bentley cufflinks. A trainee Naval psychiatrist sat next to him. Dr Beckelmann informed me the trainee was there to observe our session as part of her training, and I noticed that every now and then she would scribble something down on a pad. But I'd been assured that she was only in place to watch the working processes of Dr Beckelmann rather than making any notes specific to me or my case.

'So, Mr Fox,' started the psychiatrist. 'Tell me about what's been going on.'

It poured out of me – again. *How many times would I have to retell this story?* But there was a new aspect because the weirdest thing had just started happening: whenever I tried to recall the various tours abroad with the military, they had all become one massive, sprawling chapter in my life. Everything had blurred, each period, or year, indistinguishable from the next.

'When did you begin to become more involved in action?' he asked.

In 2002, I explained. I had been happy in the Marines,

I'd progressed to the rank of sergeant, but I was bored. I had made it through the months of training without too many problems, but beyond that nothing had really happened. The British Army experienced a lengthy period of peace. Even Ireland had calmed down a fair bit (though it could still be a little tense) and the closest I came to combat was when I played for the Navy's hockey team.

Frustration was creeping in by then. I did a signals course, and I listened, annoyed, as the older blokes in my unit told me about their times in Bosnia or the Falkland Islands. Another lad had a story about how he'd once been shot at in Ireland and everyone around him had gone into a panic, but it was hardly dramatic. At the time I remember thinking that I'd wanted to experience responsibility and control in my job rather than blindly following orders, as I had done with the Marines; I wanted to experience combat at a senior level. Given that I was considered to be good at soldiering, I applied to join the military's most elite group. I was also comfortable shooting from the hip when making life-changing decisions; I liked taking risks, though it had previously dropped me into trouble.

Examples? Well, in 1997, a week before Tony Blair won the General Election, a mate and fellow Marine called Steve and I booked a holiday on a whim. We walked into a travel agent, scooped up a cheapo trip to Cancún in Mexico and after ten days of all-inclusive boozing, we'd both gone down with alcohol poisoning, I'd hooked up with an American girl called Barbie and on the flight home Steve and I were sucked into a massive brawl.

At first the pair of us had been innocent bystanders. The flight was fairly empty and everybody commandeered a row each, stretching out and building makeshift beds before falling asleep. We couldn't have been in the air for long when I was woken up by a commotion going on at the front of the plane. Four Scousers, all of them in their mid-thirties, had helped themselves to the duty-free and were throwing a lot of abuse around. Their shouting was aimed at a pair of pensioners sitting nearby, which seemed a bit off. Wanting to avoid any trouble, the older couple had moved to the back of the plane but were trailed by one of the drunks. That's when I heard some shouting and a lady screaming. One of the Scousers had taken a swing, splitting the old bloke's head open. The air-stewarding team stepped back in shock and locked themselves in a toilet, which was when Steve and I decided to pile in. We rained blows down on the guy's head, sending him back to his mates (the pensioner even joined us to put the boot in for a little revenge) and once the situation had been calmed down by another passenger, the plane's captain made an announcement.

'Ladies and gentlemen, because of the disturbance we will be landing at Shannon Airport, where police will board the plane to sort out the issue.'

Steve and I looked at each other. *We can't go to Ireland! We're Marines and there's still a conflict on – we might disappear for ever!*

By then, one of the stewardesses had reappeared from the toilet and I called her over, explaining our situation.

'Oh, don't worry, we're not going to drop *you* off in Ireland,' she said, pointing to the lashed-up Scousers at the front of the plane, one of them now nursing a few nasty cuts and bruises. 'It's for that lot down there. You helped us out.'

Talk about a relief. In Ireland the Garda arrived and dragged away the guilty party, one of the girls screaming dog's abuse at me as she was hauled off the gangway, and when we later arrived in Manchester, miles away from our original destination, the cabin crew applauded Steve and me as we left the plane. The media were less impressed, however. By the morning our (thankfully anonymous) scrap had been plastered all over the papers, with one headline raging about a 'Brawl At 36,000 Feet'.

Barbie and I stayed in contact, and a few years later, when I'd got bored in the UK, I decided to visit her in New York on a whim, even though she had a boyfriend at the time. That relationship didn't last for much longer, however: on my first night in town I got absolutely trolleyed and woke up in her bed the next day, stark-bollock naked. Barbie was on the sofa and looked furious. 'Don't even think about acting like that when my boyfriend's around,' she snapped, and when I met him the following night he seemed like a nice dude, though he must have thought, 'What's the score with this bloke?' Barbie later introduced me to her family, who had a big fat house in Connecticut; the two of us went to Broadway shows and got drunk; and when we hooked up again she decided the time had come for her to bin the boyfriend, and would I move in with her?

I didn't think twice. 'Yeah, sure,' I said. 'But what will I do for a career if I quit the Marines?'

'Don't worry,' said Barbie. 'Dad will give you plenty of work.'

Within four days I was back in England and handing in my notice at the base. 'I'm going to America. I've met someone,' I told my senior officers when they asked me what I was planning to do instead. The blokes in my unit laughed when I later told them my idea. *You'll be back in five minutes, Foxy!* But I was determined to prove them wrong, and shortly after resigning I packed up and left for Fort Lee, a suburb in New Jersey positioned just across the George Washington Bridge.

For a while everything was cool, I was happy in the States, but Barbie soon turned out to be a control freak and her fussing did my head in. Before long I had pressed the self-destruct button, as always.

'You know what, you can poke this relationship,' I shouted after one particularly rowdy blow-up. 'I'm leaving.'

'You can't leave!' said Barbie, dramatically. 'I'm the best thing that's happened to you!'

That raised my hackles. 'Oh really? Well, for your information, every time we've had sex I've had to think of someone else.' It hadn't been true, but I'd chosen to lash out. Barbie flipped.

'Right, give me half an hour,' I said, once she'd stopped screaming the place down. 'You won't ever see me again.'

I scrambled around the apartment, gathering my stuff. It was 4 July, Independence Day (*the irony*), and because of the national holiday finding a hotel proved impossible. I ended up sleeping rough in Grand Central Station before heading back to England, my tail between my legs. I begged the Marines to let me back in and my mates had a field day, rinsing me for falling flat on my face. But at least I'd taken the gamble; I'd tried to make a massive change in my life.

The Marines were later sent to California so we could perform a series of training exercises in the desert that would ready us for the Allied Forces' conflicts in Afghanistan, and later Iraq. Though nothing had been announced officially, we could all tell that a war was coming. My final few months in the regular military had taken place in late 2001, when a bunch of blokes flew two passenger jets into the World Trade Center in New York and life seemed to change for ever, for everybody. The attitude of a lot of the senior commanders appeared to intensify. Everybody became even more serious, even more focused than usual, and when we arrived in 29 Palms, a US Marine Corps base near Palm Springs, we completed four weeks of live firing featuring eight hundred blokes from 40 Commando working alongside the Americans. I knew everybody was thinking, 'We're going to war; this is the build-up.'

The training exercises had been topped and tailed with two periods of rest and recuperation, and after 29 Palms we were let loose in Las Vegas (*What could possibly go wrong?*) and everywhere was carnage.

Ten coaches drove us there, and as we were dropped off our instructions were issued: 'Right, piss off. Be back at Caesar's Palace car park for collection on Monday at 11 a.m.' Eight hundred men disappeared into the city and I barely saw anyone apart from my immediate circle of mates. It was messy. One night we got so drunk that we couldn't escape the Mandalay Bay resort. It was so disorientating that every time we made to leave we'd stumble into another nightclub, and when I eventually checked out of my room at 10.30 a.m. on Monday morning, the door opposite opened and there was my brother, Mat, who had also been on the training exercise. He had been staying nearby me all weekend, but neither of us had known, we'd been in such a state the whole time. I hadn't slept for the entire weekend, and when I checked my bank account, I'd blown a month's wages in three days.

With a little leave on our hands afterwards, a few of us decided to hire a car and drove to San Francisco for nine days of drinking. It turned out to be one of the best cities I'd ever been to and on the first night a few of us ended up in a club called The Bamboo Hut. As we danced stupidly to 1980s music, the girls around us loved it, but their boyfriends weren't so keen and a massive brawl soon kicked off. We were heavily outgunned and beat a hasty retreat, moving across the dance floor as a body of men (like well-trained Marines), copping punches and swinging back wildly. Outside in the fresh air we legged it across the road, but I was hammered and unable to see properly in the dark and as we crossed the central reservation dividing a dual carriageway I didn't notice it had been protected with a low chain-link fence. I ran into it, the collision sending me flying to the tarmac. Luckily our pursuers had given up chase by that point, but I was battered and bruised all the same.

As I recalled those incidents during my one session with Dr Beckelmann, I realized I'd have been happy to take risks back then – but now? *Not so much.* At the age of 36, I wouldn't have gambled on my military career as I had when I joined up with Barbie in New York. Instead I would have turned the idea over and over in my head, fearful of making a mistake. Leaving the Marines for more exciting work? Had I been in my present state of mind back then, there wasn't a chance; even the thought of heading into conflict was now weighed down with a sense of serious consequence. I didn't want to go back and I had become riddled with self-doubt, which was maybe partly down to age. The feeling of being bulletproof was something that everybody lost as they got older, but I'd sussed out that my trepidation was stronger than the fallout to approaching midlife. Instead it was a scar that I'd picked up in war.

My nerve had vanished.

Where had that bloke gone?

16

Forty Commando were in the thick of it – but I wasn't. News of their involvement in Afghanistan had filtered through to me as I'd made it on to jungle training, one of the precursors to elite service. The intel annoyed me a little. By the sounds of things, they were heavily involved in the War on Terror and had been dragged into all sorts of scraps. I remember thinking regretfully, *I knew I should have waited!* I'd longed to get into action with the Marines – not to kill people, but to test the skills I'd learned in training and push my adrenaline to the limits. I went into the military for combat. When it had finally broken out, I'd been stuck on the sidelines. Even when I eventually made it to elite service during the war in Afghanistan, there was an element of missing the boat because the Coalition forces had walked in without too much resistance and the Taliban quickly went to ground, hiding in the mountains of Pakistan. There wasn't a lot for my group to do at first, apart from working on support operations. All of that would change later on.

While I was eager to see action, without war I wasn't really a violent person. I didn't look for conflict like some people did. Sure, I had been in a couple of tear-ups outside the job, though only when somebody had pushed me way too far. One of these flashpoints later left me in a community service programme after I was arrested during a night out in Portsmouth. A bunch of us had been drinking at a mate's leaving do – he was quitting the Marines. We partied at a club called Joanna's, which in those days was a real dump and renowned for being a brawling hotspot. While we were there, a couple of Dutch sailors had decided to give us grief for no other reason than it must have seemed like a fun thing to do. At first they began by barging into the group, which seemed more like foreplay than anything else, but one of them, a fat bloke, was taking it too far. So, as he leaned on the bar, having ordered a round of beers, one of my mates grabbed at his legs, tipping him forward. His wobbly body nearly upended into the optics with a force, and he was hauled over with a crash. It was hilarious. But once the sailor had regained his composure, he was quickly up on his feet, in my grill, snarling and threatening to thump me. I wasn't interested, though. The bouncers soon got involved, which was when I decided that enough was enough and announced to everybody that I was going home.

That's when the trouble began.

The two sailors followed me out as I walked along the street looking for a taxi. Before I knew it, both of them were in my face again; they were shouting, goading me. One of them shoved me in the chest, which I wasn't going to take lightly, and I immediately headbutted him, sending him to the floor with a couple of follow-up punches before decking his mate. Just to ensure the job was done, I went back to the first one – the fat lad, who was now rolling around the floor clutching a bloody nose – and gave him a hefty boot to the head. But everything had been caught on CCTV. I was lifted.

This incident marked the beginning of a horrendous episode in my life. I needed to hire a solicitor and had to pay for the legal fees with a chunk of inheritance money left to me by my nan. I then had to fight charges of GBH, ABH and affray, a claim I really resented because it suggested that I'd incited a riot or created a situation where people feared for their lives. I was told to expect no less than an eighteen-month custodial sentence, which freaked me out along with my girlfriend of the time, who then binned me. But I got lucky. The judge was impressed by a series of character references presented to the court, and despite having made claims for financial compensation the prosecution failed to show up for my sentencing. I was given three hundred hours of community service, which, while teaching me a lesson about keeping my fists down, proved to be something of a joke. I spent one day wrapping elastic bands round plastic bags for the cancer trust Marie Curie, before working for a few days as a gardener on a roundabout in Somerset, me wearing a hi-viz vest and surrounded by a number of other wallies wearing hi-viz vests. One morning a bloke showed up because he had been caught knocking through a wall in his council house without permission. He caught everybody's attention when he arrived, firstly with the grimy, broken-tooth smile plastered across his chops, but also because somebody had shaved the word 'C**T' into the back of his head.

'Mate, what the hell happened there?' I asked.

'It was my children,' he laughed, his smile a moss-covered graveyard. 'They're thirteen and fifteen. Always up to no good . . .'

I laughed, but the admission shocked me. I couldn't believe someone would crumble to their teenage kids like that. It showed a massive lack of discipline and self-respect, two qualities that would later become the cornerstones of my military career.

Should I really be admitting all this to a complete stranger? Wasn't I supposed to be an experienced soldier: superhuman and immune from negative emotion? Is this normal? Am I a loser? Have I broken some unwritten code?

The feelings of insecurity and vulnerability became more and more real as I continued to blurt out my story. Then I became embarrassed. I imagined myself as weak, as if I'd blown it in my roles as a fighter and as a man, when to everybody around me I was functioning perfectly well (the odd bad mood aside). Only the other day at the base, one of my teammates had mentioned those brief moments in the ditch on the helicopter mission. He'd been recalling how he was crouching alongside me, pinned down by fire, as we figured out how best to get to our target. When he spoke I suddenly feared my mental spasms might have been obvious and that he was now building up to The Big Reveal. *Was he about to expose the chink in my armour?*

'Mate, you were like a ball of fire,' he said, laughing.

I thought I'd misheard him at first. 'Eh? What do you mean?'

'You got up and ran across the field. You were, like . . . *unstoppable*. I saw you kicking through the bushes, taking shots. It was awesome . . .'

Funny. We had both been doing the same thing at the same time, but as different people seeing different things. In his mind, my actions had been heroic, like something from an action movie. The truth was that I had been choked up with terror and shame.

'Mr Fox?' said the psychiatrist, halting my train of thought. I had zoned out, replaying the moments in my head again. I must have looked vacant.

'Mr Fox, I think you have PTSD, mild depression and chronic burnout . . .'

The words sounded muddled, warped, as if I were underwater in a swimming pool and somebody was shouting at me from above. I imagine it would be the same for someone receiving a terminal illness diagnosis. To my mind, the conditions *were* terminal; I was mentally ravaged. Finished.

'What do you mean?'

'Look, what you've experienced in war has caused issues,' he said, 'but we can help you – though we'll need to sign you off work and you'll have to begin taking antidepressants.'

'But, mate, I don't want to be signed off!' I argued. 'And I really don't want to be taking any pills.'

'It really is the best course of action for you. You can sign off sick, which will give you a chance to right yourself through therapy, and the tablets will help you with the depression. We'll simultaneously put you on a treatment plan. We'll start with Cognitive Behavioural Therapy and a procedure called Eye Movement Desensitization and Reprocessing therapy, or EMDR.'

I nodded as if I'd registered every word, when really I hadn't understood any of it. (I later went online to learn what both of those treatments would involve – neither of them sounded like fun.) The realization that I was taking sick leave and being given antidepressants upset me – *and being told by a complete stranger who didn't know me from the next bloke!* When Dr Beckelmann handed over the prescription, I looked moodily at the paper, my identity unravelling in a soulless office somewhere in Portsmouth, a million miles away from the places where the damage had first been done. And over and over and over, the troubling, terrifying question of . . . *What would happen to me next*?

But I was all out of ideas.

17

I drove back through the grey and wet to Poole, my head in tatters. The rain seemed heavier than ever before and the water whooshed across the tarmac and surged under the cars ahead. Within the big picture, I didn't really know what was going on; I wasn't sure what the psychiatrist's plans might mean for my life and my career. The good news was that I could be fixed, hopefully. I was still sure of that. I told myself that maybe, with more sessions alongside the psych nurse, some tablets, the CBT or EMDR – whatever that was – I would be back to my old self in no time.

I glanced down at the prescription note resting alongside me on the passenger seat, a neatly folded certificate of defeat. *Those pills, though. What would they mean for me?* I was so unsure of what I was actually stumbling towards by taking medication, and what its visible effects might be, that I feared for my reputation rather than any long-term healthcare gains. In terms of priorities, getting better was almost secondary to my respectability within The Brotherhood, which was bound to take a battering if any of the other lads discovered Dr Beckelmann's treatment plan. His medical diagnosis had grabbed my ego and shaken it like a rag doll. I couldn't allow the bruises to show.

I was exhausted. The last few hours had only amplified my increasing sense of disorientation, but I needed to collect the antidepressants. I stopped at a chemist somewhere on the way to Poole, bashfully handing over the paper to a checkout girl as if I'd been requesting ointment for an embarrassing condition. *Would she know?* When I got home, the bottle sat on the coffee table for hours before I found the minerals to neck my first dose, easing myself in with a half-tablet on the doctor's recommendation. Breaking the pill apart, I scanned the list of side effects stuffed inside the box, each bullet point a reminder of my mental injuries and the mess I was now living in. Nausea, increased appetite and weight gain would be some of the less impactful consequences upon my life. But fatigue, insomnia and constipation sounded horrible, as did drowsiness and the occasional dry mouth, though not entirely impossible to manage. Most frightening, though, was one sentence which seemed to stand out from all the others:

'Might experience a loss of sexual desire and other sexual problems, such as erectile dysfunction and decreased orgasm.'

Great. Not only was I being made to feel like a loser in my job and as a man, but now my sex life was in the bin as well. I was completely stressed about it. The fear of impotence and a malfunctioning cock lay in wait like a militia ambush.

I swallowed the split pill, grimly gulping it back. And waited. Initially nothing really discernible happened, not something I could define with any confidence, anyway. I started to feel more tired, for sure, but the other side effects took hold more slowly. As I increased the dosage over the next twenty-four hours, different chemicals oozed into my system. Gradually, each pill brought a numbing sensation to my existence and I became even blurrier in the head than before. My new default setting throughout the day was one of increased drowsiness, indifference and emptiness, when feeling drowsy, indifferent and empty was already one of my biggest problems. In the rare conversations I had with mates on the phone, or when I was chatting with my new girlfriend, who I'd met recently, I noticed my mood lurching wildly up and down. At the lowest points I was a miserable sod and incredibly difficult to get on with.

Whenever I attempted to get a point across, people found it very hard to understand me – probably because I didn't really understand myself.

My sick leave was soon in place. The walls were closing in. I knew I had to escape for a while from Poole, where I felt surrounded by The Brotherhood; they were everywhere, and it wouldn't take long before people started to pester me about why I wasn't showing up at work. Someone was bound to cold-call me at the house, especially once word had spread that I'd been signed off. They would ask what was up. There would be phone calls, comments in the pub and plenty of jokes about my health and whatever socially awkward condition they fancied conjuring up for me in my absence.

Contagious is it, Foxy? Yeah, I bet it is. You dirty so and so . . .

In all my confusion I feared I might give the game away. I was scared it would take place during some random, innocuous conversation, and my pride was dented enough already without everyone knowing the truth. I had to find some way of avoiding any questioning. On those rare occasions when I was needed on base, I kept my head down upon arrival, all the while praying I could collect my things, or land at a meeting, without bumping into somebody I knew. I was mega-embarrassed. Unknowingly, I had made the first steps towards detaching myself from the military, physically at least, when in reality I should have pulled my closest friends even tighter for support, opening up to them about what was happening to me. Maybe if I'd embraced The Brotherhood and told them the truth at that point, my recovery would have started, and finished, more swiftly, but the antidepressants pamphlet hadn't imparted those vital words of advice. There were no guidelines, or protocols for how an experienced soldier should handle himself in the middle of a mental breakdown.

And so I bailed.

After a few weeks of ghosting around Poole, I became convinced that a change of scenery was my best hope for any form of peaceful recovery – but where? This feeling only intensified once my girlfriend had suggested that I take up a job at her family's bar in a seaside resort on the south coast. She reckoned I could work there part-time, earning some cash and filling my days between visits to the therapist's office back in Poole. At the thought of a temporary release there was suddenly more room to breathe, especially without The Brotherhood's intolerance to weakness bearing down on me. I agreed to my girlfriend's offer, ignoring the full consequences of my running away from the problem (partially due to the pills clouding my judgement). A couple of months after my PTSD diagnosis, I'd moved from the base's married quarters and started a new life as a temporary civilian, wiping down tables in a boozer, pulling pints and taking medication for my mental health while commuting a couple of hours every week to have my head checked by the psych nurse in Poole. The superhuman component of military existence was a rapidly disappearing speck in the rear-view mirror.

At first I convinced myself that working in a bar at a cool seaside town was a good move, *the only rational decision*, but I was in denial, lying to myself. At times, the realization that I'd been signed off from work returned and I became moodier and distanced from what I was doing. That was unsurprising, really. I was on the mother of all comedowns. Not that far back I had battled my way through the jungle. I had worked on dangerous missions and headline-making operations in all manner of bullet-riddled hellholes. Like the astronauts I'd read about in that magazine, I had seen my metaphorical Earth from Space. Now I was aiming a bottle of Cif at a grubby bar top and sweeping up half-eaten chips from under the tables for my encore. The stink of stale booze and bleach surrounded me; I was a thirty-six-year-old bloke working alongside students earning cash for their degrees and beer money. Talk about demoralizing.

One morning, as I readied the bar for another lunchtime rush, the world slowed to a standstill. I gawped at the traffic outside, my mind blurry and confused, my mouth dry. *Those bloody pills.* The memories of war swept in once again. This time I remembered that terrifying sprint to cover as the enemy closed in during that fateful helicopter mission, my legs lifting higher and higher in order to escape the suck and grab of all that gloopy mud. Bullets were churning up the ground ahead of me . . .

'Foxy . . .'

A voice seemed to be ricocheting around in the background. Somebody was calling my name.

'Foxy!'

I had been snapped into reality, as if yanked back on an invisible cord. I looked around, startled. One of the barmaids had noticed me staring into nothingness and was calling me over.

'Bloody hell, mate,' she said, sounding worried. 'Are you all right?'

'What?'

'You're on another planet,' she said. 'You're staring a million miles away. What are you thinking about?'

I brushed her off, but my freak-out moment, where I had gawped into space, caused me to wobble even more. *What had I looked like?* As I carried on wiping down the tables I realized that if a nineteen-year-old girl had noticed the state I was in, how could I possibly hide my problems from anyone within the military when I eventually got back to Poole? I hated the idea that someone could read my emotional disconnect, even if it was only for the briefest moment. I felt exposed, vulnerable. Psychologically I wanted to be safer, higher up, in a position where I could see any approaching trouble from a distance, a feeling I'd last craved after Danny had been shot in the throat. I knew I needed to shut down even tighter.

So when the next bloke from the base called up asking where I'd been, I concocted a plausible excuse, hoping it would throw him off-track.

'I've been diagnosed with tinnitus,' I lied. 'My ears are in bits from all that gunfire.'

'Really? Shit, Foxy . . .'

'I know. Mate, do yourself a favour, the next time you're heading into a scrap, wear your ear defenders.'

My alibi was believable. I'd been involved in so many head-shrinking firefights it was highly conceivable that one of my senses would have been irreparably damaged. The fact my mind had been injured was a war wound too embarrassing to reveal.

18

Drugged-up and drowsy, I arrived for another session with the psych nurse, sneaking into the base with my coat collars pulled up, a camouflage to anyone noticing my arrival as I walked along the sports pitches towards the medical offices. The work ahead had the potential to unbalance me even further, but only because of my suspicious views on mental health care: Eye Movement Desensitization and Reprocessing was a style of psychotherapy treatment designed to alleviate the chaos associated with traumatic memories. From what I'd learned online, I was about to be 'mentally stimulated' by an expert directing my eye movements laterally, from left to right, with an object such as a pen. That had sounded weird enough, but I could also expect to be questioned at the same time. While staring at a fast-moving biro, the shrink and I would discuss deeply disturbing incidents that I believed had broken me down. The idea was that within this processing, the exact catalysts for my meltdown would become clearer; there might even be an unexpected root cause that would surface along the way, though I wasn't exactly chuffed at the thought of sitting idly while a nurse bored down into my happy early family life yet again. There had been a slight shift in my mood this time, though. After a brief period of confusion and then denial, I was beginning to accept that PTSD, depression and burnout were now a part of my life, as was therapy. *I had to.* If I wanted to be fixed, I needed to be open to just about anything that might help me to rediscover my military buzz.

In yet another bland, soulless room, the psych nurse did exactly as my Google search on EMDR had described. I was settled into a chair and told to relax, which felt almost impossible under the circumstances. My innermost thoughts were about to be picked apart.

'It might be a good idea to use the mission you mentioned in our first session as a jumping-off point,' he suggested. 'How about we start in the helicopter again?'

Again?

The nurse loomed over me, his index finger raised in front of my eyes.

The bloody helicopter.

My eyes traced from left to right, right to left, following the finger moving across my line of vision.

'Think about the helicopter . . . What were you experiencing? What were you feeling?'

I went there yet again, to the memories of fear and adrenaline tumbling over and over as I remembered the first flashes of muzzle fire in green, my throbbing knees as I grabbed at the legs of the bloke sitting alongside me, and he grabbed me. I saw the helicopter riding next to us rocking with the kinetic energy, the tremors caused by an explosion nearby. The trees were bowing and bending in the rotary blade's downforce as we came in to land . . .

The nurse stopped suddenly. 'Right, Mr Fox,' he said. 'What's the first thing that comes into your head?'

'The mission, the gun battle,' I said.

'Oh, right . . . Are you sure?' replied the nurse. 'Normally, it's common for people to go back to the original source of the trauma, something deep inside that might have messed you up previously. Something from your childhood, or family, maybe?'

I shook my head. 'Look, I told you about my family,' I said, tensely. 'I had a great time growing up.'

I felt as if I was being treated in the same manner as any

other civilian patient; that the discussion was primed to deep-dive into a series of non-existent father issues, or some other form of long-forgotten psychological event, when it was combat that had been the trigger for my stress.

The nurse nodded. 'Well, don't be surprised if at some point you end up going back to your childhood in these sessions.'

I became annoyed. 'Don't be surprised if we stay in a helicopter.'

I knew I'd presented an unusual case for the military's psych nurse: a soldier of experience admitting to being thrashed by the extreme limits of war. Most people in my position wouldn't have confessed to feeling rinsed psychologically. Meanwhile, I understood the military was in a learning phase about how to handle the complicated and nuanced symptoms of PTSD, a condition that differed from one example to the next. Every case was unique in one way or another. But when it came to treating mental health issues, I was learning that most institutions had a square hole, square peg philosophy: they were going to hammer somebody towards their idea of a perfect programme, hoping it might fit, whatever the shape or size of the patient's problem. I knew the military liked things to be cut and dried and almost compartmentalized; they were always big on procedure. Thinking outside of the box in a case such as mine wasn't going to happen, which was a shame because, as I learned later, I could have explored a million different treatment options. There was no mention of me trying alternative practices such as group therapy, or something more holistic. I had been placed on a set path, a catch-all course of treatment, whether I agreed with it or not.

'Listen, Mr Fox,' said the nurse. 'Over the coming weeks we'll do this with all the stressful events that have taken place in your life so far. Then we'll see what the response is. When you go home, have a ponder about what they are . . .'

I went dizzy thinking about it all. For nearly a decade I had served in war, jumping in and out of gunfights, trying not to die. I couldn't remember a time when I *wasn't* stressed. My combat backstory also seemed like a tangled clump of wool, confusing and impenetrable. Yanking at the threads in this way was a disaster waiting to happen. Like the military, I realized that I, too, was in a new learning phase of emotion and mental health, and disorientated about how to handle my complex condition. The feelings and the processes needed to manage my wounds were new to me. I was scared. Almost immediately, the toolkit I believed the Navy medical team at Poole might have had – the one that would give me back my love for the job – felt rigid and blunted. I was frustrated at its unwieldiness. As I left the psych nurse, the thought of never going back to work again filled me with an overwhelming sense of despair.

Over the coming weeks, my downers intensified. I second-guessed every decision in every aspect of my life, even down to what I was going to eat, and then I second-guessed again. The dark moods that had weighed me down previously became heavier and more prolonged, and nothing could shake me from the darkness. When I later travelled to the Lake District for a short holiday, I drove from Carlisle to the west coast. I dropped an antidepressant after settling in and it knocked me out for three days. I felt drunk. I couldn't string a sentence together. I was exhausted, able to open my eyes – but only just, my eyelids felt lead-heavy – and I was miserable for the entire trip. The drugs had become a numbing agent. Sometimes they helped to shut out the emotions that had unsettled me in the first place, but they did little to push me towards a healthy resolution. The chemicals might have worked for some people, but not me. Instead they acted like sticking plaster covering up a chest-sucking bullet wound when I really needed surgery and stitches. I was falling deeper and deeper into a mental black hole.

I kept on jabbing at the self-destruct button when I was at home with my new girlfriend, as I had done in previous relationships. There were occasions when I would be spaced out on the sofa, the pair of us relaxing with her kid, enjoying a night of domesticity in front of the TV. She was laughing and having a good time, but I would flip out. I couldn't handle the comfort and security smothering me, I found it annoying, and often looked to escape. I tried to screw up moments of calm by starting an argument, or I'd react badly to something, exploding into a rage and then sulking for hours afterwards.

I think deep down I knew that my future was being controlled by a psychiatrist's professional diagnosis, not by me, and that ten years of military service had taken a heavy toll on my mental health – I was retreating from being a part of the elite. The realization had caused me to become a nightmare to live with – I was retreating from contact at home. I became unable to face my family and friends because I was losing everything I'd once stood for – I was retreating from the basics of life, caught in a cyclone of misery. The effect was crippling. It didn't help that I was driving along the motorway for three hours every week to visit psych nurses who seemed unable to locate the root cause of my problems. I was tired of the experience, the drab, cold and clinical rooms I had to sit in while my thoughts were dissected by an expert, by someone seemingly all out of ideas.

And then I was offered a permanent escape route into civilian life.

'The only thing that's going to fix you now is to leave the military,' said the psych nurse after months of frustration and dead-end questioning, him waving his finger around, me repeating myself in yet another unproductive session. 'Leave the uniform. Take away everything that makes you depressed. It'll be a huge weight off your shoulders.'

The idea wound me up. I was yet to falter at any stage in my military career and quitting felt like a cop-out. 'No. No way. That's not an option – I'm not doing that.'

The suggestion was enough to tip me off-balance, and during that period the idea of leaving The Brotherhood caused me to spiral down even harder, the darkest thought striking me for the first time.

Without any purpose, what's the use?

A psychiatrist had worked out what I was bringing to the party, and the answer chilled me.

I had nothing.

Absolutely nothing.

So what's the point to any of it?

*

After endless sessions of therapy, killing time became a priority. I figured it was as good an opportunity as any to holiday somewhere hot and sunny, with plenty of beach-facing bars to lose myself in. I needed a little rest and recuperation, hoping it might settle my head in some way, and besides, there was nothing better to do. Senior officers on the base had entrusted me with some minor tasks to keep me busy at home, paperwork to complete on the side, but it was a token gesture, and when I booked a fortnight in Tulum, the Mexican town which was bordered with a picture-postcard Mayan wall and a coastline that dipped down into the Caribbean, I felt vaguely excited by the prospect of creating some space between my issues and the grey and damp atmosphere dogging me in England. But not too excited. The pills had blunted my endorphins to a point where not being moody or vacant was the closest I ever got to real happiness.

For the first few days away I definitely felt *different*. Somewhere approaching OK. I rested and became comfortably spaced-out, a mood located between the pills and my mental fuzziness, the lethargy unnoticed by everybody around me as they rested and became comfortably spaced-out too, but due to booze, sunshine and adventure. From the security of a sunlounger, everybody was escaping the personal stresses and fatigue of home. Then a mental fracture proved to me that there was no fleeing the problems crushing my spirit in Poole.

I had decided to go for a morning run along the beach. It was early, the sun had barely crept above the ocean but I'd wanted to exercise, believing that if I maintained my fitness there might be a shot at re-joining The Brotherhood somewhere in the future. Plus it made me feel better about myself. Smashing out a few miles in a jog while sweating away the beers from the night before seemed like a good way to start the day. The scenery was beautiful too. An inky-black ocean stretched away into the distance, the sunrise burning at its edges. Waves lapped at the coastline and the crunch of the beach under my feet felt almost therapeutic. But having only gone a mile or so, the sight of the sand stretching ahead triggered some strange mental episode – not a flashback as such because I didn't really have flashbacks, not in the trippy sense, but a memory that created a tsunami of heavy emotions. It was the shadows, my dark silhouette shimmering on the beach in front of me. I felt the hot wind on my face, the sun in my eyes.

Like I was sitting at the back of a helicopter again.

In the moments of calm once a mission had been completed, while the troops were making for base, I sometimes sat at the rear of a Chinook, my gun trained on the desert. The chopper's shadow speckled the ground hundreds of feet below. My skin was buffeted by scorching air, my eyes squinting at the high sun. During those minutes I was often in an emotional state of purpose and meaning. We were about to land. I'd done my job. *Mission complete.* I was looking forward to showering and eating my breakfast.

Now I was on a beach in Mexico, my shadow flickering on the dunes beneath me, sweat in my eyes, the sun on my face, dreaming of a fancy meal in the hotel restaurant. And the war had caught up with me again.

Riding around in helicopters – I'm not doing that any more. I used to love doing that.

Negative thought was back. PTSD had grabbed at me again, and with it, the self-inflicted abuse.

Why am I not doing that any more?

Why don't I love it any more?

I felt hunted, tracked down to a place where I'd believed I really might be able to hide from my troubles. I should have been OK, I'd been hunted before – in war, but also in training. Back then, when I was hoping to make it into elite service, myself and several potential candidates were released into the Welsh countryside and stalked by dog trackers, on our scent for up to seven days. It was a test. The

sole job of the 'Hunter Force' was to find the soldiers running around in the darkness before bringing them back for
tactical questioning where their alibis would be stripped
bare over a period of intense mental and physical beastings.
At that time, I had found my development in the military –
and all the specialist courses that went with it – a fun
challenge. The evasion training felt like just another adventure, a small group scarpering from the enemy and, like
most aspects of military life, it mainly comprised lengthy
episodes of tedium interjected with rushes of excitement. I
remember walking through the Welsh countryside as a
group, feeling tired, hungry and bored, fed up with the
cold, when suddenly the Hunter Force moved into view for
the first of several skirmishes. We'd seen them; they had
seen us, and a chase kicked off, our gang darting into the
woods and making our escape.

We managed to avoid capture for several days and while
we were allowed to live on our wits during that time, the
one rule in place was that we couldn't cheat by engaging
with members of the public. But nobody paid any attention
to that. We had heard from other soldiers that the trick was
to break those rules without getting caught. One night,
after five days of living off food scraps, a pensioner spotted
us as we crossed her farmland. The flashlights from the

Hunter Force sweeping the skyline and their dogs barking aggressively in the distance must have alerted her to the pursuit. When she noticed us crouching by a perimeter wall we were ushered over.

'Get in here, boys,' she whispered conspiratorially, showing us inside. Nobody thought twice about taking up her offer. Through the windows her home looked warm and cosy.

'Have you eaten?' she asked, opening up her fridge and setting out a banquet of sarnies, chocolate biscuits and cans of Coke. I think cold and starving soldiers must have been regular visitors to her property because she understood exactly who we were and what we were doing. Greedily, we shovelled in stacks of food as she looked on and smiled, like the unlikeliest leader of some imaginary group of freedom fighters. But when we later left her place, fattened and happy, the show of generosity attacked us with a vengeance; our expanded stomachs, starved for nearly a week, bucked and lurched as we raced towards the woods, all of us projectile-vomiting fizzy drinks and half-digested crisps into the darkness.

When we were eventually caught, the fun and games really began. Our interrogators instilled fear in us by forcing us towards a state of shock, first by screaming into our faces and manoeuvring our bodies into agonizing stress positions, then by exposing us to a series of psychological pressures, each one designed to crack the most stubborn of personalities. Physical resistance resulted in payback. Not taking the onslaught seriously was just as risky and when I laughed at having two men in balaclavas yelling at me from point-blank range I was stripped naked and tied outside in the wintry air. Then somebody soaked me down with icy water from a hose. I was left there for what felt like hours.

Bloody hell, I thought, shivering, my bones and muscles bucking and wrenching with the cold. *I wish I'd kept my mouth shut.*

Now in the warmth and comfort of Mexico, with cocktails on tap and an all-you-can-eat buffet within reach, I realized my problems had trailed me like the Hunter Force in Wales, though the consequences of being caught were far scarier than any interrogation. This time the shadowy forces dogging me were the aftershocks of war; the interrogators a crushing sense of self-doubt working in my own head. They had crept up on me in the most inconspicuous way, the tremors caused by a morning run through the sand.

Why am I not doing that any more?
Why don't I love it any more?

JASON FOX

I got back to my hotel room, showered and ate breakfast. I then shut myself away from the world for three days and acted like a miserable bastard, knowing that I was done, believing that the doctors had been right all along and that I needed to quit the military. Preparing to make the worst decision of my life in a period of never-ending screw-ups.

19

This is not good.

This is really not good.

As I bunkered down in a luxury hotel room, unable to push away my bed covers, unwilling to face the sunshine outside, I came to an understanding that riding the emotional roller-coaster of a gun battle was pretty similar to wrestling the fallout to PTSD. Both shared the same mental push and pull. There were moments of intense stress. Often my heart seemed to be bursting through my rib cage as I became weighed down by the never-ending questions of *What next?* and *What if?* My worst-case scenarios were replayed over and over. But then faint slivers of hope would arrive, and then fade, those painfully brief interludes usually trailed by flashes of anarchy as everything around me spiralled out of control.

During that period I believed there was nothing in my power to stop a bad incident from taking place – it was inevitable. I found myself living in epic chaos where surreal, almost slow-motion episodes of drama unfolded, such as a hellish argument at home. Moments of calm collided with moments of combustion. Life felt dangerously unpredictable, 24/7. There were so many false endings. On countless occasions I sensed some fresh breakthrough or an escape route that might lead to recovery. It might have been a thread of a new idea in my therapy sessions, or a combination of pills that temporarily lifted my mood, and for those brief periods claiming resolution seemed possible. The reward I wanted so badly in those snapshots of optimism was my military mojo, fully restored and in better shape than ever before, there for me to utilize once more.

But I couldn't.

Given my experience with epic and awful battles, it would have been understandable had anyone outside the mental health profession assumed that I could carry my issues like a slightly-heavier-than-usual piece of kit. Elite fighters like myself were perceived as having been psychologically toughened; my working attitude was finely tuned to functioning within seemingly impossible scenarios. In the past I had been able to push past my breakpoint in elite training and operate in conditions so awful that only a tiny percentage of soldiers made it through. Suffering had become my speciality and no warzone had proved too tough. I once remember emerging unscathed from a seemingly never-ending battle that had lasted for over twenty-four hours – though its intensity was nowhere near as exhausting as my conflict with PTSD.

The details of that scrap still felt vivid. We had been ordered to attack a fortified position which was pitched on one side of a deep valley. We'd been informed that the place was heavily guarded with machine guns. Intelligence had warned us that a lot of senior bad dudes were camped there and the place was considered to be something of a hornets' nest. It was decided we should open fire at night. During the crazy battle that followed, the valley was bombarded for six hours, the enemy firing all sorts of artillery at us; our own troops returning machine-gun fire across the rocky expanse with no real idea of our targets' exact location as the hostiles constantly shifted position behind a wall of trees and vegetation. The shooting would go on for an hour at a time before dying down temporarily. Then a chatter of bullets would kick up out of nowhere, unexpectedly, usually at the exact moment that we'd believed our fighting was done with. The noisy encounter would rumble on until the next brief respite.

When the sun came up the shooting seemed to calm down, that's when the real struggle began, the heat scorching our skin at fifty degrees. As a body of men we made a nerve-shredding dash across the exposed land at the bottom of the valley, waiting for the gunfire to open up again, only to discover the enemy had abandoned their positions. Everyone had disappeared into the nearby mountains where we knew they would find it quite easy to vanish without a trace. Frustrated, we turned over their village, which was located nearby, rampaging through a series of tiny huts and shelters, rummaging through discarded boxes and bags for any scraps of intelligence. I kicked my way through a door and spotted the entrance to a disguised underground bunker in the corner of a small shack. Peering down into the darkness with my flashlight, I noticed a storage space was located at the end of the narrow tunnel and dozens of wooden crates had been packed inside. Accompanied by another soldier, I crawled on my hands and knees into the tight, claustrophobic space, checking for booby-traps as we investigated what might be stashed down there. When we reached the first stack of wooden crates, I prised a lid off to reveal an unexpected treasure trove of artillery shells – hundreds and hundreds of them.

'Bloody hell, mate,' I whispered to the bloke next to me. 'We're going to have to blow this lot up.'

He nodded grimly, and we set about rigging a series of explosive charges, lighting the fuse on our way out and legging it to cover as the electrical spark ignited some way down in the darkness. *WHUMP!* The ground trembled, puffing smoke and dust around us, but something wasn't quite right. Our pyrotechnics show should have been bigger, louder, wilder. *The charge hadn't gone off properly!*

Oh shit, I thought. *Now muggins here is going to have to crawl back in and redo the bloody thing.*

Like the organizers of a village fireworks display, we knew that returning too soon to an unlit rocket was asking for trouble, so we sat it out in the blistering heat for thirty minutes before crawling down into the bunker again to reset the fuses. But when we reached the explosives, my senses prickled. Something wasn't right. I raised a hand, signalling for the other bloke to hold as I assessed the situation in the gloom, flashing my torch towards the ammo stash. In the spotlight I could see that our detonation hadn't caused too much surface damage to the contents of the bunker, but the shells inside must have been unsettled or cracked open. They were now leaking a fine, yellow mist. It seeped from the slits in the wooden crates. *Could it be mustard gas?* We pulled on our respirators, the black rubber edges squelching to my skin with the sweat and heat before quickly finishing off the rewiring job, this time the bunker caving in on itself with a huge bang, burying whatever was hidden inside.

Our job had been done. But it hadn't.

Our operations that day had been played out against a backdrop of paranoia. At one point, intel alerted us that the enemy was returning – but they never came. Our air support later had to return to base because it was running low on fuel, which made us vulnerable. Every moment had been fraught with the nerve-shredding anticipation of more attacks and more gun battles, and once we had finally been extracted from the valley, over twenty-four hours later, all of us were frazzled. False ending after false ending had taken its toll. All day we had been on the verge of leaving the area, only to discover another stash of weapons. At times bullets had rained down on us, just as we'd thought the day had been decided. The action had gone on and on.

Over a year later, I was still lurching from emotional peaks to emotional troughs, but from the relative safety of a Mexican tourist resort. And as in war, there was no finishing line in sight. Just as I'd been in gunfights that had dwindled into nothing, only for our unit to walk into another ambush moments later, PTSD constantly tricked me into believing that a decision or change in my life was the endnote to a period of crushing misery.

But it wasn't.

My latest false ending had appeared on that morning run. Spinning out with the realization that there was no safe hiding place from the ghosts of combat, I was now succumbing to my biggest fear: I had finally admitted to my failure at being a soldier – an awful, self-fulfilling prophecy hinted to me after hours and hours of therapy. *The experts were telling me to quit in order to get better – they must have been right all along.* And as I wallowed in the misery of the idea, I decided to succumb to the advice of both the psych nurse and Dr Beckelmann. It was time to leave the military. Once I'd landed back in England I was going to tell the people in charge that I wanted to be medically discharged. In my muddled mind, only walking away from the job – a job that had defined me – was going to fix the damage caused by war. My time in The Brotherhood, the union I'd dreamed of being a part of ever since I was a kid, would be over, though at least a huge weight was going to be lifted from my shoulders. I could look forward to rebuilding myself into a healthy, functioning bloke again.

But I wouldn't.

*

Quitting was an unfamiliar idea. I struggled to recall the times I had walked away from anything in my professional life. Away from the military, several relationships had been ditched, for sure. I'd imagined a shrink would suggest that I was bailing out of my exams when I left school as a teenager; but I was walking away to join the Marines, which seemed to me like a step forward and a massive upgrade. I was known for my resilience and resolution in war, a stubborn bastard who liked to see challenges through to the end, as I first demonstrated during elite training later on in my career, especially in the jungle, which was a six-week test of survival designed to break anyone not wearing the toughest of mental armour. It had confirmed me as a capable soldier.

The jungle was hard work because the conditions were so hellish. It would rain every single day and the heat was unbearable, often pushing towards forty degrees. In those tropical rainforest conditions, the foliage came alive and just about everything tried to eat me while I was there, such as spiders, snakes and all sorts of grim insects. One morning I had to scoop away a leech that had attached itself to the inside of my mouth while I'd been sleeping. In such testing circumstances, a soldier really needed to look after himself physically. Any cut, scratch or blister was liable to become infected with rot, or worse, a flesh-eating bug, while bacteria infections could lead to sickness, so all wounds had to be tended to constantly. The tasks I was required to perform proved demanding: navigation expeditions, live gun-firing exercises and mock casualty evacuation drills, all of them executed in lung-sucking heat across an environment that was so claustrophobic that the sun struggled to break through the canopy of leaves and branches overhead. Meanwhile, everything we did was subject to scrutiny, our work analyzed at a distance by a group of assessors who were experts in jungle warfare and survival and were able to crawl through the foliage to observe us unnoticed. Although we couldn't see them, their presence felt intrusive and I always sensed them nearby, watching and listening. Sometimes an assessor might pop up from the undergrowth to bollock one of the lads for not having cleaned their gun properly. One morning I remember getting a tonne of grief for no particular reason, but it had been a test: the people watching had wanted to wind me up, to throw me into a mental spin, to see how I reacted in an inhospitable and oppressive environment under the pressures of doubt, the rot between my toes burning, my camouflage cream running with sweat, the battle to ensure my gun and ammo remained dry a never-ending struggle.

The fact that so many of us didn't know whether we were succeeding or flunking made it a psychologically self-destructive process. Some blokes probably talked themselves out of passing the phase through their own uncertainty.

But I had thrived. Several hopefuls around me dropped out, or were told at the end that they hadn't made the grade, but I carried on regardless. I'd proved myself to be focused and bloody minded, but I was also able to adapt to the environment I was fighting in. It wasn't enough to be the toughest, fastest, most powerful dude in the game. An elite soldier required flexibility. In the space of twenty-four hours a raid might require a unit to jump from a helicopter, moving from hot jungle terrain to urban thoroughfares, all the while remaining undetected and prepared to engage with a hostile enemy. There was no room for rigidity. Meanwhile, functioning comfortably had been doable under those unpleasant pressures; the thought of abandoning jungle training midway through never crossed my mind. Not once. I didn't understand the point of walking out, not when I had already made it so far. I had worked hard and the discovery of an unknown level of fortitude pleased me.

That satisfaction had been there on a smaller level in the Marines too, especially when I'd finished the Potential

Royal Marines Course. I had been pushed to my physical limits for a few days, climbing over assault courses and crawling through mud. When I was told that I had made it through and could join 40 Commando I'd walked boldly down a corridor at the base, feeling chuffed.

So why was I quitting now?

Because I had been scared by my own thoughts. During those darkest moments of combat or procedure, as the bombs and bullets peppered our position across that scorching valley, or in the thick of the jungle's unrelenting heat, I knew I could trust my mind. *I had control.* After that run on the beach, the complete faith in my mental strength – which had teetered on the brink for a while – had vanished. I had continually questioned my purpose for the past few weeks; I had asked myself, *What's the point?* And not just once, but on a number of occasions, which meant I was on a slippery path where suicidal thoughts might soon loom into view. I didn't want to go there. I wanted to be free of the misery.

I walked towards the psych nurse's office, across the all-too-familiar sports fields, convincing myself that The New Me was only a medical discharge away. In Mexico, just the thought of walking away from the military had lifted the stressful burden of indecision almost instantly, because the choice wasn't entirely on me. I hadn't wanted to leave the job, but I had been told that doing so would be for the best. The toing and froing, the *should I, shouldn't I?* It had brought so much anxiety that simply succumbing to the experts' advice felt like a blessed relief. Like the times when I'd had to dump a nice girlfriend because she hadn't been quite right for me. The internal debate was more agonizing than the actual break-up conversation.

I waited in the psych nurse's reception room, perched on the same plastic chair as always, habitually flicking through a crap magazine, staring at the bland decor and soulless artwork on the walls, mulling over what I was about to do. I still had time to change my mind, *so should I?* Once the nurse had called me to his office, my resolve returned. Quickly reminding myself of the relief I would feel seemed to make the process so much easier, and when I broke the news of my wobble in Mexico, the run, and my decision to quit the military, I felt instantly vindicated.

'How do I get the ball rolling on me leaving?' I asked.

The nurse nodded and smiled reassuringly. 'It might not feel like it right now, Sergeant Fox, but this is the beginning of the new you,' he said, pulling out a pad of paper. 'This is the fresh break you need to get well again.'

The affirmation that I was doing the right thing actually

excited me. *Yeah, he's right!* I thought. *This is the start of a whole new life!* I became so excited that the details of my discharge flew by like a rush of white noise.

'Look, I'll file the report and then you've got to do a med board,' he said.

'What's that?' I asked.

'Well, it's where you sit in front of several hierarchy doctors and some people in the Navy. It's usually done in an old building stuffed with antique furniture and hanging art, it's all quite official. They'll study your case and talk to you about how things are going. You'll just have to explain what's been happening and they'll medically discharge you.'

My resignation from a life of respect, purpose and military super-humanity was finalized with the swipe of a pen. Meanwhile, the official wording of my departure, the events of the past months and the process ahead, felt cold and clinical.

'Service personnel with medical conditions or fitness issues which affect their ability to perform their duties will generally be referred to a medical board for a medical examination and review of their medical grading. In clear-cut cases where the individual's fitness falls below the Service employment and retention standards, the board will recommend a medical discharge. In many cases, however, the patient will first be downgraded, to allow for treatment, recovery and rehabilitation. For personnel who do not make a total recovery, the board may recommend the patient is retained as permanently downgraded with limited duties, or they may recommend a medical discharge. The recommendation is then forwarded to personnel administration units or an employment board for ratification or decision and action.'

My career of gunfights and dangerous missions had been reduced to grading and protocol; I looked set to become just another statistic in a military medical report. But I really didn't care. A date was set for my board hearing and I worked on tying off the loose ends on my life within the job. In the weeks that followed there were admittedly one or two flashes of doubt, all of them linked to the camaraderie and prestige of working in The Brotherhood. They'd had my back throughout my career and I'd had theirs; I was about to leave that all behind, for good, but I couldn't dwell on it too much. I hadn't thought about what might happen to me once I'd left the base and moved permanently into a civilian lifestyle. Why, I couldn't tell you. At that time I wasn't thinking too hard about the consequences of my actions when it came to my career. Instead, I wasted mental calories wallowing in negative, reflective situations and the only light at the end of a dark tunnel was my medical discharge, a process that was happening quickly – *a little too quickly.*

I went back to my job at the bar in the meantime, pulling pints and cleaning tabletops. Occasionally I'd catch myself staring into nothingness, a sense of loneliness drawing in as I detached from the people closest to me. When the day of my hearing came around, I was briefly struck with nerves. Butterflies fluttered in my stomach as I buttoned up my suit, checking the tie in a mirror like I was preparing for the first job interview of my life. And as I left the front door and made the long drive to Portsmouth, I reassured myself that I had found the beginning of the end to a heavy period of personal misery. *It was done, and I would be fine.* Those words even stayed with me as I sat down in front of the medical board, a table of officials in uniform working from a fancy room in a fancy building, surrounded by busts and old portraits of even more officious figures from the Navy's illustrious history.

'Well, Sergeant Fox,' said the Naval doctor after a brief discussion of my case. 'We've heard what you have to say and we've deemed it necessary for you to now leave the military. It's for the best due to your PTSD and burnout. You will complete your final day on the fifth of April.'

There it was in stone, *my finality*. I left the meeting feeling elated, buoyed by the idea that I was now finally getting on with my life. But how would I tell The Brotherhood? Their reaction terrified me so I decided to avoid them all, ignoring the idea of a leaving party. I couldn't admit to the lads that I had been medically discharged because of my mental health, so I decided to ghost away from the job quietly, without any fanfare or announcements. There was no need for me to return to Poole ever again. Instead I could slip off, evading the blokes I had become enmeshed with over the last ten years. In the event of any unlucky encounters with someone from the base, I would stick to my previous alibi: *I had tinnitus*. My ears were banged up from all that gunfire and the condition had become so bad that my days of active service were done, so I was out – *gutted*. It was a lie, a big one. But unbound from The Brotherhood's code of conduct, it didn't really matter. Their trust was irrelevant. I was now in the cold, stuck in yet another false ending of my own making.

20

The soul-crushing familiarity of 6 April 2012 was the only thing that made it memorable. Feeling a little groggy, I'd hoped to open the curtains on a mega-sunny day, the twinkling sea view from my window stretching away in the distance, a hot girl jogging along the street, waving out to me as she passed, the birds chirping their morning chorus. All of it was a patchwork of positive images, the fantasy that I was about to live in the idyllic opening credits to some faded British sitcom from the 1970s. Instead, my morning appeared to be the same as usual, shadowed by overcast and grim-looking skies. A postman advanced moodily down the driveway, a clutch of bills and junk mail in hand; the seagulls, fattened by chip-shop scraps, squawked from the rooftops, their gloopy, mortar-blast crap wreaking havoc below. Everything was the same as it had been yesterday, and the day before. *And the day before that*. My new beginning, the one I'd believed would take place the second I'd left the war business, simply hadn't arrived.

Hang on a minute, I still feel the same, I thought. *Nothing's changed.*

In those fast-moving months since my board hearing, I hadn't addressed my next steps or thought about what I could do with my new life. It was almost too frightening. The night before, a mate had asked me what I'd planned now that my military role was done. *Where was I going to go? What was I going to be? What mission objectives had I set out for myself?* But I had nothing, so I batted away the questions, pretending I'd been considering a few leads when in reality the calendar ahead was full of blank spaces. Every morning of every day since the medical hearing had been a flight of fancy where I imagined a different career, but I hadn't acted on any of my ideas. Not even a cursory search on Google. Instead I convinced myself that something would come calling. Maybe an ex-Royal Marines Commando mate would emerge from the shadows to offer me a cool job in a high-end security company, or something similar. Anyway, I'd be fine, *I had to be fine*, otherwise what was the point in my leaving the job in the first place?

And on the morning of 6 April I thought about what the future held and saw . . . *nothing*.

The new me was no more than a black expanse of emptiness, a void stretching out to nowhere.

Just several weeks into a new life, my mornings had become a soul-crushing debrief for the soul where I asked, over and over, *Why do I still feel so down?* At night, I would be in fun, safe environments, such as a restaurant with friends, and I'd wonder, *Why does this still feel crap?* With every snippet of despair, the penny would shift downwards a little more, like a cash prize on a Blackpool *Tipping Point* machine. Every pull of the arm pushed a layer of coins a little closer to the edge, with the loot never quite reaching the moment where it cascaded in a noisy crash. The realization of my existence out of the military was gradual. Each lesson took place in domestic situations such as an argument at home, or the condescending attitude of a stranger in the bar as I pulled pints and waited tables. And the inevitable explosion, when it came, was as noisy as any jackpot in an amusement arcade.

No one's really talked down to me like that before.

Wait, I used to have all those blokes about me. They would be on either flank when things went horribly wrong. Yeah, we'd fought our way out of some hellish stuff together, losing mates in battle, not knowing if we were going to make it ourselves, but I miss those times. I had decent people around me. There was respect.

I have no one I can really rely on now . . .

I became crushed by an overwhelming sense of loneliness. Away from the military, I was left exposed to The Real World's harsh realities, where people were able to let me down without consequence, relationships built on trust could collapse very easily, and competence and ownership of responsibility was shot through with flaws and excuses. I had no one to rely on but myself, and it scared the crap out of me. Approaching friends for help was a step too far. I turned my back on nearly all of them due to the embarrassment of my new life, but they were also too busy for me, fighting away in a war on the other side of the world.

I was later reminded of a radio interview I'd heard with a former professional footballer. He'd been talking about what happens when a player retires from the game. 'The phone stops ringing', he explained. 'There's no more banter. The laughing and joking in the dressing room that filled the day vanishes overnight.' Cut adrift from The Brotherhood, I understood exactly what he'd been saying. I was an experienced soldier; I wasn't a civilian that did bits and pieces.

The military was my life, even down to the brass tacks of my day-to-day routines. The senior officers told me when I needed to go to the doctor's. My dental care was paid for. Even the jabs required for going abroad to tropical countries were sorted out for me. I had taken for granted the stuff that most people would have been chuffed to receive for free, because I was living in a bubble. Yes, it had been a dangerous bubble, but I was protected within it while working with some of my best mates. Now, the sense of an out-of-reach community wasn't unlike the life mentioned by that footballer on the radio. As a consequence, I hit a new low.

There were some vague stabs at replicating my old routines as I tried to get a handle on my changing existence. For a while I worked out in the local gym. It was an attempt to fight back, to remain physically elite, but I struggled for motivation most of the time. Without war there was no real incentive. Meanwhile, I stayed busy by working in the bar, convincing myself that I was buying time to evaluate the next steps and that what I was doing represented a positive move. My self-denying inner voice said that I'd made the right choices for my life, over and over, and I listened. But in truth, I knew it was awful.

I was also without the mental tools needed to operate

effectively as a civilian. As I'd prepared to leave the base, it had been mentioned that there were courses for me to attend, programmes focused on transitioning to a job away from the Marines. They promised to teach me the techniques needed to successfully apply for a new job, or even to write a CV and covering letter. But my enrolment was optional, so given an easy way out I'd turned my back on the offer. It was a stupid move. My only priority had been to escape the stress of military life, when really I'd needed somebody to say, 'Mate, look, you really need to take this stuff seriously. It'll help you in the long run.' I was slipping through the net and nobody was on hand to catch me. Nobody questioned the wisdom of my negative decisions.

It wasn't the fault of the Marines, though. I couldn't blame them for allowing me to retreat from their world. And with an ever-expanding and hidden war raging across the Middle East, I was the least of the British military's worries. And I only had myself to blame when the curtains of self-delusion were finally pulled away.

21

Spring 2013

What would it be like to fall?

The heavy tide frothed and churned below me as I peered 150 feet down from the cliff's edge at the jagged rocks and battleship-grey waters, the English Channel thrashing against the Devon coast in a stormy tantrum. Heavy winds and sideways rain buffeted my face. *Everything was different, but the same.* Months after leaving The Brotherhood I had a new office job, a changing life, but I was still endlessly miserable. The polished shoes I'd been wearing for work were now muddy and damp. My suit jacket and tie had become soaked through with water and sea mist, the uniform to a career I hated sticking to my skin. *I fucking despised those clothes.*

It was cold, the air felt wintry, but my personal calendar was sketchy back then and pinning an exact day, or month, to my lonely death wish was impossible. *Could it have been April? May?* Maybe. I honestly had no idea, but it was evening and the light was still dimming over the horizon, so it was probably near to being late spring. So very little of note had taken place since becoming a civilian a year previously that clinging to any snippets of happiness, or satisfying events, for reference was impossible. The happenings that most people used for orientation, like birthdays, weddings, parties or notable football results, had been muddled by depression. The only glimmer of hope in that time was the birth of my second child, but the joy from that moment was soon overwhelmed. Meanwhile, the monotony of a life away from the military was a confusing blur of soul-crushing routine: wake, work, sleep, repeat. *Wake, work, sleep, repeat.* Over, and over, and over. My eyes brimmed with tears. My chest tightened under the stress. Throwing myself off the edge would end the pain I'd sucked up for the best part of three years, all those dark thoughts and periods of worthlessness finished forever, my loneliness gone. One jump and it was done, merciful and quick – *please, let it be quick* – my collision with the rocks killing me in a split second, the tide sucking me to the bottom forever.

What would it be like to fall?

I had often imagined the scenario, even during times when I'd been really happy and fulfilled, before the onset of PTSD and chronic burnout. But haven't we all, if we're really honest? Most people admit to having stood near to the edge of a railway station platform as a fast-moving train has hurtled through, their thoughts turning darkly to the final possibility: *Mate, what's to stop me from jumping forward?* It was a perverse flight of fancy, the human condition testing its resolve for survival in an everyday situation, but on that clifftop I had consciously sought out a spot for suicide rather than being presented with an unexpectedly dangerous scenario. *But could I do it?* I definitely wanted to, I felt compelled. I was weak. Brittle. My spirit had been crushed and the resolve I'd shown throughout my toughest moments in jungle training, or during the harshest of battles, had retreated. With no purpose, there seemed very little point – I had failed as a fighter, a father, a son and a friend. The self-pity I'd hated seeing in others was now all over me like an angry burn.

I might as well die here.

Who would give a crap anyway?

I'm a waste of air.

So, what would it be like to fall?

Six months earlier

I'd been in Andy Leach's air-conditioned office for twenty minutes before realizing he was actually going to offer me a job – a proper job, my first ever civilian contract as a project manager, not that I'd known what the role had even entailed. Very little of what Andy was saying had actually made sense to me. I'd listened to his sales pitch about the company and how Sodexo was delivering all sorts of 'exciting services' and infrastructure assistance to all sorts of businesses, such as the deployment of manpower and equipment to work sites. Some of them had even been linked to the Royal Navy, so I would at least have a little connective tissue to my old gig. There was talk about my responsibilities, how it was a great chance to earn some decent money, all of it explained in a way I didn't really understand, with details on regulatory breaks and expense forms. Andy talked and I sipped on a cup of coffee and nodded, fidgeting uncomfortably in my smart suit while looking around his office, noticing the kitbag and weaponry of his position: a computer, his plastic letter trays stuffed with paper and folders, and a cupboard of stationery. It was so different from wearing a backpack weighed down with all manner of firepower, or a combat vest, the scrapping gear I'd worn on some missions. Maybe one day I'd have a similar desk, working as an MD of a big firm like this one, I thought. Then I heard Andy's concluding proposition.

'Look, Foxy, this isn't the right job for you,' he said. 'But I'm going to give it to you anyway because people in the military have vouched for your skills and the reputation you carry. So take it for what it is – a money earner. You can learn from it and make some forward steps into corporate work.'

I shook Andy's hand and smiled. Somehow, I had landed myself a position with sick pay, holiday leave and all sorts of benefits. I even had a company car. I was to be announced as a project manager in a large firm working along the south coast and throughout the Home Counties. I understood that I would be in charge of the logistical side and I would be working with auditors and drivers. It wasn't a line of work that moved at the high tempos I had been used to, and the company employees weren't as fiercely motivated as The Brotherhood, but Andy was right. It was a way of earning good money while finding my feet, even though I'd hardly applied myself to seeking out a new vocation, not with any real enthusiasm, anyway.

So how had it come to this?

Fed up with working as a bar hand and in need of a serious pay upgrade, I began sniffing around for a new career. Not that it was easy. Applying for jobs with covering letters and a CV wasn't something I'd ever done before and I was clueless about the process (thanks to ignoring the parachute courses on offer in the Navy). I wasn't sure if mentioning some of my later covert military work on application forms was even allowed, given its secretive nature. Eventually I added it into the section marked 'Employment History', and during my first (flunked) interview the guy on the other side of the desk read out the job description and my specialist qualifications. He looked at me quizzically.

'Hmm . . . That all sounds really cool, like something out of a James Bond film,' he said, unsure of what to do with the information. '*But what is it?*'

I'd heard of a lot of blokes leaving the military who were landing cool jobs, usually within security firms or personal protection roles, by manipulating their military experience and applying it to areas outside the Army or Navy. Some of them had even become bodyguards for Hollywood superstars and A-list pop singers, but my head was in such a mess that I often became overwhelmed when imagining how I should apply the skills I'd learned in war to a civilian environment. I knew I didn't want to work in personal security. It paid good money and a lot of the people I'd spoken to had loved it, but I'd listened to their horror stories as well. Blokes I knew felt uncomfortable as they became closer to the people they were protecting. It wasn't uncommon for them to be doing jobs that were out of their remit, like wandering around Sainsbury's for the weekly shopping, or carrying the kids' *Transformers* rucksacks on the school run. Is that what an ex-soldier with a serious amount of experience was really supposed to be doing?

The fact I'd been struck off from the military with mental health issues also meant I was unable to apply for a lot of the professions that might have benefited from my experience and strengths, such as the fire service or police force. At times I was reminded of a scene from the movie *Rambo: First Blood*, in which a battle-bruised Vietnam vet, played by Sylvester Stallone, breaks down in a civilian environment that doesn't understand him. 'Back there I could fly a gunship, I could drive a tank, I was in charge of million-dollar equipment,' Rambo says, emotionally unloading on his former Army mentor, Colonel Sam Trautman. 'Back here I can't even hold a job parking cars!' The fear I might eventually experience a similar fate chilled me.

Like a lot of lads who had left the military in a hurry, I'd started to flap, with no idea of what I should have been doing for work, while the little money I had left in the bank drained away. Despite the urgency of my situation, when it came to hunting for a job I struggled to move with speed or purpose. Summoning the energy for self-promotion and networking felt like a waste of time. Not long after leaving the base, a mate of mine, Mark, had invited me to London for a couple of days. Our plan was to meet with various recruitment types and industry head-hunters, people with a track record for finding work for lads who had previously served at a high level in the military. But when it came to selling my abilities, I clammed up. I didn't want to talk about my past with anyone who hadn't moved in the same line of work as myself – *the people I didn't understand.* Painting a picture of my experience and skills to complete strangers felt weird and I couldn't be arsed with the chit-chatting or small talk. That wasn't a new sensation. It had happened on previous social occasions, such as when I'd been hanging around with Sarah and her friends shortly after my final tour. Back then I'd put my reticence down to unfamiliarity with the people I was with. I'd wanted to blow off steam with the military crowd instead of a group I didn't really know, but my social insecurity was another symptom of PTSD. Cut loose in the civilian world, I now couldn't even muster the enthusiasm to talk to people who wanted to shape my future. If somebody asked me about the work I'd been involved in previously, I inevitably mumbled something about being in the Marines for a little bit. Then I'd change the subject.

'I did some stuff here and there,' I'd say, shrugging my shoulders, deflecting the spotlight away from another life.

It must have sounded so underwhelming, when instead I should have been listing the skills and achievements of an impressive career.

Jason Fox: Royal Marine Commando, team leader able to succeed under extreme pressure, determined, committed, proficient in mission planning and job execution, able to learn from mistakes and react accordingly. Say hello to your next Employee of the Year.

Finding the minerals required to big myself up was impossible, and on the train home, after two days of frustration and dead-end chats in the City, Mark had a pop at me.

'Foxy, you've got to talk!' he snapped. 'Look around, mate. Everyone on this train would probably tell you how good they are at what they do. Whether they're actually any good or not is beside the point, they'll still bloody tell you that they are. You don't need to be in people's faces, but when someone asks, "What did you used to do?" – get it out there!'

He was right, but his advice seemed to have been delivered in another language. I was unresponsive.

I became just as withdrawn at home and the relationship with my partner had become so toxic that we were drifting apart, often living separate lives. Whenever I returned from another job interview or blind-alley meeting she would head upstairs, remaining out of sight for the entire evening. I stayed in the living room, usually with a bottle of wine, staring at the telly, knocking back glass after glass, not wanting to join her in bed. Sometimes I might stumble across a war film and watch the action, the battle scenes bringing up old feelings, delivering a reassuring sense of sadness. For a long while my emotions had been hardened by combat. I was able to repress what was going on internally. Away from the military, I found myself able to enjoy the softer side of my personality. Watching battle films – movies such as *Saving Private Ryan* or *The Hurt Locker* – drew on a seam of melancholy that was previously untapped, but in an unusual way. I related to the action taking place on screen; I understood the complex relationships between the soldiers in an admittedly stylized Hollywood gunfight, and it created a swell of nostalgia for The Brotherhood, one that I soon found upsetting. I realized I was missing the lads more than ever and I longed for the camaraderie. Sometimes I'd find it hard to watch a war film through to the very end.

Given my emotional turbulence, it was a miracle I'd managed to land myself a job at all. But a mate at home had mentioned Andy Leach, the chief executive of Sodexo, a bloke with a previous career as a Naval logistical officer – or a blanket-stacker as I jokingly called him – and an employer with a habit of drawing ex-military types into his business. Something about him had piqued my interest. He had visited the bar I'd been working at on the Devon coast and asked me whether I'd be interested in joining the firm.

I nodded, though I knew it was important to be truthful about my departure from active service. I didn't want Andy to be under any illusions about what he was potentially taking on.

'I've been struck off with PTSD, depression and chronic burnout,' I said, detailing the horrific incidents that had resulted in my eventual medical discharge. I told him about my angry streak and sleeping troubles. 'I definitely need an opportunity to get myself sorted, but I don't really know what to do.' With hindsight, I was probably a little too honest. But Andy nodded. He seemed to understand.

'I can't give you an environment anywhere near to what you used to work in,' he said. 'But the company has a structure that looks after Navy and marine contracts, so there are people and situations you might be familiar with. Taking a halfway step back, but into the military environment again, on the services side . . . That could be a start for you.'

Weeks later, I was dressed in a new suit, feeling excited as I stepped towards the unknown. I drove to work in my company car, walking into a plush office for my first day as a project manager for Sodexo, a company with a nationwide staff of 70,000 people. I announced to myself that the job would make me a corporate success, when in truth the idea of working there hadn't really flicked my switch in the slightest. Instead, I had set down an emotional IED, packed with self-delusion, one that I would step on over and over and over again.

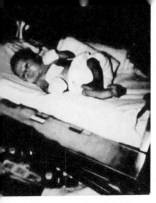

Above: A worry from the minute I was born: I died twice during my first few days of premature life in 1976 due to a collapsed lung.

Right: Preparing for a life of extremes in the British snow with my brother Mat.

Above: My life in the military seemed to have been set from an early age. Mat and I travelled around a lot together when we were kids and were later joined by my little brother Jamie.

Left: Happy but knackered after a day yomping around in the desert with my heavy battle kit.

Above: I enjoyed working in the middle of a scrap knowing there were other capable soldiers around me.

Below: Preparing to lay some demolition equipment. I rarely wore ear defenders because they often affected my other senses during a gunfight.

Above: Relaxing at the base with The Brotherhood, and The Brotherhood's best friend.

Above: The scrapping kit I often wore weighed a tonne. It was such a relief to drop it off in my bunk after an operation, feeling my back click and stretch with the release.

Above: Scaling ladders as the water churns beneath you is one of the hardest jobs undertaken by people in my profession . . .

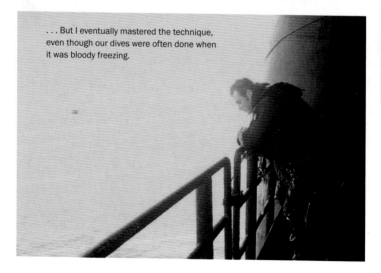

. . . But I eventually mastered the technique, even though our dives were often done when it was bloody freezing.

Above left: Moving on to target and ready for action.

Above right: Often the enemy would shoot at us from their positions as we flew overhead. Vigilance was important.

Left: The sun comes up on the desert, another mission completed . . .

Below: On the journey back to base I would sit at the back of the Chinook, my gun trained on the sand below, in an emotional state of purpose and meaning.

Above: With Jamie Sanderson, my partner in the community interest company Rock2Recovery.

Below: With underwater archaeology expert John de Bry, part of our dive team searching for Captain Kidd's lost treasure just off the coast of a small island belonging to Madagascar.

Above: Leaving the harbour in Lagos, Portugal for our 3,800-nautical-mile row across the Atlantic. The water could get a little choppy!

Right: Being part of the first team to row the Atlantic from east to west unsupported, and the first to row from mainland Europe to mainland South America, was an achievement that probably saved my life.

Above: Working with Veterans for Wildlife, a charity that combats the activities of rhino poachers. We need to wake up because the rhino is disappearing before our eyes.

Left and below: To raise money for the Borne charity – which funds research into the cause of pre-term births – I trekked to the North Pole, where temperatures sometimes dropped to a chilly -40 degrees. Luckily I didn't get to grapple with a real polar bear.

NORTH POLE
TOP OF THE WORLD

Above: From left to right: my new brotherhood – the *Who Dares Wins* team, Matthew 'Ollie' Ollerton, Mark Billingham and Ant Middleton.

Left: Sometimes leadership requires examples. Here I am fast-roping down the face of a reservoir in the Atlas Mountains, Morocco.

Below: Going behind the scenes at a cocaine lab for the 2018 Channel 4 show *Meet the Drug Lords: Inside the Real Narcos*.

22

Six weeks earlier

'I wanted to stab him,' I said, swigging on a pint, several beers in that night. After a long day in the office, a simmering anger had frothed over into a boozy rant. But I'd gone too far.

Andy winced. 'You can't do that, Foxy!' he snapped.

I knew what he was thinking, as the pair of us sat in the local boozer, downloading about another infuriating week – that I was unstable and hot-headed, which was probably right and I could almost see the question sketched across his face. *Is he dangerous?* Andy was probably picturing the worst-case scenarios too. The blood on his office floor. A dead employee – me looming over the still-warm corpse while holding a gore-covered letter opener. *Might Foxy actually do it?*

I laughed it off. 'I'm kidding, mate, I don't want to stab him really . . .'

The problem with working in an industry as regimented and perfectionist as the Royal Navy, particularly at its sharpest point, was that I found it impossible not to become annoyed with the staff working within the corporate setting of Sodexo. Some of the people there clearly couldn't give a toss about the required work ethic. I'd watch as people screwed up and then shifted the blame on to something, or somebody, else entirely, rather than raising their hand and admitting to a balls-up. People lied, cut corners and ignored rules. They promised to act on orders and then failed to deliver. (It seemed to me that this condition was contagious in the job; I feared that I would eventually succumb to the same attitude.) Sometimes instructions were disregarded entirely, and it did my head in. And all the while, life moved at an infuriatingly slow pace. From my crappy desk with my own computer, a plastic letter tray overflowing with paperwork and folders, and boxes and boxes of stationery, I became disillusioned in no time at all.

Andy had been right. Some elements of the job *were* similar to my previous role, but only vaguely and the link was tenuous at best. I was now attending meetings where we discussed how to best deploy assets, but they involved lorries and manpower rather than the tools needed to plan an attack, or where to set up surveillance cameras. At Sodexo there was all sorts of paperwork to deal with, and I was familiar with that form of rigmarole too, having experienced it within the military when requesting equipment or calling upon assistance from another wing of the war machine. And just like the corporate environment, those requests had been subjected to the machinations of office politics.

As with Sodexo there were endless meetings. Despite our heavy schedules, during war we worked through briefing after briefing after briefing, and a team leader like me went through more than most. My role required me to get up early every morning, regardless of whether or not I'd been on a frantic night operation. I'd first train in the base's gym, which was amazing: there was a space for the British, one for the Yanks, another for the Canadians, all of them carrying state-of-the-art equipment, and I was able to sweat out any frustrations. After my workout session I'd take a dirt bike to the office. The people I worked with were like Millwall to my mind – no one liked us and we didn't care – our lines placed miles away from everyone else. Once the rest of my team had arrived for work, the briefings began: our target, or targets, and their location were discussed, then what was required for us to complete our mission.

More often than not, our work took place at night. I'd be awake for twenty hours a day, every day, for six months, save for the occasional hour in which I'd find a cool spot in the shade under one of the Chinooks. When I first arrived for combat, the pace of war was fairly mellow – if you could call it that. Later, as the scale and velocity of combat intensified, more and more tiers of command were installed; there were more official procedures in place and lots more missions – and paperwork. I was soon ordered on to raids every night, even when our assistance wasn't entirely necessary. I remember feeling irked when it first happened, a commander asking me about the leads we'd been working on and what my team was preparing for.

'Not much,' I said. 'We've got nothing relevant just yet. If we go out on anything tonight, it's going to screw us up. It'll burn up aircraft hours and we'll expose our tactics to the enemy fighters on the ground, people who don't really need to know about how we work – and they've been learning quickly.'

The value of allowing some operations to bubble away for longer than others wasn't lost on us. Waiting a day or two for a little extra intelligence to arrive was sometimes the difference between success and failure, but every now and then the higher-ups became impatient. They wanted faster results.

The Commander shook his head. 'No, you're going on it at 22:00 hours,' he said.

'Bloody hell, if we go out tonight we'll get into a scrap with a bunch of fighters with AK-47s,' I said. 'Everyone in the country is poor, they're bored, and they've got a coalition force working here that they see as an invading army. If they have a chance to have a pop, they'll have a pop, because they've got nothing better to do. They're all smacked off their faces on gear anyway . . .'

I wasn't kidding. Kids had been throwing rocks at us for weeks, mainly out of sheer boredom. There were drugs everywhere and violence was often viewed as an entertaining accompaniment to a home-grown high. The British forces became easy targets, but I couldn't blame the dudes lobbing bricks about. I'd have probably done the same if I was a kid living in a warzone, watching as mobs of heavily armed soldiers walked past my house every day, people I believed to be hostile invaders, a conviction that had been indoctrinated into me by radicals. I, too, would have thrown a Molotov cocktail in the hope of starting a tear-up. It's what young blokes sometimes do in hopeless situations. They reach for the self-destruct button. Those were the very real dynamics of the war we were fighting and the Brits had been taking a bloody nose or two. But at least it was exciting.

The military meetings back then had been engaging. The buzz about the office, even the base gym, running on three hours' kip, had been purposeful. But at Sodexo I was project-managing a team where very few people gave a crap about anything other than their pay cheques or the next fag break. Tea spillages at my workstation were the closest I'd ever get to a Molotov cocktail going off, and that saddened me.

One afternoon in the Sodexo office I was called upon to help settle an ugly dispute that had kicked off during work hours. Given that I was experienced in conflict, I figured myself to be fairly handy in de-escalating confrontation, but the banality of the clash blew my mind. Two blokes were standing toe-to-toe at their workstations, screaming abuse at one another, their dispute over sloppy timekeeping coming to a head. Profanities ricocheted across the office as everybody gawped at a row that had been apparently brewing for days. But I couldn't get my head around it. As I stepped between the quarrelling colleagues, ordering both blokes to simmer down quickly, a hush descended upon the Sodexo floor. Then a smiling face popped up from behind my computer terminal. It was Mike, one of the staff members I'd grown friendly with.

'Oi, Foxy,' he whispered conspiratorially. 'What was it you used to do again?'

I'd laughed off his wisecrack, the ludicrous tiff, my role as a peacekeeping force, and the jarring contrast to my old job, where conflicts usually turned noisy, the gunfire and explosions overshadowing any personal disputes or slanging matches between colleagues. But the office flare-up was more disorientating than any military engagement and the long-term implications were certainly scarier. For the very first time, I decided that I wanted to return to my life in the military. The sense of nostalgia for the old days had been lurking around for months, and I had experienced several pangs of regret where I felt desperate to go back. The problem was that my return now seemed impossible, because of my mental health issues, and that made me miserable. *So bloody miserable.*

My days at work were a monotonous nightmare where I'd attempt to convince myself that everything was working out OK – *it's all cool*. I often drove along the motorways and arteries feeding into military towns, such as Aldershot, for hours on end, living inside my own head with only the occasional speakerphone argument with my other half for company. *But it's fine, this will all get better.* I was wrong, and working for hours in a solitary, soulless environment meant there was too much time to relive the horrors of my life in war, the stuff I couldn't unsee, and yet I was craving to be back there, which confused me even more. I kept thinking that, given the opportunity to serve on one more tour – even just a short one, say, three months – there might be a way of bringing a closure to my life in The Brother-hood. But I also feared that returning to war would plunge me even deeper into the hole I'd been living in. I became anxious again. Deep sleep was increasingly rare, my eve-nings spent fidgeting on the sofa, and I'd quit the antidepressants, figuring their side effects to be more troublesome than any of the medical symptoms I'd been experiencing. Worse, I felt like a failure on all levels. My relationships with partners, friends and work were in tur-moil, my masculinity shattered. Everything seemed diabolical. Hopeless.

Nobody around me guessed what was going on and it's unlikely they would have even cared, had they known. I was able to function easily enough, cruising through the day without exerting any real effort. Besides, my colleagues were too wrapped up in their own work to worry about my issues. (Andy was paying attention, though: he would eventually place a tracker on my car after one or two speeding incidents and this later revealed I'd spent hours in the gym on company time – not that he was too bothered.) I was even unable to ask for help from those closest to me – *my family*. I didn't want to burden them with my problems. My brother Mat was in the Marines having his own dramas within the various scraps going on across the Middle East; Jamie was nine years younger than me and, though I loved him, we had a completely different dynamic and operated in two totally different headspaces at that time. Meanwhile, Mum was a worrier, and I couldn't even find it in myself to broach the subject with my dad, even though he was cool and would have been able to advise me. Dad was an approachable bloke and fair (he still is) and yet the thought of opening up to him, admitting that I'd been medically discharged from my job with PTSD, was embarrassing. The thought of laying a heavy form of stress on any of them was awful and racked me with guilt. Besides, I was the oldest son, *I was supposed to handle the big stuff*. I decided to keep my family out of it, hoping nobody would pick up on my weird moods.

Luckily, Andy Leach had.

Whenever the pair of us went to the pub after office hours, blowing off steam with a few beers, our work conversations were always relaxed. Andy had come to understand why I was so intolerant of people who couldn't work as effectively as me, and at times he shared the same frustrations. He also knew I was under pressure in my personal life. Elsewhere, our chats occasionally drifted across the emotions I'd experienced during my time in the military, until eventually all the horrors seemed to tumble over one another, pouring out of me as if I had been going through therapy again. During one late-night session, I even told him how much I missed fighting in war.

'I liked being in the middle of a scrap,' I said.

I hadn't meant that in regards to killing people, it was more my reflection of the thrill of having a superhuman purpose under high-risk circumstances. I missed fighting on dangerous operations. I missed being in the thick of military action, knowing that I was protecting people back home, and I missed the risks we had to take on a daily basis, the life-or-death decisions that often happened in the blink of an eye. But my nostalgia came with symmetry and its balancing point was rage. I was angry with myself for having pretended to want a job that was a million miles away from exciting. I was angry with the psych nurses who had forced me through a rehabilitation process that, with hindsight, seemed unsuited to my personality. Most of all I was angry at the Navy for accepting my resignation so quickly when I had been in the wrong frame of mind to make such a life-changing decision for myself. I believed they could have easily encouraged me to take more time over such a big decision, with or without their help. But there was confusion to unsettle my thinking even further. *How could I miss my job when I was angry at the military?* I was so disorientated. Nothing made sense any more.

Andy looked at me with concern. 'We need to do more for you, Foxy,' he said. 'I mean, much more than me just giving you this job. Have you considered going through therapy outside the Navy?'

I shook my head. 'I dunno, mate. Haven't I gone through all that crap already? It'll just be the same as before, probably.'

But Andy wouldn't have any of my excuses, and explained how he'd had his own issues with mental health following a stressful divorce. He then detailed how to seek out an expert that best suited me, rather than one employed by the military, which had been my previous, hellish experience. I was still unsure. My experience of a psychiatric care programme had left me more suspicious than when

243

I'd gone in, and I'd been pretty sceptical in the first place. But I also knew that talking to someone, to an expert, was becoming imperative, with one incident in particular alerting me that I was stuck in an increasingly precarious spot.

During my early weeks at Sodexo I'd befriended a company account manager, a woman called Debbie Smith. We'd shared several mutual acquaintances from the military and I often turned to her for help or advice regarding the job. But as I slowly disintegrated further over the following months, my troubles seemed to stretch beyond any immediate support. Debbie often remarked that I looked sad. She sometimes took me away from the office for a coffee so we could discuss whatever it was that had brought me down that day, the issues dogging my life, such as a lack of sleep, or the stresses and anxieties at home. Whenever we spoke on the phone, which occasionally happened after I'd come through an argument with my other half or endured a lonely day in the car, I often found myself sobbing by the side of the road as she tried to instil a sense of peace in me. My situation troubled her; Debbie became a shoulder to cry on, though she often found herself out of her depth as I slipped further into depression. Whenever we discussed my feelings, Debbie often described me as looking 'troubled' or 'haunted'.

One afternoon she was called out to the Navy barracks in Plymouth to talk me down from a potentially explosive situation. I had been asked to conduct a Sodexo meeting earlier in the day, but my head was a mess and my whole personality seemed to be on edge. Somebody had spoken in a way that had annoyed me and my reaction was volatile, not that I'm able to recall what happened exactly – that's how disorientated I was back then. The words would only have been throwaway, a glib comment or something dismissive, an attitude that would have grated against everyone in the unit had it happened within a Royal Marines setting – but I wasn't in a Royal Marines setting and my hands were tied. I couldn't shut the annoying comments down, and releasing my frustration on the problem would have probably seen me charged with assault. Instead I followed protocol and procedure to the letter, and it angered me. For a project manager there was so much red tape to get through just to make the smallest of changes that, at times, it seemed to work against everything I'd been used to when operating in conflict. There, the aim was to execute a job as quickly and as effectively as possible, no matter what. When Debbie eventually found me, I was pacing the corridors, wearing out the laminated flooring with my heavy footfalls, unable to talk. My frustration had been sealed in tight, and when I finally found the words to speak it poured out of me in a raging torrent. She listened patiently as I raved about the mess I'd got myself into at home, the experiences screwing with my head at work and the awful things I'd seen in war. At times it must have sounded like gibberish.

My eyes brimmed with tears. 'I'm pretending to be someone I'm not, Debbie. I've been lying to myself, making out that I've been happy all this time at Sodexo, which is bollocks. Now nothing's working . . .'

I became angry. 'I gave my whole life to the military,' I said. 'Why didn't they care about me more? Did they have to let me go so quickly?'

Then I sucked in a deep breath, blurting out an idea to Debbie that I'd previously kept tightly locked away.

'I've seen some terrible things,' I sighed, looking down at my feet in shame.

And then came the words that suggested my thinking had become more distressed than ever before.

'I don't deserve to be happy,' I said.

'I don't deserve to live.'

23

Six days earlier

The sound of angry AK-47s and their muzzle flashes were now distant memories tinted in rose. I drove around the Home Counties, visiting offices in provincial outposts such as Aldershot, Farnborough and Plymouth, checking on stationery orders and lorry deliveries. With only the radio for company, my long hours on the road became even more tortuous as the dark episodes of my career were replayed over and over. The good times were mourned as well. By that stage in my depression I sometimes missed the dice games on tour that decided whichever poor sod had to get the drinks for the whole mess, or our chats under the helicopters away from the baking sun. I even reminisced about the sound of the coffee machine that crushed the super-strong beans at breakfast, everyone piling in after a night raid to grab a freshly brewed cup. The opposing forces of nostalgia and fear pulled me this way and that.

Most of all I missed the action. I felt alive in a gun battle and my endorphins charged up. Excitement grabbed me; I became adrenalized, my heart pounding hard, the hair on my skin prickling. Like any adrenaline rush, where dopamine flooded the brain, a massive comedown followed soon after, but the high of engaging the enemy in contact always dropped off especially quickly, sometimes before I'd even returned to base, the downer landing as I gathered my thoughts during the helicopter ride home. I found that in the hours after a battle I often looked to discuss the action with other blokes in The Brotherhood, not because I wanted to brag about any moments of heroism but because I wanted to be back there, in the thick of it, reliving a life played out at the extreme ends of emotion. Some soldiers I knew compared the sensation to taking drugs, once they'd left. Maybe the rush of snorting a line of gear might have come close to being shot at, and shooting back, but for me there were more similarities with a one-night stand. Yeah, the sex had been great at the time, but afterwards, once the high and the comedown had passed, I'd think, *What was that all about?* And like the Monday morning after a weekend of heavy partying, I sensed a grubbiness in the fallout from a battle where lives had been lost and my adrenaline had been sky high in the thick of it all. My entire life in war had seemed like a succession of brief peaks and sobering lows.

It had been the same as a young lad in the Marines. Having started my career at the age of sixteen, when I finished my training I was elated, as if I'd already made it. To some degree I had, I guess: I'd proved Dad wrong, after all – I *did* have the guts to follow in his footsteps. The next morning, as I buttoned up my uniform for the first time, the mood was weirdly underwhelming and I felt just a little bit deflated. I looked in the mirror at my immaculately pressed kit, my boots shining with polish, and thought, '*So . . . is that it? What about those feelings I'd had yesterday when I was marching about the place believing I was the dog's bollocks?*' There were identical roller-coaster moods after making it through some of the toughest tests the British military hierarchy could throw at me, and having received congratulations in the immediate aftermath, I was soon yanked back down to earth by my colleagues just twenty-four hours later. *Right, Foxy, get off your high horse and let's get shit done.* The changing moods sometimes became disorientating.

The experience of killing enemy fighters could be just as unsettling because I felt so detached from the process. Did it make me sad? *No.* Did it make me happy? *Not at all.* But the lack of emotion around it seemed strange, even though it was part of the job. I had a mission to complete for the British government and I needed to protect the people around me. Whenever I was caught up in a firefight I found it was the risk that excited me the most; the fact that I could have died, but hadn't, in a dangerous situation, rather than the specific act of dropping someone – I wasn't a psychopath. Sometimes the kills didn't feel real, and there were times where I wasn't even sure whether we'd hit anybody in the chaos of battle, or if any of the rounds I'd fired had suppressed the movements of an enemy target. On other occasions I was distanced from the absoluteness of war, especially while working from the base. Then, an enemy target might have been hit by an air asset from hundreds of miles away and the experience was always surreal, almost fictional, the monitor, which showed the filmed footage, acting like a filter between me and the black and white explosions blossoming on the ground, my emotions disconnected from a stranger's life ended in battle.

The only person who bothered me was somebody whose smug face I can still see smirking at me as we hauled him on to a helicopter. He had been a big player in our attempt to suppress a guerrilla militia as they wrecked shop and planned suicide attacks on the local army. My team had first engaged in contact with him when several gunmen took aim at us from a car as our forces came in to land at a village, and as we swooped down the fighters abandoned their vehicle and ran off into a nearby field of tall grass. We gave chase, the rounds whistling around us as the fleeing enemy opened fire in a vain attempt to scare us off. In the chase, two enemy targets were shot dead, and once we'd searched the bodies, discovering radios and weaponry, there was the confirmation that we'd actually collared some senior bad dudes rather than a group of angry locals shooting at us for giggles. A cordon was set up and the unit searched the area for more intelligence when, suddenly, a shout went up from a nearby clump of reeds. One of the local police officers we were working with had found a 'person of interest' cowering in a ditch. I walked over, my gun raised. The guy was dressed in red robes; his hair was long and lank underneath a headdress and he was waving his arms in the air as if to prove he had been unarmed, just another innocent bystander caught up in the madness. I kept my weapon trained on him nonetheless, and when we shortly discovered a gun and radio that had been thrown into a nearby bush, we made the call to take him in for processing.

When moving in warzones, the British military only engaged with enemy fighters if they posed a serious threat, either to us or to others. Every captured but unarmed target had to be detained and questioned before moving into the country's judicial system, which we all knew to be flaky. Corruption was rife and detainees probably spent only a week or so in their cells before being released shortly afterwards, usually due to a lack of evidence. From there they were free to pick up an AK-47 and take more pot-shots at any passing helicopters, over and over, until their next capture, when the sorry story was replayed. Working through the legal processes in anarchic countries was infuriating to us all, a real waste of time, but the same realization dawned on our prisoner as he was being tagged and plasti-cuffed. The scumbag knew he'd be let off the hook shortly after his capture and there was a visible change in his demeanour. Knowing he was safe from lengthy imprisonment, the captive became arrogant as the helicopter lifted him away, which was irritating as hell. I sensed he was a serious player in the conflict and felt the sudden urge to grab him by the shoulders, launching him from the back of the chopper to his end, but I calmed the rushing blood. Weeks later, after his disappearance into the legal chaos, I learned that he *was* a leader in the war we were fighting. It turned out the cocky bastard had been responsible for killing a number of local soldiers, but even after our dossier of evidence had been expanded, it wasn't enough. We were told he'd been set free, an announcement that bothered me for a long time afterwards. I reassured myself that I had done the right thing at the time, that the situation had dictated my behaviour, and that I'd acted correctly. After all, what else could I have done? But any random attacks that took place across his turf in the months afterwards often made me wonder.

Why did he have to be the one that got away?

The grim realities of war fighting were something I had to deal with all too regularly, but the sight of the seriously wounded or dead never really bothered me until that final tour, not emotionally, anyway. I was able to compartmentalize it as an unpleasant but everyday occurrence in my line of work, mainly because I didn't have the time to process the horror of it all, a bit like a detective working through a murder scene. Whenever we stumbled across a dead body in a car or house, it often seemed like an almost surreal discovery. An incongruous snapshot of death set against the day-to-day happenings of everyday life. I'd notice weird details about the deceased's appearance – *His trousers don't even fit properly*. Or struggle to grasp the realities of their mortality – *Is that a homeless person and he's actually asleep?* Maybe it was a defence mechanism, my brain raising a partition of plausible alternatives to soften a very grim experience.

I remember that during one patrol a gunship ahead of us attacked a fighter who was strafing our unit with mortar fire. I watched as the bullets chopped through a field of high grass and trees, splintering branches and burning at the vegetation. When our gunner announced that the target was down, it was our job to head into the undergrowth to find him, creeping in like *Children of the Corn*, understanding that our target might still be alive and in possession of a weapon. My heart pounded as we moved into an area where the grass tips had been scorched with gunfire. In the middle of a small circle of hacked-to-bits vegetation was a body, or what was left of it, the fighter's face caved in by shrapnel, and as one of the unit wiped his empty eye sockets with DNA swabs, I realized that what theoretically should have been a disturbing sight hadn't bothered me at all. Whenever I'd looked at the dead, their bodies didn't seem real, as if I'd been watching them in a film, or on TV, instead.

The only death I remember as being *really* unsettling was a suicide bomber who had clacked himself in a partial detonation. Thankfully, nobody else died, but the explosive vest he'd been wearing had delivered enough damage to burn its wearer alive. As we cautiously approached the smouldering figure, the general consensus on comms was that he'd probably been killed in the blast and there was no saving him, though we weren't entirely sure. Suddenly, the body's top half heaved violently, sending the cadaver into an upright position as the remaining air from his lungs escaped loudly with a whistling sigh. Everybody freaked out, jumping back with the shock before the corpse slumped back to the dirt. It didn't so much as twitch again.

Kids were my kryptonite, though. I hated seeing families in distress, which was something the military had to deal with all the time, and this fallout from war was always heart-breaking. I later felt remorseful at upsetting the innocent. Enemy bombs obliterated houses; our forces attacked back. And while the aim was to avoid all civilian injuries, homes were sometimes destroyed and communities became fractured. Occasionally, hunted enemy fighters hid behind their families or walked among people who were totally oblivious to their intentions. Our job was to extract those significant targets and the efforts sometimes became unpleasant. Having my own family at home meant that the emotions caused by a screaming child or terrified family caught up in a battle resonated with me far more deeply than it did with some of the other lads, even though I'd become quite a hard-hearted parent. If ever one of my girls started crying or grizzling, I had very little patience for it; I'd tell them to stop moaning, though I still wanted to protect their innocence for as long as possible. And so the sight of kids in war broke me up. I knew their childish naivety had been ripped away forever. It became another price to pay in conflicts played out during close combat and within built-up civilian areas. Once I'd returned to a peaceful, British life and the pace of my day-to-day slowed considerably, I couldn't shake off the sense of despair. Some of the horrors that war had inflicted upon good people were just too awful to ignore. *That kid and his dark eyes on that impactful mission, clinging to his teddy. A mouth shaped into a blackened scream in my NVGs.*

As I drove across Hampshire and Surrey, moving from meeting to meeting for Sodexo, my thoughts became shadowed by his distorted, screaming face, all grainy green-and-black through my optics. In those intense moments I always wondered about his whereabouts. I felt pangs of remorse whenever I imagined what he might have experienced that night, the sounds of gunfire and the people around him dying, bombs and bullets ripping through the air. *Had he got to safety? Was his life wrecked for good?* I understood I'd only been doing my job, but the worry for a vulnerable young life in the midst of war tweaked at my thinking. All of the victims caught in our crossfire did, and sadly there were too many of them to remember. We were always interacting with locals, wherever we were, so the chances that bystanders might experience psychological damage as we worked were high. Families might witness extreme violence. Kids understandably became terrified at the sight of a raised weapon. As I spent more and more time driving around from Sodexo client to Sodexo client, my thoughts seemed to be invaded by every single face over my ten years of violence, a collection of demons chattering away in the passenger seat, a running commentary on the terrifying job I now wanted back.

I'd also noticed how those experiences of conflict were changing me politically. During my time away from the war life I became more liberal, my perspective shaped by the impacts of Britain's combat record. When I was younger, working through training and embarking on the early phases of my intense, battle-filled career, I probably would have been marked down by mates as having a slightly right-wing attitude. I certainly hadn't been able to get my head around the former Liberal Democrat leader, Paddy Ashdown, a one-time member of the SBS. *Why is he sitting on the fence about our military choices?* I thought. *That's weird.* But having gone through war myself and then witnessed the resulting carnage, I realized a lot of our efforts had been for very little. *What had we actually achieved? Was the world really a much safer place afterwards?* It was hard to tell.

Ultimately, the two sides in any war carried radically different opinions, both halves engaging in hardcore violence, regardless of how or where the dispute had started. I realized that I didn't want to see people killing each other in battle any more, and definitely not over a set of ideological beliefs or political agendas; it seemed ludicrous. War had taught me to be more tolerant of others; I began to think differently towards narrow-minded people and I wanted to listen to varying opinions and viewpoints so I could reach a balanced conclusion for myself when debating the rights and wrongs of a particular issue. Of course, I was still very much of the opinion that if a foreign power had acted like an arsehole by oppressing, threatening or killing innocent people then they needed a slap from the military. I was all for that; it went back to my long-held feeling that bullies needed to be taken down. But my attitude became more considered: we shouldn't send our troops into dangerous conditions simply to further the selfish, personal gains of people in power. I hadn't become involved in the military for those reasons anyway; I wasn't there for somebody's political plans. If I were to distil my motive it would be this: *I was in the job to do good work and to stop good people from being crushed by aggression.*

This rationale couldn't hold back the growing tide of remorse that seemed to be dragging me under during those awful months at Sodexo. The images and emotions rushed at me when I least expected them and my guilt was amplified when I remembered how much I'd once enjoyed being in the thick of a gunfight, shooting at enemy targets while forgetting the innocent lives that were being ruined for ever in the fallout. My mourning for a loss of adventure and purpose was now in conflict with the ghosts of war. *How could I miss it and hate it at the same time? And how could I resent the military for letting me leave and yet yearn to be back in their embrace?* To my mind, those things seemed mutually exclusive and the contradictions inevitably caused me to crack.

On a Monday morning as I made it to the office, I noticed that Debbie was walking towards my desk. She looked ashen and was staring at me fearfully. As she beckoned me over, I knew that something was seriously wrong. Had I screwed up at work, big-time?

'Foxy, how are you doing?'

I felt confused. Was she asking about my weekend, my workload, or something else? I didn't get it.

'Yeah, fine,' I said, shrugging my shoulders.

'Really? I was so worried after all those phone calls.'

The sentence seemed to slap me across the jaw. Paranoia prickled at my flesh. Phone calls? *What phone calls?*

'Debbie, I don't know what you're banging on about . . .'

She looked confused. 'Foxy – Friday night, we spoke on the phone for ages. You were in such a state. I was so worried.'

I was rocked at the blanks in my memory as Debbie relived several lost hours, me calling her at ten thirty p.m. from a motorway layby in tears, sobbing uncontrollably as I told her how my misery had become too much to handle. There was the worthlessness, my burden to others, a crushing guilt, and the frustration. All of it was swirling around, an overwhelming weight of despair I couldn't carry any longer. The confusion of wanting to go back to a life that had broken me was even more destructive.

'Debbie, I'm looking for a tree to hang myself from,' I'd said.

She had freaked out. 'Where are you?'

'I'm somewhere in Devon.'

And when she'd offered to drive from her home in Woking to get me, I had drawn back. I'd not wanted her to help. I'd not wanted her to find me. I wanted to die. Somehow she kept me talking on the phone, bringing me round, calming me down, calling me every couple of hours throughout the night to ensure I'd not done something stupid on the drive home. I'd been at the emotional extreme, on the verge of suicide, a moment in life that most people would have been scarred by. *And yet I couldn't remember any of it.*

24

Six minutes earlier

What would it be like to fall?

The thought first flashed across my radar as I approached the clifftop car park, another day of crawling the motorways and A-roads done, dark thoughts strapped to my chest like body armour. I knew the trails there led to a coastal pathway. Popular with hikers and dog walkers, the route that topped the cliffs was peppered with flimsy perimeter fences and local authority signs that warned of an awful fate if anyone strayed too close to the edge. *But I'll take that.* I stepped out of my car into the drizzle, and headed towards the precipice with purpose. There was no one around in the crappy weather and so I was going to fall, unnoticed, ending it all with a running leap into the dark sea and heavy clouds, a scene so similar to the psychological sensations that had trailed me since that first day back in Poole – me staring into nothingness at a pedestrian crossing, the world rushing around me at a million miles an hour. Today the water could take me. If life wanted really to swallow me whole then it was welcome – *if it'll only end the fucking misery.* As far as what might happen to my rag-doll corpse on the rocks, I couldn't have cared less. Once my body eventually washed up on a beach somewhere, I figured nobody would really mind. I told myself that the misery and mood swings of the last couple of years had been a burden to the very few people still in contact with me. Suicide would probably be as much a relief for them as it would for me.

There was a second or two for contemplation. I'd wanted so badly to get shot of the negative thoughts and confusion, but what was coming next? The stomach-lurching plummet for sure, a flash of pain probably, but only if I hadn't passed out on the way down, and then . . . *Blackness.* But as I looked out to the English Channel, the unknown suddenly scared me even more than the unpleasantness of living through another day. Death was going to numb my anguish for sure, but what about afterwards? I wasn't a religious bloke so I didn't fear the afterlife or some judgement by an all-seeing power, but imagining the finality of noth-ingness suddenly seemed to unnerve me. Did I really think that death was going to suck me in and spit me out again a happier, well-rounded, box-fresh bloke, gagging for another shot at a fulfilling life? Because finality didn't come with a money-back guarantee and there was no returning from whatever lay in wait.

I sobbed, crumbling with fear once again in an existen-tial meltdown. Even the thought of escaping from a depression that had brought me to the edge of this cliff, the ejector seat button, had filled me with terror and indeci-sion. *But wasn't it supposed to be the easy way out?*

I laughed darkly.

I'd even become a failure at suicide. How does that happen?

Could it get any more shit?

I peered down at the rocky teeth and frothing tide beneath me. The drop seemed greater now, longer, even more terrifying, as slowly I came to realize that going through with suicide was beyond me, for now at least. Instead I stood there for who-knows-how-long, staring into noth-ingness before trudging back to my company car, the status symbol for a job that hung around my neck like a dead weight. I dried my eyes and got on with my shitty day before driving home, where I sat on the sofa and swigged my way through another bottle of wine, alone, trying desperately to push away what had happened on that cliff edge, while fearfully thinking about what might come next.

Had the person who eventually pulled me away from the brink of self-destruction not turned around my way of thinking, I might have found myself writing these pages from prison. The anger bubbling away inside would have finally overflowed into something more terrible than my earlier flashpoints, such as a simple dispute with some colleagues at work, or an explosion of road rage on the A38. More likely, an early death was the finishing post for me back then; it was only a matter of time before I summoned the guts to pull the trigger on myself. The cliff edge had been a test run, a warm-up for my final act of desperation. But I was about to be turned around by an outsider who would help me to help myself while reshaping my thinking, reattaching me to a way of life that I'd eventually come to find fulfilling.

Alex Lagaisse was a clinical psychologist working from a practice in Devon. After weeks of nagging from Andy and Debbie, my moodiness having taken a noticeable dip in the office, I'd eventually relented and a session was booked for me by one of Andy's colleagues. Once it was set, Andy assured me that if it didn't work out with Dr Lagaisse, we'd try another therapist. Then another. And then another. In order to get me fixed he was willing to play the long game. It was just about the best tactic for a bloke in my state of mind.

'Foxy, we just want to get you right,' he said one night in the pub. 'It'll take as long as it takes.'

I hadn't told either Andy or Debbie about my moment at the cliff, but just by watching me at work, both of them understood that I'd ended up in a dangerous place, and neither of them was in any position to plan my escape route without an expert's help. Dr Lagaisse's website was the first result in an early search and apparently offered 'evidence-based assessment and treatment for people experiencing mental health difficulties', but when I drove towards the clinic a few days later, to say I was pessimistic would be an understatement. I couldn't see beyond my experiences in the Navy's mental health care facility, and I convinced myself that Dr Lagaisse would be no different from the psych nurses in Poole and Portsmouth. I dreaded more sessions of EMDR and CBT, those endless pen-waving episodes and deep dives into my family life, and when I arrived at the clinic, which was a GP's practice, my worst fears were reinforced. The place looked cold and sterile. *Medical*. Its exterior reminded me of a building from Ricky Gervais's BBC TV comedy *The Office*, and inside its prefab walls and cheap furniture only added to the inhospitable atmosphere. *More Ikea, more beige.*

I sensed my day was going to end with another frustrated and miserable car ride home, but eventually a young woman arrived to take me into the doctor's office. She didn't look like one of the receptionists I'd been used to in Poole. A real hippy-ish type in her early thirties, she wore a long dress with a brightly coloured and flowery pattern, a string of New Age-style beads draped from her neck. She was relaxed, smiley. My introduction to Dr Lagaisse's working practice seemed a million miles away from the Navy's psych ward, where the treatment I had been used to was very rigid and formal. This was at the other end of the spectrum. Sadly, the positive mood faded quickly, my heart sinking as she showed me into a room that reminded me of an oversized stationery cupboard. *Here we go again*, I thought, settling myself on a sofa and waiting for the doctor to arrive. But then, to my surprise, I discovered the same woman had followed me in and was taking a seat on the chair opposite me. I must have looked startled because she smiled, knowingly. Then the penny dropped.

'Wait, are you . . . ?' I said, feeling both embarrassed and mega-rude at having expected Dr Alex Lagaisse to be a man. 'I'm sorry, I just assumed . . .'

'Dr *Alexandra* Lagaisse,' she said, laughing, shrugging away my blunder. I recovered my composure, knowing I'd come over as a clumsy, sexist idiot. I drew in a deep, settling breath and took in my surroundings. The mood of the place had already depressed the hell out of me. Nothing brought to mind the concepts of wellness or recovery like a dull office stuffed with empty filing cabinets and boxes of stationery. I looked at Dr Lagaisse again. I was worried she wouldn't understand me, or my life in war.

This isn't going to work, I thought. *But what the hell, mate, just go along with it.*

'So, Jason, do you want to start by telling me what's brought you here?' she said.

We settled in to an easy conversation. I detailed the unpleasant circumstances that were tearing me apart and the nature of my departure from the military. I went into the crazy events of the past few weeks and how I was regretting my resignation from a job I'd loved, but weirdly I was more haunted than ever by what I'd seen in conflict. I told her of how I felt guilty at the lives that had been damaged by war, but how I'd been yearning for the adrenaline rushes experienced in a gunfight. Dr Lagaisse nodded sympathetically while taking notes. She seemed so easy to talk to. Her manner was friendly and open, and I felt at ease in her company almost instantly. Without the Navy's shadow looming over us, I was unshackled, secure in expressing my true thoughts and feelings. I'd also realized that I had nothing left to lose as far as my career was concerned. There was no Brotherhood or senior officers to judge me. I could trust her.

'I'm shit,' I said, eventually. 'I'm shit at everything. I can't keep my partner happy, so that's going down the pan. I've got a shitty job and I really don't like it, but then I'm feeling guilty because Andy, my boss, is great and he's given me a company car, a decent salary, a lot of perks – I'm allowed to do pretty much what I want, but I'm still unhappy. He even encouraged me to come here. The thing is, I'm supposed to be a soldier, but now I'm not a soldier. I'm a nobody.'

I was slowly building up to my most worrying confession of all, the one I hadn't admitted to anybody. 'I do understand why blokes take their lives,' I said.

'What makes you say that?' asked Dr Lagaisse.

'Well, they're literally at the end of it all thinking, "What's my purpose?"'

I paused, wondering whether to confess everything before spilling it all.

'The other day I even walked to the edge of a cliff and stared down wondering what it would be like to die,' I said sadly. 'But I bottled it. I couldn't throw myself off, even though I'd wanted to . . .'

She nodded. 'So how do you feel most days?'

I sighed. 'I'm in this fuzzy head-fuck and I've got this whirlwind going on and I'm not sure what's happening, and I think I'm doing the right thing by working this job when actually my judgement is skew-whiff because of the fuzzy head. And I don't have anyone to talk to. All that unwritten stuff in the military, that you shouldn't open up about your emotions because it's not good for you . . . That's bollocks, isn't it? If you feel unwell, or you think there's something wrong, or you notice yourself acting spaced-out or experiencing dark thoughts, you need to be brave and talk, don't you? I needed to chat to other lads, but as a bloke working in an alpha-male environment, I'd been conditioned not to do it.'

'Other lads?'

'Well, when I say lads, I mean friends, mates, the people that I'd been fighting alongside,' I explained, 'whoever it was – but someone I felt comfortable talking to about what was going wrong with me. Instead, we'd been encouraged to give it the stiff-upper-lip treatment, so I avoided them. Yeah, I chatted to some of the boys on the phone, maybe three or four blokes I knew well after I'd left, but it wasn't all the time, and I definitely wouldn't talk about what was going on with me, about my thoughts. Chatting to them was probably more of a distraction than anything else, it certainly wasn't what it should have been: me, opening up about traumatically leaving a job I'd done for so long. I even told them I'd been struck off with tinnitus rather than telling them the truth. Looking back, quitting was a massive deal for me and I had no one to talk to about it.'

As we spoke, I noticed that Dr Lagaisse was interested in my upbringing, but not to the point where it was the only thing she focused on. I later learned that she'd arrived at the early conclusion that – despite everybody having their own unique patterns and conditioning from family life – my issues were a direct result of the experiences in war. But I'd been free to lead the conversation; she hadn't even announced some grand plan of how I could expect to be healed within her care, though I should have guessed a more holistic approach was coming. When I'd first looked her up, Dr Lagaisse's website had promised 'the practice of clinical psychology'. Her introduction continued, 'I work with individuals and groups to alleviate suffering, and I work with professionals in the healthcare system. My work with individuals involves using mindfulness and presence, and nature-based work . . .' She rounded up our session by asking me what I liked in life, to list the things that made me really happy.

'Adventure,' I said. 'Having a purpose, being part of something with meaning. Taking risks and pushing myself.' These were the career goals that Sodexo hadn't been able to deliver in the slightest.

'Jason, you're not broken,' she said. 'This is a process about discovering again who you are, beyond these experiences. You're having a normal reaction to extreme events. You don't need *fixing*, just the chance to be who you are. A space where you can be honest with yourself and deal with the truth of it. Is that something you think you'd want to do?'

I nodded. There was nothing for me to hide any more, my secrets were out in the open and nothing I might say was going to worsen my position. I'd already hit rock bottom. Yet for the first time in ages there was a shot of optimism, an idea that my escape from emotional tumult was a very real possibility, and I began to feel more and more comfortable talking to Dr Lagaisse. The only thing that bothered me about our work was the surroundings – not that this lasted for long. After a few sessions I was informed that we'd have to move rooms due to logistical issues. Dr Lagaisse wanted to know whether I'd like to change clinic spaces or shift into what she called 'an even worse meeting place'.

'Well, what about somewhere else?' I said, looking around at the drab office. 'Is there any way we could do these chats outside, like on a park bench? This place does my head in . . .'

'Well, actually we could,' she smiled. 'I'm happier working outside this office, too. Next time let's take a walk through the woods instead.'

25

Author's Note

So much of my time spent in therapy with Dr Alex Lagaisse is very hard to recall. I was a mess back then, a fish out of water in a corporate job, trying to be a person I was never meant to be. Having re-examined such a heavy episode from my life during the writing of this book, it now seems detached from my current reality, like a parallel universe, one completely unrecognizable from where I am now. It's as if I was watching my time in therapy rather than actually living through it. I reckon it might well be a self-defence mechanism, my mind distancing itself from what I was going through. Weirdly, my career in the military now seems nearer to me than that period in my life, which lasted for around a year from 2013 to 2014. Because of that, I've had to ask for Alex's help in piecing together what actually happened to me during our year or so working together. The following two chapters have been written by combining each of our recollections of the events that took place, plus a series of patient notes.

> 'Mr Fox describes how his problematic experiences have greatly improved over the course of time but he still struggles with the number of difficulties. He describes still being very emotional and crying easily and becoming distressed by things that would not have previously bothered him. He said his emotional state is more volatile in general, becoming tearful at times and angry at others . . .'

Patient notes: Jason Fox.

We arrived at the woods, the path beyond leading into an expanse of overgrown bushes and trees. This was much more calming than the office we'd been working from previously. I could take in the fresh air now; I felt safe, and my senses relaxed with the scent of the damp breeze, dewy grass and wet bark. The chemical smell of a medical building, the air-freshened waiting room and the unfriendly plastic furniture seemed a million miles away. Even stretching my legs as we talked seemed therapeutic; natural, engaging. But after chatting to Alex – she was happy for me to call her by her first name – I'd come to understand why so many other patients *were* comfortable when meeting with their therapist in a GP-style practice. The vibe was supposed to make them feel reassured. People went to their doctor in order to fix whatever sickness was cutting them down; they naturally associated clinical environments with help, cure and a source of sympathy. Any psychologist operating from a building like the one Alex and I had met in during our first sessions was aiming to deliver a sense of confidence and safety to someone that might not have experienced therapy before. A reassuring arm around the shoulder; a calming whisper that said, 'It's OK, mate, you're moving into a place of healing.'

But the clinic hadn't felt like a safe space to me. Instead, those rooms reminded me of Poole and a time when I'd first realized I was losing my identity, when I'd first admitted to someone that . . . *I had a problem.* Alex would later tell me that the environment had helped to crush my sense of self. It had tricked me into thinking my body was failing, like a sweating, feverish patient in a doctor's waiting room. It made sense that I would respond better within a more natural backdrop because I'd spent most of my adult life outdoors, running through jungles, harsh mountainous terrain and deserts.

'Just notice that you're entering into a different kind of space here, Jason,' said Alex.

A trail led towards a steep incline. On one side its edges were lined with a bank of looming redwoods. Standing upright in neat rows like a drill parade of soldiers, they looked identical, packed in together so tightly that the leafy armour prevented a lot of light from seeping through. The other side was less dense and brighter. Sun dappled its vegetation, which had become wild and knotted, as branches and thorny vines tangled over one another. The wood was a public area, so dog walkers and runners occasionally passed by us on either side of the pathway.

'It's really valuable to recognize we're in a place of purpose,' Alex continued, stepping along the track. 'That way you can put intention into taking something seriously, to giving it the attention it deserves, otherwise it's just another jaunt in the woods, something you might do with a mate.'

I walked on, making mental notes of the paths that led away in several different directions, the clearings ahead, and a steep hill on what looked like a stretch of private farmland. Over the coming months we'd explore those woodland routes together on a weekly basis, Alex encouraging me to talk about what had happened in the days since we'd last met and how those events had affected me.

Essentially, she wanted me to observe my emotional state; the process was in place so I could return to my wholeness by noticing what I was all about. *The real me.* The bloke I'd been before my mind had crumbled.

One of her observations was that I'd built up a series of limiting beliefs through my time with the military, assumptions about myself that had halted my progress and were fundamentally wrong. I could go along with that. My shame at being medically discharged was certainly a massive weight upon me and it challenged the image I'd previously created for myself. The idea that I was a man operating with kudos was dissipated by the events that led me to leaving; from there I assumed I was a failure in a profession I'd loved. As a result, my view was that I'd become weak and worthless in all aspects of life, but Alex was teaching me the value of unconditional acceptance. During our early talks I was given a framework in which to share my deepest thoughts and fears without judgement. At times, Alex offered practical advice or ideas on how to manage a certain situation. At others she challenged me to explore my own thinking.

'I'm just wondering what's going on for you right now . . .' was a line I'd hear whenever she wanted me to delve deeper, particularly if my moods were revolving around the idea of shame. 'Look at what's being evoked in you during that moment. What's your fear? What are you running away from and avoiding? Let's stay with it for a bit and look at what it's like to feel shame, or the fear of rejection . . .'

The problems moved more clearly into focus. I was definitely struggling to overcome the contradictions in my life – they were spinning me out. My fear had been so great on some of my final missions that it had created a dangerous level of anxiety, and yet I wanted to return to combat, the root cause of my issues. Then there was the mourning for camaraderie. I believed that re-joining the military was the only way to experience the powerful levels of union I'd shared with the men serving alongside me. But because I'd been institutionalized in my work, I'd decided the two issues of a yearning for that bonding and my fear of combat were mutually exclusive and couldn't be reconciled. I was scared and weak, so the concept of The Brotherhood seemed out of reach. Feeling like an outcast, I'd moved into the civilian, corporate lifestyle, building a new story for myself, but the pressure to fit in had made me feel inauthentic. I clearly couldn't live with the imbalance; I'd felt like an alien. Meanwhile, the actions of my former employers bothered me more and more, especially regarding their speed in binning me off so quickly. Had they just wanted to be rid of my issues?

'That's not what life is, though,' said Alex, as I tried to define the blurred lines and inconsistencies one day. 'Not everything is black and white. Just because you've lost a brotherhood in the past, it doesn't mean you can't find a new one again. You can rediscover another purpose, too. You just need to work out what it was that you really valued in the military. You can then create that for yourself somewhere else.'

I was finding it hard to take in. 'I don't know, Alex,' I said. 'I'm just so angry about everything that I can't see how I'd get into that headspace.'

'It's OK to be angry at the military and to miss that environment, to need that brotherhood and to want to have that experience again. But the test now is this: how do you find that feeling – that crucial sense of belonging – in a *different* way?'

It was obvious that responding to those challenges in the months ahead would present the route map to a changed and hopefully renewed life – one with serious purpose. But arriving at that point wouldn't necessarily happen overnight.

There was so much work to do.

'Agreed to do mindfulness practice through the woods and walked mainly in silence for about half an hour. Then

Jason began to narrate what he saw. See paths he hadn't noticed before. I asked him to narrate his emotional experience and he said he felt quite calm and was able to notice things he would usually find himself distracted by.'

Patient notes: Jason Fox.

From the outset, Alex observed that PTSD had forced me into a state of hyper-alertness. This, in layman's terms, meant that I was constantly scanning for threats. I wasn't assessing the woods for any snipers that might be lurking nearby, or looking under fallen logs for signs of an embedded IED. Instead I was subconsciously searching for obstacles that might hinder the task at hand, not that I actually knew what that task was at the time – it was a vague sense of urgency, one that shadowed me everywhere, and anything that distracted me from it was viewed with annoyance, which then quickened my temper. According to Alex this was a common PTSD symptom, and totally understandable in my situation. For years, I had been trained to work within a constant state of extreme arousal where all my senses were ramped up in order to assess situations for danger and risk to life. My fight-or-flight mechanism was constantly in operation. Once removed from the combat environment, I hadn't settled down, which, unsurprisingly, had frazzled my nervous system. No wonder I couldn't sleep. No wonder I'd been wound up tight. No wonder I remembered every awful war experience in painful detail.

Over the next few months, Alex asked me to practise a new habit of attention, a method that aimed to bring my thoughts to the present, making me active in the moment and shutting out the stresses of the past and my fears for my future. 'You feel irritation because you're overstimulated,' she said as we prepared to walk in silence for thirty minutes, noticing the sights and sounds of the woodland around us. 'Bringing a mindfulness approach for a period of time is where you calm your nervous system and put your conscious attention towards the things close to you. If you're in a hyper-alert state, you're scanning for threat. Mindfulness is different. You're looking at things as they are; you're asking yourself to notice the environment and everything that's happening *now*. Not five minutes earlier, or five minutes into the future.'

As we walked, I definitely felt calmer; I became immersed in a sense of stillness. I heard the rustling leaves and branches above, the tweeting birds perched in the treetops. A dog barked somewhere along the trail, and every now and then my thoughts were punctuated by the sound of quickening footsteps somewhere behind us, a runner panting their apologies for disturbing our tranquil mood as they swept past – but the interruptions didn't matter. It felt good to live in the now. *I felt good.* A brief sense of peace descended upon me for the first time in ages.

'I feel connected to myself here, in the woods,' I said after our session had ended.

'Nice, isn't it?' said Alex, smiling. 'We'll try mindfulness more often. It really helps to quieten a lot of the chatter in our heads.'

From the very beginning of our work together, there were certain images from the past that I couldn't push from the 'now' so easily. Some of the horrors I'd seen were eating away at me constantly, as did intrusive, painful thoughts about the people affected by my actions, or the consequences of war. The kids and families whose innocence had been stolen by conflict still tore me up inside, and nothing could shift my remorse. 'I've been involved in some grim stuff, Alex,' I said, once I'd come to trust her implicitly. 'Stuff that young children have seen me do, or mums and wives. When the shooting started, we often hadn't realized they'd been there in the first place. They'd got caught up in it, and I'd see them afterwards, cowering in a corner and crying, screaming. It didn't really do my head in at the time, but the thought of what might have happened to them afterwards . . . now it's breaking me up.

'I remember the worst one. We'd snuck into the building, when suddenly a door sprang open directly in front of us and a bloke lurched towards me. He must have been alerted by a noise because he had an automatic weapon in one hand. With my NVGs on, I could see him, but he couldn't see me, and in a split second I had to assess whether he posed an immediate threat to my life. Was I able to take him down without shooting? Then a quick movement forced me to act. He'd raised his gun in my direction and I couldn't hesitate. The room lit up, there was all this noise, and our target was down, dead. It was only once I'd turned around that I noticed the blowback. A woman and three kids were ducking down behind me, huddled up. I saw them in my NVGs, all of them wearing the same deadpan expression of shock. I can't forget it.'

I tried to recall how I'd felt in the immediate aftermath, to experience the emotions again. I remembered that at first the incident hadn't bothered me. I'd chalked the encounter down as being something that happened in my line of work. I imagined what the enemy gunman might have thought had *he* killed *me*. Would he have shown a moment of remorse for the mental wellbeing of those witnesses? No chance. But later, as I'd found myself with too much time in which to reflect upon my war experiences, the grim memories of those children upset me. And there were others too, like the kids we'd once discovered in a compound, chained up and abused by a mob of feral gangsters.

'I feel so guilty, I just want it to stop,' I said. 'They're the thoughts that made me think about killing myself . . . I'm haunted by them.'

Alex nodded sympathetically as we spoke, but I'd come to understand that the issue might not be resolvable – not immediately, anyway. She also had pre-conceived notions about those situations. Prior to my approaching her for therapy, Alex had helped the survivors of torture as they came to terms with their painful war experiences, people seeking asylum from some of the countries I'd been fighting in. She was honest about her past work, and I realized it would be down to me to manage the complexities of my feelings.

'I've brought quite a lot of judgement and the pain of witnessing others' misery to our therapy relationship because of that,' she admitted one afternoon. 'Jason, I don't buy this narrative that the enemy are bad and you're the hero. I don't.' I understood why. Alex had been witness to the survival stories of so many innocent victims that it had affected her, too. Suddenly I'd presented a vivid reminder of those damaged lives and their cries for help. Their distress and pain had been directly caused by the conflicts I was involved in. Now I was asking for assistance in salving my own wounds.

'I don't think my task is to help you to resolve your guilt,' she eventually reasoned. 'But I'll sit with you in those feelings. My task is to help you stay in the complexity of the reality, and the reality of the complexities – because it *is* complex, isn't it, Jason? You get sold a story that everything is black and white: "Here's the enemy; this is your job; you're the good guy. Your job is to do this and the reason you're doing it is because we're going to save people." And when you get there, the reality reveals the complexity of the situation. So you're telling me you've shot someone and then seen the guy's family? Well, in my opinion what you've been faced with is the stark reality that, in life, not everything is as simple as the narrative you've been sold . . .'

Alex was right; it had been complex. And throughout our work we'd decided that my tendency to continually relive certain incidents from my past – alone or during our sessions – hadn't been helping either. Alex was always happy to bear witness to my moments of regret and shame when we walked. Opening up had certainly helped to quicken the healing process, but only for a while, and if it became obvious that replaying those awful experiences wasn't delivering any positive, progressive movement, she would change tack, knowing the past was pitching me backwards. Talk about my kryptonite, the vulnerability and guilt at seeing innocent lives in distress was re-traumatizing me again and again, on and on. I had to anchor myself to the here and now instead. From there it was my job to work alongside the past because there was nothing I could do to change it. My time in war was done, gone, and analyzing my actions to the nth degree wasn't going to move me forward.

And then the breakthrough arrived.

26

It had happened one afternoon. The pair of us were following a new path, a route I'd never explored before, when we stumbled across a little girl playing with her mum in a clearing ahead. She could only have been two or three years old, and as she kicked her way through the leaves and puddles, laughing as her mum became grumpy because of the mess she was making of her clothes, Alex was struck by an idea.

'Look at her,' she said. 'Children don't care about what's happened previously, or what's happening in the future. Children just care about now. They follow their own feelings. I want you to look at her playing. She's not governed by anything. Why can't we all be like that? Well, we can . . . Jason, you *can* be like that. You *are* like that.'

I looked back at the little girl again, observing her in the now. Her coat was muddy, her hair tangled up with leaves. I slowly began to grasp at what Alex was saying – kind of. Previously my psych nurses had told me that, 'Yeah, you're screwed up – and that's because you've done a lot of crazy shit.' But Alex was giving me a new way of viewing the dark life I'd inhabited for so long. I wasn't broken. And now a window was opening that hadn't been there before. I could see that I had to live in the moment because there was really no other choice. And from that point I should make the decisions that felt right to me – not someone else. I'd come to understand that where I went in the future was undecided, an exciting mission ahead.

Was I finally seeing progress?

'Met Jason and he described how he's been thinking about big things, big questions such as who he is and what he wants to do. We talked about all the things that he enjoys. He talked about being outside and also about helping people. He talked about how he's begun to do personal development plans for people at work and he's realized he likes helping people.'

Patient report: Jason Fox.

*

She gets me.

She understands.

The thoughts crossed my mind every time we walked through the woods together, Alex asking me the same questions over and over. *What is it that brings you aliveness? What is it you like doing?* She might have changed the wording on a weekly basis, but her enquiries usually carried the same thrust; they pricked at my psyche and stimulated a new way of thinking because there was a plan in place. Or so I thought. All along, my belief was that she knew that I'd needed to feel whole again and was gently coaxing me towards a stable future. In actuality, it was me that knew what had to be done. I just hadn't relocated my truth yet, though it wouldn't take for ever. And when it landed, the penny-drop realization of what I had to do was both powerful and life-changing. The idea of that little girl playing in the woods, splashing around in the mud without a care for what had gone before or what was coming next, had pushed me there.

'Have I just been thinking about things in completely the wrong way?' I said one afternoon. 'The way I should be thinking about life was the way I used to think when I was younger, before PTSD had set in: "Don't stress too much about stuff because when you do, life gets problematic. Don't overthink things because life gets in the way." I've lost that sense of doing that, haven't I? I joined the military without worry, I pushed myself towards dangerous challenges in the job, and I didn't stress. I even moved in with a girl in America that I barely knew and didn't flap! When I eventually had my dramas, and then afterwards, I'd ignored my youthful attitude to risk and danger, so I'd got scared. But I'm *good* with risk and danger. It was always good for me not to be worried. So I've basically painted myself into a corner where I'm not being me, through fear, and it's caused some proper damage. Now I'm angry at the world because I've been angry with myself all this time . . . *for not being myself.'*

'What would feel like an authentic next step for you?' said Alex. 'What would feel more aligned with what you really want?'

'Maybe run adventure courses that help people?' I said tentatively, tugging at an idea that had been with me for a while.

'Just do it!' she laughed. 'You can do that, Jason! You can choose, you don't have to live and work in the corporate world for ever. You could do something that combines what you loved about the military – the camaraderie, being outdoors – and this notion of men struggling with not having a brotherhood . . .'

The thought had certainly been formulating for a while. I'd wanted to work in a role that was more suited to my personality than simply driving around the country for Sodexo. It needed to be something with excitement and risk – maybe an outdoor course for people who wanted a taste of military life so they could discover something about themselves.* At times I felt that a project where I helped people in a similar situation to me would prove inspirational, too. I'd recently completed a number of personal-growth plans for some of the staff at Sodexo and the experience had been rewarding. I'd discovered a sense of purpose in listening to their aspirations while figuring out a way to help them achieve those goals. The sense of satisfaction surprised me.

There was also an idea for a community interest company called Rock2Recovery that I'd been working on with a former Royal Marine commando sniper called Jamie Sanderson, who was discharged from the military with

---

*I later started working with Matthew 'Ollie' Ollerton (a soon-to-be member of the *Who Dares Wins* team on Channel 4) at Break-Point, a company running outdoor adventure courses that took their cue from some of the work we did in military. It turned out there was some good money to be made in putting civilians through their paces and teaching them the skills required to survive in the wilderness.

PTSD around the same time as I was. I had previously seen Jamie at the base while I was still in service. I later learned that, at his lowest point, the poor sod had attempted to hang himself.

Linked together through mutual acquaintances, Jamie and I got in touch, moaning about our respective treatment programmes within the military healthcare programme over a few pints – *This was crap. That was crap. Why didn't they do that for us? Where were they when we'd needed help?* – until eventually it was decided we should begin a project of our own making. The plan: a programme helping other military personnel to face the problems brought on by a life in war, and without the stigma associated with mental health care. With PTSD, Jamie had temporarily lost his memory, but playing music had helped to pull him through. (This was where the name for our venture came from.) He was undoubtedly set to be the engine of the project, later climbing Kilimanjaro to raise money for its expanding work. Even though I was still in therapy, I'd decided to take on an ambassadorial role within the organization, watching as it slowly grew in scale and former soldiers began to speak up, encouraged by our efforts. Upon introduction, they could chat freely about what was bothering them; it was our role to help them get their lives back on track. We might suggest therapists or help centres for assistance, while encouraging them to realize a life beyond the military with charity expeditions and exciting challenges, or even a new career path. Jamie and I were both blokes of experience. Our aim was to avert the disasters before they happened, and when it came to understanding the psychological roadblocks that could appear when seeking professional help, we were better equipped than most.

My only concern was our respective CVs: at Rock2-Recovery we hadn't a scratch of clinical training between us, which made us incredibly well-meaning but totally underqualified. My first thought was that maybe Alex would want to help, but when I'd hinted at the idea – without blurting it out fully – during one of our sessions, she sensed my intentions and declined (though she'd understood why I'd asked in the first place). The knockback surprised me initially, but it didn't take long to realize it had been an inappropriate idea.* Somewhere towards the beginning of

---

* Alex's report from that session makes for interesting reading: 'He said he's still committed to working with ex-servicemen and rethinking PTSD,' she wrote. 'I noticed (to him) that he seems to have a very good idea of what he wants to do. There seems to be a clear picture and I wondered what he was scared of. He agreed and said he thought he could do wilderness training stuff and he thought he would be good at it. He said he felt anxious because he didn't have clinical experience or

our patient–therapist relationship, Alex had mentioned that a time might arrive where I'd mistake what had been a chapter of assisted self-discovery for something else; that I might view her work as a crutch to lean on for *all* my decisions.

'You'll think I'm the bee's knees at one point,' she said afterwards. 'You'll think my support will be important for everything you do . . . But it won't.'

I'd laughed it off at the time, but the inevitable had happened. After a year and a bit, I'd attributed the lightening of my emotional burdens solely to her wisdom, rather than the two-way process we were actually working through. And Alex was right. I didn't need her help in everything I did. Taking risks without support was now a reward for all the hard work I'd put in on my thinking. The fact that I was happy just to take bold and unsettling choices again, without assistance, was something I couldn't have

---

training and would want someone involved that was qualified. I felt that Jason was intimating my involvement and I stated explicitly that I was wondering if that's what he meant. I felt like he was saying something without naming it.

'I explained those things were generally not appropriate dynamics of a therapy-to-patient relationship because sometimes it's easy to become disempowered, believing that you need that person for everything. But I noticed why it would make sense to him, knowing the work he did.'

imagined a year previously. I'd recently broken up with my other half, too, and was now in the process of rebuilding a whole new life from scratch. The time had come to go it alone.

Often we worked through an hour of cognitive behavourial therapy – we always conducted these sessions outside – and I was trying other methods elsewhere, as well. Alex wasn't the only one I was visiting for help. Around the time of our very first meeting, I'd also been introduced to Malcolm Williams, best described as a 'life coach'. Malcolm had built up several years of experience working with military veterans and his website spoke of how issues such as PTSD, habit-breaking and overthinking were fixable within his care. Elsewhere, the techniques he'd used included mind-programming, and he was known for working on body language and interpersonal skills. In short, these methods often helped a client to reboot themselves. Overall his modus operandi was one of rewiring. Malcolm wanted me to recognize that my brain was a tool I could use to help, rather than hinder, myself. He was also able to bring me the toolkit needed to achieve this aim, something I'd hoped would happen upon first entering the military's psychiatric care programme. With his assistance I was able to come to terms with the darker images that were forever lurking in the peripheries of my thinking.

Malcolm had been recommended to me by a mate in the military, and I clicked with him almost immediately. Our first session was a little clunky and awkward, mainly because I was clunky and awkward back then, but I really liked the bloke. He was mega-engaging. His face reminded me of the Rolling Stones guitarist Ronnie Wood, though Jamie Sanderson and I would later joke that he was more reminiscent of the *Star Wars* character Yoda, given the pearls of wisdom he would often impart to his clients. Malcolm was key in helping Jamie to dig himself out of a scary place, too. Like Alex, he helped to shift my focus away from the bad memories of the past, treating them as things that were simply there, *being*; thoughts I was unable to change, so I shouldn't try. And like Alex, Malcolm understood that I needed to be more juvenile, that I shouldn't dwell too much on what had happened in my military life – it had gone. Instead, both Malcolm and Alex encouraged me to determine how I experienced my life in the future. My past was the military's for sure, and it was welcome to the horrific memories it had created, but what happened next was all about me, my choices, and my ideas.

*

Alex and I had never made it as far as the river before, but there it was, opening up to us as we walked the trails in the spring sunshine. The water twinkled in the daylight, rippling into small rock pools at the edges. A dog splashed about in the cold water, its owner throwing sticks from the bank.

'It's an easy place to get lost in,' said Alex as we found a spot to stand and take in the quiet. 'It's why I like coming here. You can walk around for ages and never see the same path twice. After all this time, we've only just made it down to the water.'

We looked at the river for what felt like ages, chatting about the future, and what I wanted to do beyond working at Sodexo. Together we were locating the permanent sense of purpose I so desperately needed. Rock2Recovery was making small strides and seeing results. (Malcolm agreed to fill the coaching role that Alex had felt was inappropriate for her to accept.) To both of us, a reassuring reality was coming into view. I had advanced enough emotionally to not need Alex's help for much longer, though I was taking to the idea more slowly than she was. I'd grown to enjoy our walks; the sessions were something I looked forward to each week. But she reasoned that we should move our meetings from weekly to fortnightly – so I could ready myself for a time without her assistance – before eventually arranging to talk in a couple of months. The process was called a staged ending, and I felt gutted at the suggestion. I thought, *Hang on. You can't say that! You're an awesome person and I like being around you* . . . But the break had been coming for a while and a closure to our work made sense. I'd made so much progress in her care that I was able to cut loose without help. After around a year of sessions, my anger and anxiety had faded. I was able to sleep without being haunted by the faces of terrified kids and families. I could see past the gloom of depression to a future that had once seemed so dark.

'This sounds funny, but it will be good for you to experience life on your own,' Alex said. 'Without having these sessions to rely on.'

It made total sense. I was stronger, healthier, and Alex had helped me to get to that point, though leaving her behind felt like a painful break-up. *What would happen without her? Who would I turn to for advice?* Then the idea of regained purpose pushed me forward again. New trails stretched out ahead of me. There were other paths to walk down, each one loaded with new possibilities as I took in the now.

Author's Note

The following is a recent note written by Alex Lagaisse when asked to summarize our time spent working together...

Reflecting on the work that Jason and I did together, which started five years ago, and hearing his account is a touching thing. Rarely, if ever, does a therapist get to do that. As I sit down now to write this I ask myself how can I best describe what happened there in the woods to give people a true account? How can I, as a clinical psychologist, shout out and give hope to the many people who have felt utterly betrayed and disappointed by the help offered? How can I justify the choices I made here with Jason?

But all of these, I know, are pointless. If anyone has had therapy they will know that the nuances and moments that make change are nearly indescribable. For example, it might read that the breakthrough moments happened for Jason when realizing his need to live in the present, or seeing the little girl and understanding that he needed to find a path forward that fulfilled him and moved him in the way the military once had. But these moments were built on many weeks of struggle and pain. Wandering down different paths – metaphorically, and literally – through the woods, often not knowing where we were going, sometimes getting lost or finding ourselves in unexpected places: it was hard work and the journey took us into dark spots. Going to those places with someone you trust, rather than going round and round in one's own mind, is like having a guide. To experience PTSD is, as Jason alludes to, like losing one's touch with the world and finding yourself alone in your thoughts. For some people it manifests as anger and irritability, for others as shame, and for many, a hyper-vigilance to fear that cannot be switched off. But to reach out and be allowed to be, just as you are, can help you find the way out.

Reading Jason's account of his previous therapy in the military was not a surprise to me as I had heard it before, but I am so glad that he has shared this because I feel it is sadly so common. To feel pathologized, to be made to feel like one is 'broken' or 'ill', is to immediately undermine the healing process. These kinds of experiences – whether they come from war, witnessing the death or injury of a loved one, or having endured things as a child that one shouldn't have to (amongst many other things) – can cause wounds. But the responses are always, in my experience, understandable given the context; they can, within the right environment, become a gift. Both EMDR and CBT, the therapies that Jason tried, can be effective and transformative. However, in my experience that happens only when a person feels understood and truly seen. No one will fit a round hole if they're a square peg.

This book has juxtaposed Jason's experience of war with being in the woods and this is something we did frequently in our sessions: reflect on the striking differences between being *there* and *here*. I remember distinctly that he gave an account of being in the desert, of being out there for days on end, before returning to a base camp in the middle of nowhere. That was his world. And then there we were in Devon, clambering up a bank of slippery mud and fallen leaves. He was struggling so much in the corporate world, which was sterile and revolting to him; full of politics, hierarchies and ways he didn't understand. The time we spent in the woods was the only time he wasn't at work, wearing a suit, doing a job he hated. It was purposeful choosing to be there, in the wilderness. It is, for many reasons, the best environment in which to find oneself; a sense of calm, presence and belonging come much easier. For Jason, many ex-servicemen, and indeed many others, it is where they feel most at home. The natural world has a calming influence on our nervous systems, which gets hyper-activated in the case of many veterans. It is, after all, our original context and most fundamental place of belonging. I recall Jason noticing that he was beginning to feel safe again in those woods for the first time.

For people struggling with mental health, finding a place of comfort in the uncomfortable – or, in other words, to be OK with where you are at – can enable change to happen. The war within can fall away and wholeness can return, leaving a person wounded in all the right places.

Alex Lagaisse, 2018

27

My inner kid was reclaimed with the help of Aldo Kane. A former commando sniper who had served in the War on Terror, the pair of us crossed paths during my early days in the Marines, at a training course where everyone was expected to be physically on-point. The night before our work was set to start, most of the lads were mega-keen to succeed and had hunkered down for a quiet night of rest and some sensible preparation for the arduous horrors to come. But Aldo and I went out on the lash. I'd warmed to him straight away. His character immediately put me at ease and everything about Aldo was genuine – there was nothing mystical or secretive going on and we would later become pretty tight mates. Neither of us managed to grab any sleep after our heavy session, and the following morning, the group was ordered to run around for hours on end, sprinting through miles and miles of muddy fields during a time trial, heavy Bergens strapped to our backs. Somehow, miraculously, Aldo and I passed, puking up into the grass when the punishment was done.

While I'd been enduring my medical discharge from the military and rebuilding my life through therapy, Aldo had turned himself into a modern-day Indiana Jones, setting up a business in which he disappeared on safety missions for TV production companies hoping to move within some of the world's most dangerous locations. In military terms, Aldo was the dude kicking down doors, ensuring that remote rainforest environments were accessible enough for film crews to work in, meeting with tribal elders and native fighters, while smoothing the way for battle-hardened TV presenters. He had lived in Ebola zones and helped toxicologists to find venomous snakes and spiders in the Amazon. At one point he even travelled into the Congo, where a camera crew had wanted to film from the edge of an active volcano. Aldo had nailed that particular job and after that the work flew in at him from all angles. It seemed only a matter of time before he required some assistance.

Given that the pair of us had stayed in touch since we'd met, Aldo had learned that I was working through a sticky spot. It was obvious to everyone that I was keener than ever to get away from Sodexo, and Andy Leach understood my desire to move on. Actually, he was only too happy to see me go; he wanted me to discover my purpose as much as Alex and Malcolm did. Various grand ideas had come and gone. There was an idea to apply for a job flying drones, but I knew it wasn't enough to give me the much-needed spark I craved. Meanwhile, I'd been knocked by the collapse of a potentially lucrative security gig.

An Italian oil executive required personal protection as he travelled the world in a private jet, and I was invited to make up part of his bodyguard team. I put aside my scepticism about the downsides of that particular profession, mainly because the pay was so great, the perks were awesome, and I knew the role might involve some James Bond-style work. Being attached to a high-risk individual often involved assessing the personal logistics of their day-to-day life. For example, knowing exactly where the person was sleeping in a hotel, and who might be staying in the rooms around them, was imperative so that any risks could be headed off quite quickly; I was also required to plan escape routes should the need arise. Cyber-security checks were often a major issue. Sometimes, when the CEO of a high-value company was looking to close a deal, rival firms would hack into the company's online infrastructure, seeking out weaknesses that could alter its position. Worse, they might seek compromising material which, if accessed, could deliver enough embarrassment to blackmail the company into signing away an asset for considerably reduced sums. I needn't have thought about my workload too much, though. Having passed a bodyguarding refresher course, the oil industry went belly-up and my contract was cancelled. Eventually, I took it to be a blessing in disguise. Even though I was fast going broke, guarding a wealthy businessman as he met with other wealthy businessmen was hardly bringing the risk and adventure I'd craved. I needed to put Alex's theory into action: *to think more like a kid.*

So when Aldo called, some time in 2015, offering a temporary job, I jumped at the chance.

'Of course, mate, what is it?' I said, imagining the possibilities.

'It's a job in Madagascar,' he said, barely able to hide his excitement. 'We're working for an American explorer called Barry Clifford who's doing a documentary on sunken pirate ships. Five-star hotels, five hundred pounds a day. It's going to be *awesome.*'

Not long afterwards I was diving into the Indian Ocean's sparkling waters, surveying the rotten husks of old boats rumoured to be the vessels of some of history's most notorious pirates and old-time bad dudes. As well as being dive buddy to Sam, the project's underwater cameraman and series producer, it was my role to guarantee that the air tanks were operational and that safety was on point at all times, ensuring that nobody suffered a nightmare while they were working. The location was amazing, real picture-postcard stuff, but I soon realized that the work could be quite dull. Watching a bunch of old archaeologists becoming over-excited as they scoured the sunken wreckage, bringing up fragments of what looked like ancient tea sets, wasn't the riskiest gig in the world. But with each piece, I smiled enthusiastically – *It's another teacup, mate* – while reminding myself of the five-star scenery I was living in.

By the third week I'd become really bored, but my mood was about to change. As I waited on the edge of the dock with Sam, our feet swinging over the side, I noticed a cluster of bubbles below. Barry Clifford was emerging from the water. As he broke the surface I knew something had happened. The archaeologist looked really excited, more buzzed than he'd been at uncovering those old teapot pieces.

'I've definitely found something down there!' he shouted, waving up at us.

For weeks, Barry had been adamant that one of the

wrecks we'd been swimming into was the *Adventure Gal-ley*, a ship used by the famous seventeenth-century pirate Captain William Kidd. Kidd had really riled the Navy when he once sailed down the River Thames, and on pass-ing a Navy yacht he failed to salute, which was a major balls-up in maritime etiquette back then. The Navy fired a shot across his bows, a warning for him to act respectfully in future, but his crew responded by turning their arses towards the yacht and spanking themselves, which, from what I could tell, was the seventeeth-century equivalent of giving it the middle finger.

Barry's claim had got me excited for the first time in days and as he climbed up to change his air, Sam grabbed his camera and quietly suggested that he and I should swim down for a look of our own. 'Shall we just do it?' he said, and I nodded, hoping for a bit of action. The pair of us dropped into the water, swimming towards the bottom, the turquoise glow turning to inky blue as we moved through what we thought were the wooden guts of what might, or might not, have been the *Adventure Galley*. In the dark, silt and mud swirled around us, so it was hard to dis-cern any definite shapes, but I knew Barry had excavated a makeshift tunnel leading into the heart of the wreckage. Once I'd located the entrance, we moved in, feeling around in the darkness for the source of his enthusiasm. *There!* In the roof I felt a large metallic block, rectangular with curved edges. It was cold to the touch, and once I'd pulled at it forcefully, the object dropped to the floor like a brick, puffing up plumes of dark sand. Whatever Barry had found was bloody heavy. (It later turned out the discovery had weighed around 50kg.) I could barely pick it up and after I'd waved Sam over, I began wrestling it from the floor, his footage later revealing what looked like a *Looney Tunes* cartoon fight scene: my hands and flippers disappearing in and out of a swirling brown cloud as I dislodged Barry's discovery from the seabed. When I'd eventually prised the slab away it seemed to be a block of dark grey metal. The letters 'T' and 'S' had been engraved on to one side. And then I realized what had just happened: *We'd decimated the old guy's historical dive site!* Panicking, we threw whatever it was back into the hole and rose to the surface, Barry passing us along the way. Sam gave him the thumbs up as if nothing had happened, and the pair of us climbed to the dock, hoping our unauthorized dig would pass unnoticed.

There was no chance of that.

Thirty minutes later, as we sunbathed with the crew, Barry stormed up to us angrily. 'You two – over here,' he snapped, pulling us to one side. 'You found it, didn't you?'

'Yeah,' I said, realizing the block must have carried some major significance. 'What is it?'

'I'm telling you, that's the lost treasure of Captain Kidd.'

According to Barry, the archaeology team had sent off photographs of the block to a series of experts around the world* and early signs suggested his claim was going to be confirmed. My heart raced. I'd helped to find a serious chunk of pirate loot, and for a few hours afterwards the story ran across every major media outlet in the UK and beyond. All the newsflashes were accompanied by a video image of my hand as it grabbed at the dark grey metal slab in the gloom. Apparently, it was a silver bar, the largest ever found and a piece of booty that could be traced back to a Bolivian ship once attacked by Kidd as it sailed across the Atlantic. The story even knocked the news of the 2015 General Election from the BBC News homepage, and the

---

* Barry's claims that the silver ingot was part of Kidd's infamous treasure haul were later dismissed by a team from UNESCO – the cultural wing of the United Nations. 'What had been identified as the *Adventure Galley* of the pirate Captain Kidd has been found . . . to be a broken part of the Sainte-Marie port constructions,' claimed the report. 'No ship remains have been found. Also the metal ingot, recovered apparently from the above site, is not a "silver treasure", but is constituted of 95 per cent lead. It does not contain silver and has been identified as a lead-ballast piece.'

knowledge that I'd played a small part in the discovery of a sunken treasure haul gave me the kick I'd not felt since my time with the military. *I was reconnecting with my old self.* When Sam had suggested swimming down to check the wreckage, I hadn't flinched. I'd instinctively taken a risk and the rewarding burst of adrenaline that tingled through me afterwards was all the affirmation I needed that Alex had been right. I could be like that kid. I *was* like that kid! The recognition felt more lucrative than the contents of any swashbuckler's treasure chest.

At times, the television business seemed more close-knit than the military. Once word had spread that I was the diver involved in the *Adventure Galley* project, my name was brought into discussion for a new Channel 4 series that explored the physical attributes of the military at its highest level. Entitled *Who Dares Wins*, the show pushed a group of keen civilians through their paces rather than a team of battle-toughened soldiers or Royal Marines. The production crew were looking for four ex-military dudes to fill the role of directing staff (DS) – the assessment team, who pick out which recruits have the minerals to pass through to the highest level. Once I'd been identified as the diver on Barry Clifford's latest haul, my name was chucked on to the short-list. Initially I'd thought they'd wanted me to go in as an off-screen consultant, but when it was mentioned that *Who Dares Wins* required me to present a visible front and centre position with three others – Matthew 'Ollie' Ollerton, Colin Maclachlan and Ant Middleton – I wasn't sure if getting involved was such a good idea.

'Are you going to disguise our faces?' I asked nervously.

I knew the Ministry of Defence weren't overly keen on ex-soldiers like myself revealing their identities on the telly, and landing myself in trouble was the last thing I wanted, but Channel 4 remained adamant that our personalities should feature in the show. Meanwhile, I was stressing about what my old mates in The Brotherhood would think as I pushed a mob of civvies through their paces. I'd be putting my head above the parapet – getting shot down in flames on social media by ex-military and the public wasn't my idea of fun – but when I explained my plans to some of the blokes I'd kept in touch with, their reactions had been fairly positive. People seemed cool with it. Meanwhile, I'd become more relaxed about my reputation, after Andy Leach dragged me along to a military boxing gala some months previously.

It was meant to be a fun night out, but when he'd first mentioned it my gut instincts warned me not to go. 'The people I worked with might blank me . . . They might not let me in,' I half-joked when Andy showed me the ticket. The event was a black-tie do at a fancy London hotel and as the date of the gala approached I became fearful of a rejection from my old teammates. I worried that somebody might say something out of order when I walked through the door, a cheap crack about me being weak, and I felt embarrassed to see everyone after what I'd been through. I was being paranoid and Andy knew it. He wouldn't take no for an answer.

'Mate, your buddies are going to be delighted to see you,' he said. 'I can't believe they wouldn't be.'

He was right, too. Once inside, I spotted several familiar faces in the crowd and moved towards them nervously, wondering how my arrival would be received. 'Foxy!' shouted one of my old friends, grabbing me by the arm. *'Mate, where have you been?'* I honestly wasn't sure what to tell him because, despite Alex's help and my recent moments of self-discovery, I still remained cautious about how to act in social settings. I didn't know what to do around people I used to fight alongside, or how my condition might manifest itself in a big gathering of The Brotherhood, blokes that probably wanted to relive their memories of war over a few drinks. Sucking in a settling breath, I figured that honesty was the only policy.

'Listen, I got struck off, medically discharged, but you probably know that bit,' I said, steeling myself for an unpleasant backlash, some piss-taking maybe. 'What you don't know is that when I got binned I told everyone I'd developed tinnitus from all the gunfights, but really I was mentally shot. I had PTSD, chronic burnout, depression . . . it turned me into a miserable bastard.'

The words seemed to tumble out of my gob without thought, as if someone else had been speaking for me. There was a pause, a flash of confusion, as if the group were wondering how to react around someone who had just admitted vulnerability and weakness. *Was Foxy mad?* And then, release:

'Mate, why didn't you say something at the time?' said one of the boys. 'We could have sorted you out . . .'

The words I'd longed to hear for ages followed soon after. '*We're here for you, pal.*' I felt relief and warmth, as if I'd taken a sip of healing medicine. I also experienced a pang of regret at not having opened up in the first place. It wasn't quite The Brotherhood's warm embrace, *the life jacket*, but just knowing that other people were able to deal with my flaws and meltdowns gave me a sense of security. It represented another sign that I was moving in the right direction. Even Danny was there, able to move through the crowd towards me in his wheelchair, cracking a few jokes with the lads as he appeared at my side. Seeing him like that, unable to move from the neck down, was tough. I'd expect most of the blokes who knew him from his time in active service would have felt the same way. His injury was yet another reminder of just how close we'd all been to copping it in war.

'Who was that?' asked Andy, once Danny and I had finished catching up.

'A long story, mate, but basically he went through the door first and got shot. It was my turn to go first later on that night. That's just the way it was . . .'

Often the difference between life and death in war seemed like a coin toss. Emotionally steadied, and with The Brotherhood rallied round for support, I was now more determined than ever to take charge of the odds. I wanted to grab that TV gig. Even more encouragingly, I felt compulsion, a sense of urgency.

I needed to grab it.

28

Emboldened after my meeting with some old friends, I decided to press ahead with *Who Dares Wins*, though the Ministry of Defence weren't so keen at first and initially requested I reject Channel 4's offer. But I wanted the job so desperately, having realized it would help to push my mind towards a healthier place. I would have purpose again, a sense of adventure, kudos; I'd be surrounded by a team of ex-elite soldiers, each one fully aware of the demands and pressures of our work. There was also the question of money – I was flat broke.

I understood the military's need to retain its secret practices and none of the people on the show wanted to discuss covert tactics or reveal the technical details of any operations we might have been involved with. All of us knew that discretion was key. So when I was contacted by the officer tasked with overseeing ex-military members' media involvement, I worked hard to explain this and eased his concerns.

He still wasn't convinced. 'I'm advising you not to do the show,' he said.

'Mate, I can't get bloody work,' I moaned, my patience straining. 'It's hard for me to get employed when people know I have an underlying mental health problem. I won't get a sniff at most of the jobs best suited to my military experience, not when people find out I've suffered from mental health issues, and I can say goodbye to those big contracts in maritime security where I'm expected to be carrying weapons on ships. Unless it's a very good friend who's willing to take a risk with me, I won't get a gig. Police force? No chance. Fire service? No chance. They're all jobs that someone like me should be perfect for, but I can't do any of them.

'So what the hell *am* I supposed to do? I'm fumbling around here, wondering where my next pay cheque is, and I'm not seeing any help coming from the bloody military – and I shed blood, sweat and tears for you. So sod it, *I'm doing this.*'

Once production was underway, Ollie, Colin, Ant and myself worked with the TV crew to ensure that everything was done with authenticity and within the boundaries of what we could, and couldn't, say to a public audience. Set on the unforgiving terrain of the Brecon Beacons, which is used by the military for training exercises, we ordered the recruits to embark on long runs over the peaks while carrying huge military backpacks. We pushed them through 'The Sickener', a gruelling test of the body and mind where the group was forced to run for hours on end, breaking out to perform a series of endless push-ups or long crawls through icy-cold streams. The challenge ended only when several candidates had dropped out, not that we informed them of that particular detail. The thrashings went on all day. As in war, the finish was seemingly never in sight and there were plenty of false endings.

The tests lasted for over a week, and at the end of every day, the directing staff would gather to discuss the merits of each individual, via debriefings and assessments, in what was called 'The Prayers Meeting'. Some recruits might quit on their own accord, handing in their armbands – each bearing the recruit's number – once a particular challenge had splintered their spirits. Others might be deemed unsuitable for the next session's efforts and were binned off. But over the eight days, a shortlist of individuals came to the fore as being elite, physically and mentally, and there was a major transformation in several of them.

Jon Callaway was cocky as hell when he first turned up on the scene. A good-looking bloke who obviously spent way too much time looking at himself in the mirror, his ego was out of control. At one point he told us he'd wanted to emulate the Hollywood actor Jason Statham in a film or TV career, and almost immediately the DS had taken a dislike to him. Jon was too flash, and ego wasn't something we ever tolerated in the military elite. But after every beasting – a verbal assault, or physical punishment, such as a gruelling extra set of sit-ups – he seemed to learn a little. His attitude changed, and by the end of the series he'd discovered self-control, choosing not to react aggressively when ordered to do things he didn't like, and surprisingly even a little humility. He became one of four candidates who made it through to the infamous final phase where the recruits were sent on the run, as a team, for twenty-four hours, the 'Hunter Force' eventually tracking them all down through the woods, where they were then captured and exposed to an unpleasant form of interrogation, though not as bad as anything I had experienced in my training. It was still pretty tough for them. For the next twenty-four hours, with no respite, they were placed into stress positions, forced to listen to white noise and dragged into questioning sessions, where they were screamed at by a team of skilled inquisitors.

One lad, Freddie – 'Number Five' on the show – nailed the final challenge with class. A bloke with a high-end job in an oil firm, he'd surprised everyone in the interrogation phase by remaining totally switched on after a week of physical exertion and long stretches of sleep deprivation. Each recruit was given an alibi for why they were wandering around the Brecon Beacons in standard-issue military kit during that final stage, and it was the interrogator's job to rip those alibis to shreds. Rather than giving 'Yes' or 'No' responses, however, Freddie made vague, non-committal statements. He'd say, 'I believe so', when presented with a questioning statement, or 'I think that's what happened.' This was an impressive way of stalling the people in front of him, instead of pissing them off with straight denials or hemming himself into a position with a definitive answer. At one point during the episode, a camera even caught him wincing after he'd accidentally nodded and responded 'Yeah' to a particular line of enquiry. Fatigue had caught up with him.

Still, Freddie remained focused, perhaps more focused than we'd expected, and at one point during the final episode (in a moment that wasn't aired) he even managed to escape from the interrogation process. Having asked for a toilet break, Freddie locked himself in a cubicle for a few moments, which was allowed. Five minutes passed and when a member of the production team – a former soldier dressed in a black balaclava – knocked on the door to check on his timekeeping, there was a worrying silence.

'Bloody hell,' the bloke exclaimed. 'He must have fallen asleep.'

When he peered into the cubicle, Freddie was gone. His trainers had been left on the floor and a pair of combat trousers had been draped over the toilet seat, the ends of the legs meeting the shoes to give the impression to anyone peering under the door that someone was still sitting in the stall. Above the toilet an open window was the gaping evidence that Freddie had chosen his moment to get away half naked, later running into the production office, which had no direct part to play in the events unfolding. Instead, a team of TV crew and office managers stared as Freddie ran into their Portakabin, dressed only in his pants and a T-shirt.

'Er, are you handing your armband in, Number Five?' asked one of the crew in a vague attempt to stick to protocol.

Freddie shook his head. 'No, I'm happy to go back in. I just thought I'd try to escape . . . That was the whole point, wasn't it?'

It turned out Freddie had everything required of an elite soldier: plenty of brains, strength, resilience and determination. He was a cheeky bastard, too. I'd have been quite happy to scrap alongside him, had he chosen a very different career path earlier on in life.

As part of *Who Dares Wins*, each ex-soldier was required to chat on screen about various psychological aspects of the challenges being faced by the show's recruits. I knew that talking about my mental health on the show would be an important step for me; I wanted to open up. Retelling my experiences to a national audience was something I felt would quicken my healing process. The confessional might even help viewers when coming to terms with their own issues. At some point I felt the platform to discuss my experiences with PTSD was too big an opportunity to pass up, so I told the show's producers that I wanted to reveal what I'd been through. My aim? To show anyone watching that experienced military personnel were vulnerable, too. But when the moment came for me to get it all out on camera, I stressed about how I should come across, what I should say and how I should say it. I waited in a hangar, the team preparing their cameras, lighting and microphones, the debate raging in my head. *How should I tell this story?*

What image do I want to present? In the end, I told myself, *Just be you. Be yourself, be brutally honest and talk about what really happened.* I acknowledged that deceiving myself in the past had contributed to my becoming dangerously depressed. I certainly didn't want to fake it again, like I had at Sodexo, pretending to be somebody that I wasn't. Besides, there was no need for me to play a role. I'd actually lived what I was about to talk about.

It was time to teach myself about being myself.

I took a deep breath. 'There's a night that I'll always remember,' I said, looking directly into the camera. 'We got into a firefight, and it was a long night anyway, and there were a lot of bullets flying around, on both sides. I remember thinking to myself, "This is quite hairy, this is one of the hairier situations I've been in . . ." I remember getting into a ditch and feeling so fucking tired and drained that I actually wanted to be at home, to be back as a kid and be with my mum. That feeling was momentary because I suddenly realized, "It's not over; it's not over yet," and that I had to keep pushing myself. No matter how drained you are, if you're someone who quits when bullets start flying, or people start dying around you, you're not the sort of person we need. That's why we test it.

'I don't really believe that there's such a thing as a

completely weak person or a completely strong person. The weak point for me is that I'm overly self-critical. I've recalled certain things, decisions made, and they've had an adverse effect on me. It's obviously to do with killing people in front of other people, which is something that happens a lot – we're in such close proximity to civilians – or it can be women and kids seeing stuff that's just violence, basically. I got medically discharged when they diagnosed me with PTSD, so I had to leave a few years before my time was up. A strong person is someone who knows their weaknesses and knows how to control them, or at least manage them. They're someone who knows themselves to a certain degree.'

As the film crew captured every word, I found it had been easy to talk in front of the camera. I viewed it as just another tool to get the job done, and apart from the odd muddled line here and there, I'd quite enjoyed it. Throughout, the *Who Dares Wins* experience had given me a renewed sense of excitement, camaraderie and adventure. With the final interviews filmed and the crew packing down their gear, I started talking to one of the directors. He wanted to know if I'd got a buzz from the job.

'Yes, mate,' I said. 'And you probably won't believe this, and you'll cringe and flinch at me for saying it, but fundamentally the people in this industry are no different from experienced soldiers at the top end, apart from the fact that people stereotype you as a bunch of left-wing sods and us as a bunch of right-wing hooligans. I'm generalizing in a very bad way, but you're people who like to be busy, you like to have a lot of things on, you like to pressurize yourselves, push yourselves out of your comfort zone. You get itchy feet, you're always travelling, and when you get a chance to let your hair down you go ahead and let your bloody hair down.'

I had found a new calling, a way of operating away from my life in the military that delivered comparable shots of adrenaline. The work had been fun, a better version of being in active service, and we had creative licence over what we were doing. Essentially, we were our own bosses, too, operating with a little guidance from the production company, Minnow Films. But none of us knew just how well the show was going to do and the high audience ratings and reviews were something of a surprise when they landed, even though one of the producers had warned us: 'You lot are going to be bloody superstars, mark my words.' And once the first episode of *Who Dares Wins* had been and gone, and the accompanying hype began to build for episode two, the moment of my very public confessional, I went into meltdown. I fretted over how people would view me afterwards. Clearly, the lads on the show had been portrayed in certain ways to amplify their characters, and I became anxious that my profile would come across as weak or incapable. For a brief moment I regretted my decision to open up. At home, as the Channel 4 screening time approached, I became grumpy and irritable, arguing with my new girlfriend when I should have trusted in myself, realizing that it was too late for me to do anything about what I'd said or how I'd acted.

When episode two went out, it was everything I'd wanted it to be. The feedback on social media was instantaneous and overwhelmingly positive. People tweeted me with their recovery stories from PTSD, some asked for advice on how best to move forward in getting help. The cathartic confessional had been invaluable for others as well as for myself, and over the coming months fans of the show approached me to say, 'Mate, that helped me to sort myself out,' or, 'My son decided to join the military because he needed that purpose in his life.' My anxiety over the show had served as a personal lesson, too: *Nothing's ever as bad as you think it's going to be*. And when I met up with Jamie from Rock2Recovery for a pint in South

London the following day, he gave me all the affirmation I'd needed.

'Foxy, that was on point,' he said. 'That was a brave thing to do. Thank you.'

I had made another bold stride into an exciting and rewarding new life.

29

The Ellida pitched upwards, a small five-man rowing boat dwarfed by the churning Atlantic waves. We were 2,000 nautical miles into a seven-week journey, with another gruelling 1,800 to go, our team battling hypothermia, sleep deprivation, dehydration and now one of the hairiest squalls I'd ever sailed through. The boat rolled this way and that. From the safety of our cabin at the end of the vessel, Aldo and I desperately tried to secure the crew's possessions, bailing out water from the small hatch in the side during a vain attempt to keep the equipment dry. Outside, the three blokes whose shift it was to man the oars – Mathew Bennett, Oliver Bailey and Ross Johnson (our complete crew working under the name of Team Essence) – wrestled against the forces of nature. As we took a much-needed break from rowing, Aldo and I watched through the Perspex wall that separated us from them, and laughed nervously at the storm's gathering power as it swirled around us. And then the water ahead lurched violently, taking us with it, the boat rising up, up, up against a wall of wave, slowly cresting, Mat, Oliver and Ross pulling hard to avoid disaster.

But we hadn't enough momentum.

The black ocean became steely sky as the boat twisted upwards and over. For a second the world seemed weightless, the horizon spiralling above us, and then . . . *Crash!* *The Ellida* had flipped back, landing at the base of the wave, its fury washing over us. Through a porthole I watched as the wreckage of our capsize floated past: I saw at least two pairs of shoes, a box of protein bars, a water bottle, and then a pair of milky-white legs swimming towards the upturned hull of the boat, our craft – so insignificant against the vastness of the Atlantic Ocean – slowly righting itself. I pulled myself upwards and looked around. Aldo was OK, drenched but unhurt. Our cabin was a watery wreck, though, pulped into a slopping soup of sleeping bags, kit and clothes. Outside the three lads pulled themselves back on to the oars, heaving their spirits into another battle with the next oncoming wave, then the next one and then the next. Our mission – an attempt to set the world-record row across the Atlantic by travelling from Lagos in Portugal to Venezuela in a boat measuring 8.5 metres in length and only 1.2 metres in width – had become as dangerous as any mission I'd served on in war.

With our belongings gathered and the crew in OK shape, Aldo and I huddled up for warmth, moving through the procedures we knew would help us to stay fit and healthy under such testing circumstances. And then? *A video blog.* In the footage that was recorded moments later, only after the boat was back in action, I looked rough – my clothes soaked through, the skin around my face becoming gaunt due to weeks of regimented nutrition and a work routine that operated around the clock: two hours rowing, two hours rest. Surrounding us was an unpredictable environment that threatened to swallow the boat whole at any moment. All of us were ragged, the transcript of our to-camera chat revealing the stresses we'd been put under.

Aldo: We're absolutely battered . . . We managed to row for about twelve hours throughout the night, and then four hours ago we rowed in to what can only be described as one of the worst squalls I've ever been in. Probably I was near hypothermic, without doubt. [Turning to Foxy.] I don't know if you were?

Foxy [Laughing]: I was cold, yeah ... There were phenomenally strong, 30–35-knot winds. We then tried to put out two sea anchors to steady us as we headed through the winds and keep us on course, but the wind was that strong, we lost both of them. We now have a power anchor that's stabilizing us and we've battened down the hatches – again. We're now eating and waiting for this to blow through. It could be three hours, it could be three days – we're not sure at the moment.

Aldo: And at the minute, our cabin is completely drenched, we're completely drenched, so it could be another night of spooning, Mr Fox.

Foxy: Lucky me!

Aldo: But it's the only way we're going to stay warm in this cabin. It's been an epic [adventure] so far.

As we hunkered down, I wondered if the challenge put in place all those months ago – five men in a boat, battling with the Atlantic – hadn't been a bloody stupid move. The adrenaline was flying around. *Had we bitten off more than we could chew? Is this boat strong enough? Are we gonna fall apart?* I was holed up in a tiny cabin, shivering, listening to the boat as it creaked and groaned under the tidal pressures swirling around outside. Certainly my younger self might have been surprised to see me in that situation: during my twenties I'd experienced a recurring dream where I was caught up in a massive tidal wave, the water looming up over me, turning everything dark as I awoke in a flap, assuming I'd died; I was always petrified by that scenario.

I had overcome my fears, though, because I needed the challenge.

Now, in *The Ellida* we were being battered and our fragilities were exposed to the elements. The chances of us emerging from the situation in one piece were worsening with every passing wave, but I wouldn't have traded my position in that cramped, watery coffin alongside Aldo for a pint in a warm boozer at home. *No chance.* I had followed on from Alex's advice to listen to my heart, and my heart had told me to seek out adventure. Now I was toiling through a treacherous expanse of water that could crush us in an instant. But in the near-death *I felt alive.*

Team Essence's formation began with Ross Johnson and Mat Bennett. Ross was an ex-Royal Marine sniper. Mat had also been in the military, operating as an RAF copper, but following their service the pair of them became brokers in the City. Apparently Mat had always fantasized about rowing an ocean, and the original plan had been to cross the Atlantic as a four-man team on the Talisker Whisky Atlantic Challenge, a race involving around 30 teams from all over the world sailing from the Canary Islands to Antigua and Barbuda. At that stage, Aldo and Oliver – a bloke who was openly afraid of water, and of both open and confined spaces (which might have dissuaded some crews from taking him on) – made up the foursome; he had previously worked in advertising and film production. I was an unknown face to some of the team. But having all met up on Aldo's stag do in the run-up to the race, the four became five and I was installed in the set-up. We soon became inseparable, later referring to ourselves as the 'Rogues of Ocean Rowing'.

The only snag was that the race organizers hadn't been entirely happy with us changing our team's personnel. We'd tried to reapply as a five-man crew but Talisker weren't accepting of the alteration and for a while I became fearful of losing out on my place. Following on from the work with Channel 4's *Who Dares Wins* and the dive expeditions in Madagascar, I knew that a rowing adventure, brimming with risk and reward, was the perfect end-game to my therapy. I'd need to train, and train hard, in the build-up. There were mission-planning sessions to execute. And once on the water, the work was likely to be as arduous as anything I had undertaken in the Royal Marines, given that it required us to be crossing the ocean for nearly two months. When I thought about it, the mission wasn't unlike a military job: we'd figure out our roles in a planning phase, before moving into training, and then muddling our way through when everything inevitably went south during the operation. It sounded ideal to me. So I was worried that missing this therapeutic dice with death – through an administrative detail – would set me back emotionally.

'Nah – they don't own the ocean,' said Ross, having realized that Talisker were opposed to reinstating our team. 'We can do whatever we want . . .'

A new mission brief was set. Forget the race: this time we were to row the Atlantic, alone, unsupported, and having heard that somebody had already done it in 52 days, our competitive spirits soon spiked. *Right, we'll do it faster, then!* We later learned that the first attempt hadn't actually made it to land; they'd hit a rocky outcrop in the middle of the sea which ended their adventure. But that news only encouraged us further. A competitive timer had been established for the team: beat 52 days and set a world record – that was all that mattered. We soon involved ourselves in training details, rowing around the Essex coast in *The Ellida* as a warm-up before taking on a slightly bigger challenge, the five of us traversing the North Sea to fully familiarize ourselves with the boat's workings.

What should have been a fairly stern test of our resources was actually quite easy – perhaps too easy. The trip was supposed to last five days and should have been gnarly as hell; we'd expected to receive a taste of the sea's perils. Instead the water was flat and glassy and the journey only took forty-eight hours, but it did give us a glimpse of the monotony awaiting us on a much longer voyage. Three men had to take on the oars for a two-hour shift, while the other two rested. We soon discovered this to be a grind: the time between work stints rarely allowed enough time for any considerable recuperation, and there was the possibility that people might become irritable and tempers would fray.

Still, I was confident the crew would hold together. Mat had been the schemer behind the operation, having funded the trip and entering us into the Talisker Whisky Atlantic Challenge in the first place. He was a dedicated bloke. I knew Aldo to be practical and experienced from his time in the Marines, and his role as a trained medic was likely to come in handy, too; he'd become adept at patching up all sorts of ailments and injuries. Ross seemed to operate in permanent flippancy, but his unshakable attitude of not giving a crap was likely to be a positive, and sitting next to him when one of the other lads was having a meltdown would later prove a psychological lifesaver for me. The only one of the crew I'd become concerned about was Oliver – he didn't like the sea or open spaces, claustrophobia was a problem, and the challenge was a million miles away from his comfort zone. Everything about the row had the potential to send him into a flat spin, but the bloke seemed eager to press ahead. The group was strong. Whenever the five of us had got together for drinks, to discuss the mission logistics or training details, our evenings were lit up by hours of boozy planning.

At times, I worried about how I might cope for such an extended period of time on the water. Not long before we embarked for South America, I'd taken a short holiday to Ibiza and for a day or so I'd looked out to sea with apprehension.

Hang on a second. What's going to happen to us on the water? I thought during one idyllic sunset at the beach. *This is quite a serious thing. We could get into all sorts of trouble.*

I visualized *The Ellida* rowing away from a land mass that was safe and secure, our small vessel nothing more than an insignificant speck in the Atlantic, slowly moving towards an expanse of nothingness. I pictured what everything might look like once we were stuck, alone, in the middle of the map, the water stretching out around us for thousands of miles. It seemed like a daunting prospect – intimidating, even. Thankfully, those moments of self-doubt only appeared in flashes and the stress rarely lasted too long. Any dark thoughts were overwhelmed by a need to operate within a tight-knit team that carried a hardcore focus. I knew if one of us were to get into trouble at any stage on the voyage, the others would immediately fall in line to help. As in The Brotherhood, an unspoken bond had formed within the five-man unit, and I knew that I could trust in every dude on *The Ellida* – even Oliver, with his fears, was regarded as a highly capable crew member. I might have been rowing away into the void, but it was a step I needed to take if I was to really reconnect with my juvenile self. I had to become comfortable with the uncomfortable again; I needed to find out about myself under extreme pressure. The time had come to forget about the past and stop worrying about the future. *It was about living in the now.*

The North Sea training mission did give us one episode of terror, when our small vessel was nearly capsized by a gigantic container ship. We had been rowing past a series of oil rigs when we noticed a tanker heading towards our path. The vessel dwarfed ours and would have sunk us without realizing had we been unfortunate enough to collide with its hull. Our crew powered on – *We need to start rowing, now!* – but the ship seemed destined to strike us; even the concerted effort to increase our speed couldn't shake the sense of dreadful inevitability as our courses aligned. As its large, steel bulk moved slowly into our route, its exterior missed us with only 500 metres to spare – that might sound like plenty, but in nautical terms it was very much a near miss. We had been given our first lesson that even in moments of calm, the ocean was a dangerous adversary.

30

The flying fish first struck us a couple of weeks into the trip after we'd pushed into the heart of the Atlantic. Sleek and silvery, they looked fairly harmless as they propelled themselves in and out of the waves, but at night, as the water's larger, scarier predators hunted them down, their movements became more rapid. They darted around at greater velocities, sometimes landing in the boat, where they usually slapped into whoever was working on the oars at the time – *Aghh!* The yelps always had the team laughing, but everyone dreaded the moment when it was their turn to take a wet hit. When the sun rose in the morning *The Ellida* would resemble a fishmonger's shop, as several fish carcasses would be littering the deck, their stink of rot attacking the nostrils.

Unsurprisingly, given the trail of dead we were throwing

into our wake, we were later accompanied by some more sizable wildlife. For a while, the dorsal fin of an oceanic whitetip shark followed in our slipstream, silently moving alongside *The Ellida*, presumably to check on what was edible and what was not. On another occasion an even more ominous shape seemed to loom in the wave behind us – broad and bulbous, I could have sworn it was a great white. For a short while there was an extra effort not to tip our fragile boat into the drink, where one of us might lose a leg or two should the dinner-bell ring.

At times, daily life resembled a 3D episode of the David Attenborough documentary series *Blue Planet*. We watched humpback whales breaching and blowing in the distance; a pod of orca later moved past us as we approached the South American coast, landfall still several days ahead of us. At other times the horizon was peppered with hundreds of dolphins as they raced across our path. I remember one morning where an army of what we thought were sailfish cruised past, their purple and pink fins drifting on the surface like discarded crisp packets, a strong breeze moving them purposefully through the water. *Oh, they're really colourful*, I thought. *I really like those* . . . It was only once I'd returned home to England and settled in front of *Blue Planet* for real that I learned the horror of what the 'crisp packets' really were: Portuguese man-o'-war jellyfish, their signature tentacles killing any unfortunate prey with whip-like stings. While they are rarely fatal to humans, in some cases the stings can cause severe aftershocks, such as heart problems or difficulty drawing breath.

Our time on the water was gruelling, but my military training helped to keep me calm under pressure. Often it was my job to navigate, and both Aldo and I were relied upon to perform a lot of the seamanship duties – if anything to do with safety came into play, or the power anchor needed to be operated, it would become our responsibility. Via our radio I was in regular contact with my dad, who constantly scanned the weather reports for the crew, warning us of any incoming storms while commenting on *The Ellida*'s course. Meanwhile, I was sometimes having to give advice to the less experienced rowers. *Do this, do that; tie this off, tie that off.* For the first couple of weeks I had to keep a handle on everything, but by the end of the trip Mat, Oliver and Ross were up to speed and able to take on the more technical work themselves.

The capsizes were usually horrendous and there were several dunks during the journey. The Atlantic could birth some hellish storms, and during unpleasant weather we tried to position the boat on the top of a wave as we travelled along, rather than attempting to climb its face. We'd found it was the most effective way to ensure momentum was always with us. Whenever we were caught out, the whole crew would move to the rear of the boat to add more weight, enabling it to stay on the tip of a crest, rather than sliding backwards. Disasters were inevitable, though. On one deceptively bright, sunny day, the ocean pitched and tossed, moving us along on a watery roller-coaster where we attempted to maintain our balance. From the cabin, as Aldo and I rested, we watched as *The Ellida* moved up the front of a huge wave. We could feel its power as we shifted – and it was getting bigger and bigger and bigger, until we were tipped at 45 degrees. Through the Perspex I saw the faces of Ross, Oliver and Mat. Their silent screams of terror were hilarious – at first. As they raced as a team to the back of the boat I knew we were in a messy situation – we were sliding back! No transference of weight was going to help us. The boat flipped and in an instant we were upside down and floating in seemingly picturesque, crystal-clear waters, while a violent wind raged around us.

In the moments of chaos after a capsize, I was always reminded of a gunfight. The adrenaline raced; instinctively, muscle-memory and the experience of working under pressure came into play. My attitude was always the same in the thick of a near-disastrous incident: *Right – that's happened. Move into action: what do we do to fix this?* Once the safety of the lads had been ensured, my first instinct after any overturn was to check on our electrical equipment, wiping it down and using a diffuser spray to clear any water from its internal workings. Nothing could fix the misery of a sodden mattress, though, or those layers of thermal clothing soaked through before another freezing-cold shift had even begun.

The first time we capsized was at night. As I opened the door to swap positions, a wall of water rose up and smashed me into the cabin. I screamed like a twelve-year-old girl. Often during rest periods, we sealed the hatches on the side of the boat so securely that when we awoke we'd lurch upright, gasping for oxygen. Whatever the weather outside, one of us would open the nearest hatch quickly again, allowing a rush of air into the cabin. We might have been suffocating, but it was reassuring to know our windows were firmly shut.

Miraculously, nobody was injured during our adventure, though all of us at some point succumbed to dehydration or hypothermia. Meanwhile, boils became an issue for every member of the crew. Oliver developed a deep abscess on one of his toes, which Aldo had to clean out on a daily basis, eventually packing the wound in an attempt to save it from amputation. We lived off freeze-dried food and supplements; my daily treat was a hit of Berocca vitamins in the morning, the effervescent tablet dropped into a glass of desalinated water that always delivered a slightly briny taste. But by the seventh week, with Venezuela appearing as a dark line in the distance, all of us fell apart at the seams, like mountain climbers entering Mount Everest's infamous 'death zone'. Everybody ached. My knees were in bits having been continually smashed against the oars as I rowed, and I was unable to sit down, such was the pain shooting through my arse cheeks whenever I took a seat. Aldo eventually located the source of my embarrassing ailment. A boil had formed on the edge of my hoop. It had to be cleaned daily, otherwise the infection might have turned into a dangerous abscess, and so the poor bloke tended to the sore every morning, applying an antibacterial ointment as the rest of the crew howled with laughter, my backside parked over the side of the vessel. 'You owe me for this, man,' complained Aldo, every time he set about his unpleasant task.

Once we finally made it to land at Macuro on 28 March 2016, we were all close to breaking point. No flab was left on our bodies; whenever I moved to row it was as if I'd perched upon a slice of sharp bone, such was my malnutrition in the final stages and the lack of strength in my glutes. I wasn't the only one, and whenever somebody fashioned a decent cushion to sit on, the people alongside him would plead to borrow it, hoping for a few moments of precious relief. Once the cushion had eventually sunk like a poorly made soufflé, another one was constructed, and the process went on for weeks. But throughout the journey there was no let-up in our performance. Our pace even quickened as we approached land; stripped bare of weighty provisions and love handles, *The Ellida* had become a much lighter vessel. The relief as we stepped on to dry ground for the first time in seven-and-a-bit weeks was incredible, my body readjusting to the stability of steady land and fixed surfaces, a sense of accomplishment washing over me.

Fifty days!

Team Essence had set world records for being both the first team to row the Atlantic from east to west unsupported, and the first to row unsupported from mainland Europe to mainland South America. The self-proclaimed Rogues of Ocean Rowing later cruised, in *The Ellida*, to Port of Spain in Trinidad to party. And amongst the celebration and euphoria, the stress of pushing ourselves to the limit taking its toll upon all of us, my mind had found a place of calm and tranquillity. Living a million miles away from the anguish that had so nearly killed me, there was now room to move.

I could breathe – finally.

There have been times of late when I've almost forgotten about *The Ellida*, as the emotional peak of our success fades from view. Then, out of nowhere, I'll remember . . . *Bloody hell, we rowed an ocean together!* The sense of achievement is almost impossible to describe. But the actual experience was more tangible; the medicine I'd needed to pull myself from an all-enveloping dark place. I had found the right path to explore. I had lived in the now and rinsed life for everything it could give me, though the techniques that worked for me might not work for everyone. (And there was no fix-all method for treating depression. I knew that from my time spent working with Rock2Recovery.) But reclaiming ownership of my life had certainly helped to sort me out. I was allowed to be myself again, moving honestly through my seconds, minutes and hours as the person I wanted to be, not someone appeasing the whims and expectations of others. I had stopped pretending.

By setting the world record I had rediscovered kudos. A sense of unity was back, too. With a new team around me

I was wrapped up in another safety blanket, one to match the warm embrace of The Brotherhood, and a support network I could rely on in episodes of life-affirming risk and danger. In those moments when *The Ellida* had tipped backwards, spiralling its crew under the momentum of yet another powerful wave, Aldo, Mat, Ross and Oliver had been on hand to help me, and me for them. Should my emotional state have suffered a fate similar to before, I knew they would have stopped me from going under. Friendship was my greatest weapon in what was now a quietening war with my mind. Overall, though, I had found happiness in my work again. The Team Essence project had required hard effort and graft – and I loved hard effort and graft. I wasn't the sort of bloke that wanted to run 100 metres as fast as I could. I wanted to be the force that busied on in life, with strength and purpose, maybe smashing a knee along the way, in a row across an ocean, while getting there determinedly. I liked working through testing episodes of drama. Previous to my meltdown, I had enjoyed the grit of military existence. *Climb over that mountain, carry a tonne of kit and then jump into a gunfight when you get there.* Now I realized that with serious challenges in my life, shouldered by the people I trusted, that same emotional drive could be recreated.

I sat on the dock at Port of Spain alongside Aldo, Ross, Oliver and Mat – the Team Essence crew – drinking beer, laughing, and nursing the weeping sores and tender bruises dotted across our broken bodies. I felt happy and at home.

'Lads, you've bloody saved my life,' I said, in a moment of clarity. I wasn't joking in the slightest.

The Ellida bobbed and swayed below us in the water, a vast ocean stretching away beyond it. Gulls squawked overhead, the trees nearby swaying and rustling in a quickening breeze. A band of fast-moving clouds was fading into the bright blue horizon. This was a scene I'd once darkened, associating the slate-grey sea and skies with terror, shame and despair, as my mind crumbled under the heft of PTSD. Today the tides were glassy calm, the heavy clouds white and fluffy, a line of them retreating rapidly from view – *hopefully for ever.*

Postscript

A Walk in the Woods

It had been four years since I'd last seen Alex Lagaisse, our staged ending having taken place in 2014, and the personal changes in my life since then had felt huge. I'd advanced so much. My thinking had changed dramatically, too. The new adventures shaping my life had given me plenty to be excited about. By the time of writing this book – in the summer of 2018 – I'd finished three seasons of *Who Dares Wins*, trekked to the North Pole for the Borne charity (which raised money for research into the causes of pre-term births) and worked to help combat rhino poachers with Veterans for Wildlife. I was only a few days away from the launch of my new Channel 4 series, *Meet the Drug Lords: Inside the Real Narcos*, for which I'd travelled to Mexico, Colombia and Peru to go behind the scenes with the cartels and authorities in the cocaine-trafficking wars. My day-to-day existence was so very different from the moment when I'd first stepped in to Alex's practice, my mind breaking apart.

There was so much to tell her.

I'd sensed a hesitation in Alex's voice when I first suggested we meet up. My plan had been to revisit the woods we'd often walked through together as I'd offloaded my stresses. After taking some time to consider whether us having a session outside the boundaries of our therapy work was appropriate, she agreed.

'But I would just say it's quite a thing to do psychologically,' said Alex. 'It's something I'll do incredibly thoughtfully. You're doing this for a specific project, your book, but if anyone contacted me to see me, I would bring a good deal of attention to that.'

I'd not thought of any mental implications to our meeting. I'd simply wanted to check in with her, to reflect on our work together and bring her up to speed on my new life and the subjects I'd been exploring within the book. A lot of my recovery was down to Alex's help, after all.

When we met at the train station, it was nice to see her. We hugged and caught up, then drove to the same car park where we'd so often set off from before walking into the woods. Nothing had changed. It was still the same patch of scrubland, the same grassy square framed by a row of small houses. A kids' plastic slide was plonked in the middle, tipped on its side, just as it had been several years ago. And yet everything was different. *I* was different.

The late-afternoon sun was creeping through the trees as we stepped on to the muddy path, through the gate and into the lush green, our shadows lengthening in the light. Some of the vegetation had been cut back, but the woods were as I remembered them. I mentioned the last time we'd been here. The talk had been bittersweet. I'd known I'd reached a position where I was able to function properly, but our conversations were so enjoyable that I hadn't wanted the weekly meetings to stop.

'From my recollection, we reflected on what it had been like, and what it felt like to end,' said Alex as we spoke about that final day.

'I think I might have been dreading it a bit.'

'Why?'

'At the beginning, I obviously knew it was something that wasn't going to go on for ever, but when it started becoming useful to me, I was like, "I don't want this to finish yet . . ." It was like a comfort blanket, I suppose – if that makes sense? It was a good excuse to go for a walk, as well.

I was driving way too much with work at that time, living in my own head. I don't know how I did it.'

As we advanced along the trail, Alex paused. I'd been making friendly small talk, joking, and taking the piss a little. But I sensed she wanted to bring a bit more purpose to our meeting. 'You would do this a lot,' she said. 'We would arrive and you would do this thing for about ten minutes at the beginning where you would talk quickly . . . And then there would be this moment where you'd slow down a bit and . . .'

'What do you mean?'

'You were having a really stressful life. I think most conversations happened at a certain level. It didn't matter what you were saying, but you'd arrive and you'd still be charged with the same kind of pace as you were going at in your external world. There would be a point where I would say, "Shall we take a moment and just arrive?" And I wouldn't have remembered this, but it's because we're walking again. Today, I would say the same thing, because there's a different pace. You've come up from London . . .'

'You're noticing I'm hectic? But that's because you're from *here*. I'm still hectic, I'm a fixed hectic.'

'And also, how are you doing? It's good to see you . . .'

It was my turn to laugh. I could feel myself settling

down. It *was* good to be in the woods, away from the rush of home. Everything seemed so much more peaceful. Even the nearby train station where we'd just met didn't seem like a proper train station, more like a shed with tracks. 'When I come out of London, I can breathe,' I said.

'A lot of the work you and I were doing was on noticing the different levels of stimulation that you're used to,' she said. 'There's the one level that you're inhabiting in your normal life. When we first met you were always *Bzzzzzzzzzzzzz!* And in the GP practice I remember you saying you were super-jumpy and hyper-alert. So there was the jump from war life into civilian life that you were experiencing. But there's a whole other jump that happens in civilian life – it's the quietness and stillness that you get in woods, where you *can* literally breathe. I'm making you stop because you're—'

I became defensive. 'I'm not! I like it . . . I still get out into the wilderness.'

'Do you feel like I'm attacking you?'

I shrugged. 'No, I don't think you're attacking me. I probably don't get out into this environment as much as I should do. I don't know, actually. I'm sometimes down in Sussex in the woods [working for Break-Point], and I'll occasionally make my excuses, disappear and sit on my own. I've got comms I can listen to in case I'm needed. So I do get out and about. Then I'll take it to the extreme where I'll go to the North Pole – that's pretty peaceful. I suppose it's more of a binge than a regular event, though. I dunno, it's been difficult to get into that environment recently because I'm being pulled from pillar to post, but that's the nature of the beast.'

Alex Lagaisse doesn't have a TV. She isn't into social media. So it came as a surprise to her that I'd found a new career working on the telly. She felt uncomfortable learning of both shows – *Who Dares Wins* and *Meet the Drug Lords: Inside the Real Narcos* – and when she watched an episode of *Who Dares Wins* from season one, when the recruits were captured and 'harshed' during the final exercise, it made her edgy, as various individuals were placed into stress positions and exposed to intense interrogation (though they had all been made aware of what they could expect prior to the show's beginning).

'There are actual *torture techniques* used in this programme,' she said disbelievingly as we neared the river. 'I work with people who have experienced torture and for me there's a strange thing happening in our culture at the moment. The glorification of that makes me feel really uncomfortable; there's an implication that if you get through this, you're the tough guy . . .'

When I explained the behind-the-scenes workings of *Meet the Drug Lords*, Alex seemed intrigued. The positions I'd placed myself in during filming had undoubtedly been highly stressful. We'd met with gunmen and assassins, witnessed the discovery of a torso in the streets of Acapulco – hacked to pieces by fifteen-year-old killers in a 'chop house' – and feared for our lives when heading into the Peruvian rainforests to meet cocaine cooks. During the promotion of the show, I'd been interviewed by a journalist from a broadsheet newspaper. The response online had been pretty favourable, but one or two comments poked at my history with PTSD. Some people were annoyed, saying, 'What the fuck does he think he's doing taking himself there? I thought he'd got discharged with PTSD?' It had annoyed me, no doubt about it. But I hadn't responded.

'Well, I kind of have to agree with them,' said Alex when I told her.

'No! This is the thing! Everyone's like, "You've got PTSD, you've got mental health issues, that's you fucked for life . . ."'

'No, not like that,' said Alex.

'I know. It's just that everyone is different, but everyone

has different things that they need to do to keep them busy. Keep them happy busy. *Busy happy.*'

'You're addicted to that,' she said.

'But it's a different kind ... Yeah, OK. I'm going to dangerous places and meeting interesting people. Because I've been on a journey and it has involved mental health, I'm intrigued to know what makes these people tick. Do they suffer from the same things I've suffered from? Because, essentially, if you think about it, they're born into those environments, they're not exposed to them in small doses. For them, it's like a lifelong war tour, so they must be somewhat conditioned. But they all have their own fears and emotions that go with it. It's good to see different people and learn how they get on with different situations.

'There's a CSI guy working in Acapulco and he picks up twenty bodies a day, and they're not in good shape. I went back to his flat and asked, "How do you decompress?" And he said, "Well, I sit here on my own, listening to music, getting ready for the next day . . ." He loves his job, but he doesn't solve anything, because the people who kill over there are usually dead before the police have figured out who has done it. A fascinating bloke – a fascinating place.

'But I feel that coming through this journey – of which you are a part – I am more in control. I know "in control" is a ridiculous thing to say, but I know what I need to do to keep myself in a good place. I know that I can see lots of different and bad things, like the cut-up body in *Meet the Drug Lords*, and I'm in the right mindset now to think, "That incident's not great, and I don't want to see that all the time, but I didn't have anything to do with it . . ."'

Once I'd finished talking, Alex lobbed an interesting question my way. 'Are you still coming up against people – because you decided to admit that you had PTSD – who have a sense of it being almost *contagious* . . . like you get some virus and you have it for ever?'

I nodded. 'Before we went out to film *Meet the Drug Lords*, I got an email saying, "We need you to see someone before you go and we want someone to be there for you at the end of the phone because we're worried about your mental health." I said, "You fuckers. Have you asked any of the other crew about this?" It turned out they hadn't, which made me even more upset. I said, "Right, we'll do this. We'll go through this process. Mark my words, I'll—"'

'". . . Be the last person to need help." I know.'

'And lo and behold, when we came back it wasn't me who needed help.'

Alex stopped me. 'But now you're judging whoever it was who needed help? *Hang on . . .*'

'I'm not doing that! I don't do that. I want to help people to understand. Hopefully, the readers of this book every now and then might think, "Bloody hell, I can draw some parallels here." I did an interview mentioning PTSD the other week and I got an email from a fireman shortly afterwards saying, "Thank fuck you wrote that, because I've just come out of the fire service and I've been having a major drama. I thought it was because of this, this and this. And it's not. It's my mental health." All I did was talk about *me*. Well, not me, my issues . . .'

We stood by the gate again, our ninety-minute chat having passed by so quickly. Both of us were pleased to have recapped my journey through what had been a hellish episode within a 'fixed hectic' existence; both of us understood the impact of our work together. Alex seemed to realize that she might not have taken a sufficient amount of pride in the brilliant job she'd completed with me. That brought a strange parallel to my previous line of work: I couldn't recall the lives I'd saved in the past either, but clearly remembered the way in which she'd saved mine.

'And are you happy?' she asked finally.

I nodded.

It felt so nice to say yes.

Appendix

A Rock to Recovery

I finished writing this book knowing I wasn't alone – that my mates were there to support me through troubling times, no matter what I was going through. I've also come to understand that my story, sadly, is far from unique and that there are just too many people out there like me. Their circumstances might be wildly different – the symptoms of mental health manifest themselves in a variety of ways – but at their core, the issues of PTSD, anxiety, depression, addiction and stress all carry the same stigma, especially for blokes. Mental health is an issue that most men struggle to open up about through embarrassment, a false sense of pride and machismo. But keeping quiet is dangerous, as I discovered to my cost. Others haven't been as lucky as me. Please don't let that be you.

If reading this book has rung an alarm bell or two regarding your own state of mind, there is help at hand – people you can call, organizations to help you and methods and techniques that will assist your long yomp out of what can feel like a waking nightmare. A lot of the time, the solutions aren't solely found in a bottle of antidepressants, though clinical treatment can help. Jamie Sanderson and I often encourage the people visiting our Rock2Recovery clinics to try complementary methods of therapy – these include one-to-one coaching and intervention work, carried out with a qualified practitioner, someone our clients can connect with and relate to as they construct a new life. This work can be reinforced with exercise, therapeutic projects, challenge and creativity. These outlets often draw a person away from their darkest thoughts.

What follows here is Jamie's personal story of recovery from PTSD, plus the lessons Rock2Recovery have learned when treating the mentally injured. No two cases are the same, and no escape routes are identical. But the first step is always to pause and then open up about the problem. Once that's happened, the next step becomes much clearer.

Music, Mountain, Water: Jamie's Story

Foxy and I were sitting at a pub table, staring at one another, our conversation darkened by talk of suicide.

We'd both hit rock bottom, the pair of us discussing the ending of it all as if that was the inevitable conclusion to our military careers. You already know about Foxy's issues. Mine began when I was a Royal Marine Commando sniper, my mind ravaged by war and a lifetime of stress, my body battered following a scrap in Afghanistan where I fell from a roof. I returned home from that tour in 2007 and broke apart shortly afterwards; my head became fuzzy, my thinking muddled. Nobody seemed to know whether my symptoms had a physical or emotional source back then.

And I suffered, big time.

Six months later, after a period of physical rehab, I went on a promotion course with the Marines, where the pressure to succeed was high, and I lost my memory. It was so weird. Everything seemed to be beyond me, even the basics of my military work, stuff I used to be able to do in my sleep. I was unable to deal with the simplest disciplines of being a sniper, even though it had been my life for the best part of eighteen years. And I was good at my job, too. The role of a Royal Marine Commando sniper is highly skilled; the training had been intense. But with all that experience, I couldn't even read a map during my final weeks of full-time work. I wasn't able to find my way across a military base that had been a second home for much of my career. When my sergeant major discovered me wandering across the site, hopelessly lost, he took me to the doctor, where I was eventually diagnosed with PTSD.

It took eight months of waiting helplessly before somebody was able to treat me – there was no intermediate work in the meantime, no intervention and no valuable coaching. I was cut adrift, without the knowledge that I could have sought out extra help, because mental health issues were all new to me. As Foxy has explained, they were new to the Royal Navy too during that period, when stress cases from the wars in Afghan and Iraq were only just beginning to flash up on their radar. Besides, 'crazy' was the kind of thing that happened to other people, not to a professional sniper. Breakdowns struck Lottery winners who had blown all their money and ended up broke, not disciplined warriors like myself. Depression knocked people who weren't tough enough to handle real life, and in becoming a Marine Commando I'd already passed one of the toughest training tests the military could throw at me. But that was all crap. Mental health issues had taken me down too.

Over four years, the Navy provided me with a programme of clinical healthcare in line with that offered by the NHS, and I was put on meds until, eventually, the therapy sessions became destabilizing events in their own right. Reliving my terrifying experiences during Eye Movement Desensitization and Reprocessing therapy, and Cognitive Behavioural Therapy caused me to fear the next appointment. In the days after each meeting I was often racked by depression, and when I finally informed my nurse that I was unable to handle her techniques, she closed the file on me abruptly.

'There's nothing else to try,' she said. 'I'll recommend that you go to the medical board and you'll be discharged.'

The parting advice from my superiors was even more chilling. I was told I'd have to figure out a way to handle my problems for myself. Apparently there was nothing that could be done for me. I was screwed. Alone.

And that was when I first started talking to Foxy about my situation. He had experienced a hellish time of it too, and together we created a mutual support network. Whenever he was struggling and questioning his worth in life, he would call me for help. I'd already experienced an attempted suicide of my own – luckily I messed it up – but whenever my dark thoughts returned, I'd ring him for assistance. Together we were creating mental sticking plasters for ourselves, usually through endorphin-raising physical activity or something creative and mentally stimulating. Foxy was working with his therapist, and the mental health coach Malcolm Williams (as was I), while branching out into TV work and a series of impressive physical challenges. I began writing music and later climbed Mount Kilimanjaro.

Meanwhile, lads from all walks of military life contacted us, because we were well known as senior figures within the Marines and beyond. They started asking us for advice about what they could do to dig themselves out of a mental fix. Most of the time, we encouraged them to see Malcolm. And as we began to rebuild our own lives, the pair of us understood – even in our frazzled states – that we could be a force for change. We established clinics and arranged meetings under the banner of Rock2Recovery. Our aim? To give troubled people some of the tools that had never been presented to us during our clinical treatment. We told them what had saved our lives: talking to an expert was vital; exercising was key, too. And working towards a challenge and finding a creative outlet were great ways of calming down a mind in chaos.

As Rock2Recovery began to grow in stature, we were

contacted by a group of scientists from Oxford University. They'd been working on the theory that the brain needs a support system to heal itself after a distressing incident, in pretty much the same way as a broken limb has a plaster cast. According to their research, mental trauma required 'music, mountains and water' in which to heal. Or, in other words, creativity, activity and therapy – the very techniques that Foxy and I had been using under our own steam. To our thinking, 'music, mountains and water' was the key part of Rock2Recovery's methodology, which we later developed into a four-point programme entitled, 'Stop, Talk, Act, Refocus', or STAR. Sometimes these steps were taken individually, one after the other; on other occasions they might operate concurrently – it varied from person to person. But we found them to be valuable cornerstones when helping others recover from their mental health problems.

Stop

No matter who we are, what we do, or what path our life has taken, we carry mental baggage around with us. Think of that load as a glass of water. The ideal liquid setting would be around the half-full mark, but our depths can change constantly – hourly, daily, weekly, monthly – and drastically. Should the vessel become overloaded – say, with a mental injury – the water level is likely to be near the brim, where adding the smallest of drops can be enough for the glass to overflow, which then throws us into a spin.

In Foxy's case, war had topped up his glass. The final spillage began with those endless days on the road working in a job he hated, living with his demons from combat. In situations like that, it's important we pump the brakes and reduce any immediate or manageable stresses in life: that imminent house move, the plans for a career change, or any other situation that might cause our glass to spill over. Pause. Find some space to breathe. Then plan the next step.

Talk

Foxy and I always recommend that a new client first visit their doctor. Why? Well, issues such as depression are sometimes the symptom of a serious medical condition, such as diabetes, and it's imperative to rule out any underlying physical issues that might be causing a mental health problem. Often, when a client returns to Rock2Recovery after their first healthcare appointment, it's with a medical prescription. That's fine. Pills can help to reduce the symptoms. After that, the most necessary challenge is to tackle the all-important root cause, which is where talking becomes imperative. Finding a therapist who works for you is vital. Think of the process as being like buying a house: everyone requires something different, so look around until you locate someone who makes you feel comfortable. Meanwhile, loved ones – partners, family and friends – are all vital outlets on what will be a journey of self-development, and one that may well last for the rest of your life. Remember the cliché about a problem shared being a problem halved? Well, it's true. Opening up to the people most important to you is a huge step in managing the issue at hand, and each shoulder to lean upon becomes a pressure valve which can be used to reduce the stress.

Act

The biggest factor always in creating change is taking the action required. Go to the doctors and follow their advice, but also consider your options and try alternatives. Finding a person, such as a mentor, who might help someone take responsibility for their mental health and personal development is invaluable, regardless of what label they are given and what treatment plan then follows. Having good thoughts, meditating and relaxation are all things that can be used to get the mind working for a person, not against them, whatever the problem. Don't settle for the 'you cannot recover' attitude.

There's also a whole raft of life circumstances to manage on top of the mental health issue itself. These could include coping with family or relationship complications, handling bills, or tackling a breakdown in communication at work. People face different social and economic problems in different parts of the country, and none are likely to be solved in a fifteen-minute appointment with the local GP. This is where a good counsellor or coach can come in: they'll organize the changes a person needs to make in life. They'll also give them an idea of the work they can do on themselves when moving forward. Meanwhile, it's good for a person to involve themselves in the 'music' aspect of our three-pronged therapy, the creative processes that distract the mind from stressful chaos. For Foxy, his outlet was located in TV and media work; I learned the guitar and began turning poetry into songs. Shortly afterwards, I had a CD with a bunch of studio-recorded tracks on them, performed by another artist. *I was a songwriter.* The work proved a rewarding release.

Refocus

Once a person has come to understand that they're on a self-development journey, it's imperative they reset their goals and ambitions in life – we need to stop living with one foot in the past. Being present and considering the new journey through life is vital. In some ways it's like starting again but with a different set of software. This isn't a lowering of bars, or a reduction in expectations – if anything, it's quite the opposite.

At this point, a person needs to find an individual, goal or challenge that will motivate them into working through the mental fog that's clouding their thinking. This is their *rock*. For some people it might be the person closest to them, a partner or family member. Music became mine. For Foxy, the thought of seeking out new adventures pushed him forward, and when I followed suit and climbed Kilimanjaro, the experience proved enlightening. It was my biggest lesson in life.

Previously I had been told that my mind was in bits. But after I'd climbed to the top of the world's tallest freestanding mountain, the guide who had led us to success looked at me and said, 'Do you realize the one thing that you thought was broken was the only thing that got you here?' He was right, too. For long periods in my life I feared my head was failing me, that it was leading me to an early grave. But when I'd really needed it, at the climb's toughest point, my mental strength had helped me to push past fatigue, pain and self-doubt. Altitude had slowed my body, but my mind had thrived. I understood that my thinking was still strong. The realization gives me a lift every single day.

Finally, no matter what we go through in life, and whatever story we're told about our situation, ultimately *we* decide how best to manage the issues facing us. We can give up, sure. We can settle for the 'it is what it is' attitude. Or we can use the neuroplasticity our brains possess to redesign and reshape our lives for the better. Striving to become the best version of ourselves is an option available to everyone, so why not keep working towards that goal? That's a real personal development, no matter what the past may have done to us.

Positive change is always possible; rethink your thinking.

Jamie Sanderson
Rock2Recovery
London, 2018

Acknowledgements

A lot of people have helped to pull me through the low points of my personal story. Even more have been alongside me for the highs. Most of them have been introduced already in the pages of *Battle Scars*, but some deserve an extra mention. Among them, my therapist Alex Lagaisse, Andy Leach and Debbie Smith at Sodexo, my coach Malcolm Williams and Jamie Sanderson from Rock2Recovery. Mum, Dad, Mat and Jamie have been so important and so supportive of me, and, of course, my other half, Jules, who has been alongside me through some of the biggest changes in my life. Some of those changes were completed with the other lads from *SAS: Who Dares Wins* and Team Essence. Then there are the others who can't be named: the fighters from The Brotherhood who gave me the support network and camaraderie I needed to survive in some of the most dangerous places on earth. Finally, the making of this book wouldn't have happened without the efforts of my agent

JASON FOX

Charlotte Walker at M&C Saatchi Merlin, Jon Elek at United Agents, my editor Henry Vines, and writer Matt Allen, who helped to turn the black and white of my story into colour (and NVG green).

Foxy
London, 2018

Jason Fox joined the Royal Marine Commandos at sixteen, serving for ten years, after which he passed the gruelling selection process for the Special Forces, serving with the Special Boat Service for over a decade and reaching the rank of sergeant.

Today you are most likely to find him gracing our television screens and giving us a taste of action and adventure around the world.